# Animation with Scripting for Adobe
# Flash Professional CS5
## STUDIO TECHNIQUES

**Chris Georgenes and Justin Putney**

Adobe

# Animation with Scripting for Adobe® Flash® Professional CS5 Studio Techniques
## Chris Georgenes and Justin Putney

This Adobe Press book is published by Peachpit.

**Peachpit**
1249 Eighth Street
Berkeley, CA 94710
(510) 524-2178
Fax: (510) 524-2221

Peachpit is a division of Pearson Education
For the latest on Adobe Press books, go to www.adobepress.com
To report errors, please send a note to errata@peachpit.com

Project Editor: Susan Rimerman
Development Editor/Copy Editor: Anne Marie Walker
Production Editor: Hilal Sala
Technical Editor: Amy Petersen
Composition: David Van Ness
Proofreader: Scout Festa
Indexer: Karin Arrigoni
Cover design: Peachpit/Charlene Will
Cover illustration: Pascal Campion

ISBN 13: 978-0-321-68369-4
ISBN 10:     0-321-68369-2

9 8 7 6 5 4 3 2 1

Printed and bound in the United States of America

# Contents

## Acknowledgments

This book would not have been possible if it weren't for the tireless efforts of my coauthor Justin Putney. His knowledge of designing and animating in Flash mixed with his Action-Script prowess make for a rare combination of Flash talent.

Thanks to my wife Becky who for weeks tolerated my absence from most of our family-related events. She continues to raise the bar of patience year after year, and for that our marriage remains intact and my gratitude unparalleled.

Thanks to Thibault Imbert for his Sausage Kong ActionScript and overall generosity. Thanks to Amy Petersen for her technical edits. Thanks to Pascal Campion for gracing the cover with his strokes of genius. Thanks to Adobe Systems for providing the tools that allow us to create endlessly.

—Chris Georgenes


Several years ago, in my first days of learning Flash, I emailed Chris for assistance with one of his beginner-level tutorials. I was amazed not only that he wrote me back, but also that he was so enthusiastic about helping a total stranger. His willingness to share his skills with the Flash community has remained a source of inspiration, and I'm honored to have coauthored this book with him.

I'm thrilled and honored that Pascal Campion created the beautiful cover. Thanks to John Smick for graciously lending his voice talent.

Thanks to Anne Marie Walker, Susan Rimerman, and the entire team at Peachpit for their flexibility in the course of making this book.

Thanks to my family, especially my mother and sister, as I worked on the book through most of our shared vacation. Thanks to my mom and my grandfather for supporting my drawing and computer interests. Thanks to Carole Petersen for her enthusiastic encouragement along the way.

Thanks to my wife, Amy Petersen, who not only did a fantastic job as technical editor, but also served as my sounding board for several elements in the book. She was very patient as she and I spent long hours at the computer. She gave me my first copy of Flash as a birthday present and encouraged me to start animating my drawings. I would not be where I am today without her.

—Justin Putney

# Introduction

This book assumes you have a working knowledge of Flash, meaning that you have probably already drawn with the Brush tool, converted artwork to a symbol, created a tween, personalized your Flash workspace, and published a SWF file. If you are not yet familiar with these tasks, it is recommended that you read a beginning-level Flash book before attempting the exercises in this book.

To best understand the approach to animating with Flash in this book, it helps to know a little bit about Flash history.

## The Nature of the Beast

In 1996, FutureSplash Animator was released with a basic set of editing tools and a Timeline, which at the time was one of the few ways to create animations for the web. That same year, Macromedia acquired FutureSplash Animator and renamed it Flash. Over the next three releases, a Library was added, the Movie Clip symbol emerged, and basic scripting was built into the package. In Flash 5, Macromedia introduced ActionScript 1.0, XML support, and HTML formatting. Flash 6, known as Flash MX, included video capabilities and user interface components. Version 7, known as MX 2004, introduced ActionScript 2.0, an extensibility language, more video support, and many other features. Flash 8 expanded on the previous features and added additional mobile support. In 2005, Adobe purchased Macromedia. In 2007, Flash Professional CS3 was released as part of the Adobe Creative Suite and included ActionScript 3.0. Flash is now a platform capable of exporting to the web, television and film, mobile devices, and computer desktops (as native applications). Adobe has introduced a developer tool, Flash Builder (formerly Flex Builder), and a designer tool, Flash Catalyst, which also author Flash content (SWF files).

The Flash we use today is not unlike a *chimera*, the beast from ancient Greek mythology composed of parts from several different animals.

## Who Should Read This Book?

This book is for you: the aspiring animator, motion designer, or graphic designer who seeks to exploit the chimeric nature of Flash to get the most out of your animating experience. If you're interested in creating animated shorts, video games, mobile games, or websites, this book can introduce you to parts of Flash that you may have previously shied away—or even recoiled—from, or that you simply didn't know about.

What makes Flash Professional different from the other tools in the Flash platform is that, at its core, it's still an animation program. The nonanimation components can be used to radically improve your animations, as well as your animating experience. Although activities such as writing ActionScript and extending Flash can feel daunting to nonprogrammers, once you have completed a project or two using these techniques, much of that original hesitation subsides.

You may have been working in Flash for a little while, and you might feel like you've plateaued at a certain skill or productivity level. If you find yourself at such a juncture, it is our hope that this book will provide some novel techniques. The book also includes several "best practices" for working in teams and may provide insight into the roles of your colleagues who may be using Flash in a different way.

You may have noticed that the titles of many professional Flash users (as well as those seen in job postings) contain "hybrid slashes" (e.g., animator/designer, designer/developer), and even more eccentricities (e.g., Flash *guru* and Flash *ninja*) are becoming increasingly common. This book will help you wear any combination of hats you find necessary while you're on the job animating.

After you have completed the exercises in this book, you will probably be pleased to find yourself off that plateau and onto a higher level, and you and that Flash beast will be playing a whole new game.

## What's in This Book?

We've compiled a mix tape containing some of Flash's greatest hits. Here's a rundown of the playlist:

**Chapter 1: Getting Started.** This chapter covers some "best practices" for file setup while introducing a few important animation concepts.

**Chapter 2: Character Animation.** This chapter covers the basics of creating a character and animating using inverse kinematics or "bones" in Flash.

**Chapter 3: Introduction to ActionScript Classes.** This chapter reaches right for the most powerful developer tools. Don't worry; we'll provide the safety goggles. If you follow the exercises, you'll create some beautiful, reusable effects that can be repurposed for as long as you like.

**Chapter 4: Workflow Automation.** This chapter focuses on speeding up some of the otherwise time-intensive tasks common to most animation projects.

**Chapter 5: Sharing Your Animation.** In this last chapter you'll assemble an animated portfolio to showcase your creations made in previous chapters. The chapter also provides additional ways (broadcast, video sharing sites, mobile, and desktop) to share your animation.

### Conventions Used in This Book

This book uses Mac OS X for all the figures. Fortunately, there is little difference between using Flash on a Mac and on a Windows PC. All shortcuts are listed with the Mac version first (e.g., Command+A/Ctrl+A). Because the average Mac mouse has only one button, Ctrl-click refers to accessing context menus on Mac systems that lack a right-click mouse option.

Code within the book is displayed in a `monospaced font`. When new code is added to existing code, it is highlighted in blue as follows:

```
//old code
//new code
//old code
```

A return character (➥) in front of a line break is used to designate continuous lines of code.

## What's on the CD?

The CD included with this book contains finished versions of the exercises for each chapter, as well as the assets necessary to complete the exercises. The CD also contains an Extensions folder that provides you with free Flash extensions to support your animation workflow.

## Beyond This Book, Where Can I Go?

If you have the print version of the book, your copy comes equipped with a tracking device. If you're reading the electronic version, we're already monitoring your location via satellite.

As a Flashstar, Chris is famously accessible. You can follow him on Twitter, Facebook, and/or via his blog:

- ▶ **Twitter.** @keyframer
- ▶ **Facebook.** http://www.facebook.com/chris.georgenes
- ▶ **Blog.** http://www.keyframer.com
- ▶ **Portfolio.** http://www.mudbubble.com

You can find Justin at one or more of the following locations:

- ▶ **Twitter.** @justinputney
- ▶ **Blog.** http://blog.ajarproductions.com
- ▶ **Portfolio.** http://putney.ajarproductions.com

There is also a special landing page for this book at http://animflashbook.ajarproductions.com.

# 1

# Getting Started

If you've picked up this book, you probably already know a thing or two about Flash. Most likely, you also know that Flash is a multifaceted application, and there isn't a single, linear way in which everyone learns to use Flash. What you learn and what you retain depends greatly on how you use Flash. This book is largely aimed at aspiring animators who want to expand their skill set and learn how to add interactivity. Even within the world of Flash animation, there are numerous techniques and styles that you can employ. This first chapter will serve as a primer and a refresher to ensure that everyone is on the same page (so to speak) before moving forward in the book.

In this chapter, we'll cover some basic animation concepts, production techniques for Flash animation, and how to begin planning an animated project. The techniques covered are applicable to animated stories, animated games, interactive applications, and in some cases, live-action movies.

The goals for this chapter include:

▶ Learn file setup basics

▶ Learn production techniques to keep your files organized

▶ Understand different types of narratives and how they can be created in Flash

▶ Learn to simulate camera movements in Flash

▶ Study the basics of storyboards and animatics

▶ Walk through an existing storyboard for an animated game

The remaining chapters in this book will apply the techniques found in this chapter to create dynamic characters for animated and interactive projects. Before bounding forward, let's look at some best practices for your Flash files.

## File Setup Tips

When audience members are immersed in a fantastic piece of art, a well-executed magic trick, or a mind-bending special effect, they are generally too distracted to think about how that particular experience was created. As an animator, it is of the utmost importance that you understand how to create a particularly engrossing experience—the successful execution of which depends heavily on what occurs behind the scenes. In Flash, there are several choices to be made (regarding Library symbols, document settings, ActionScript, and so on) that your audience will never see, but these choices will nevertheless affect your final product.

This section introduces (or reviews depending on your experience-level) some settings, techniques, and templates that are designed to save you time and energy.

### Title Safe and Action Safe Guides

*Safe* areas are used in television to ensure that important information is not lost or distorted at the edge of a viewer's screen. As such, safe areas can be considered as margins for visual content that is intended for broadcast. There are two types of safe areas: *action* safe and *title* safe. The action safe area indicates the outer edges at which important graphics can reside and actions can take place. The title safe area exists within the action safe area and indicates the outer edges at which text (i.e., titles and credits) should be displayed.

Even though most of the technology in people's homes has changed significantly since the inception of television (i.e., many television and computer screens are now flat), and most modern televisions do a great job displaying content at the edges of the screen, it's still a best practice to use safe areas. In most cases, it will also be desirable for the visual composition of your movies to keep your content away from the outer edges of the screen. Of course, action and title safe areas are generally not a concern for web content because in most cases, the width and height of the movie will be maintained and viewable in most cases across all browsers.

Most video editing software includes the ability to add action and title safe areas. Flash also offers several templates that contain ready-made guides for action and title safe areas. To create a new file with action and title safe guides:

1. Choose File > New.

2. In the New Document dialog box, choose the Templates heading at the top, and then choose the Media Playback category at the left.

3. Select from any of the template files that include Title Safe Area in their name, and click OK to create a new document from that template (**Figure 1.1**).

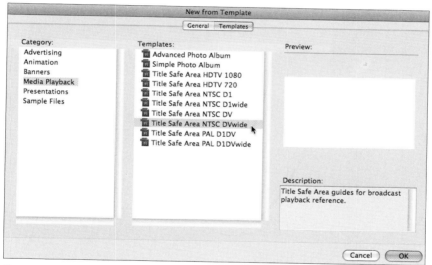

**Figure 1.1** Selecting a template with action and title safe guides from the New from Template dialog box.

A new document will be generated from the selected template (**Figure 1.2**). This document's Timeline will contain two layers: a "title / action safe" Guide layer and a "content" layer (**Figure 1.3**).

**Figure 1.2** The Flash Stage showing title and action safe guidelines.

**Figure 1.3** The Timeline contains the "title / action safe" Guide layer.

A *Guide* layer in Flash allows you retain content in your FLA document that will not be published in your final SWF (or video). Guide layers are useful when you want to keep certain objects on the Timeline or Stage while working, but you don't want them included in the final exported file. This is very handy when you have reference material in your movie that you need for production but don't want to delete the materials entirely from the Timeline when you're done. The content on Guide layers can be used as guidelines to easily align objects or as a rough sketch to trace over (as you will do for the character created in Chapter 2). A Guide layer can also be used as a motion guide to direct a classic tween (also known as a *motion tween* pre-CS4) along a specific path.

To convert a layer to a Guide layer, Ctrl-click/right-click on the layer name and select Guide (**Figure 1.4**). In the case of the template file, the title/action safe layer is already a Guide layer, so you don't have to worry about changing it.

**Figure 1.4** The context menu allows you to convert an existing layer to a Guide.

Guided content can be used as reminders to yourself or as notes to other animators that may be working in the same file. The sections that follow will touch upon several other methods available in Flash to organize your content and communicate with colleagues.

### Frame Labels

A *frame label* in Flash is a unique identifier given to a keyframe. Frame labels are great for adding notes to specific points on your Timeline. Additionally, frame labels can be utilized to easily target a specific frame using ActionScript.

To add labels to the Timeline:

1. Create a new layer to house your labels that will remain separate from your artwork.

2. Name the new layer **labels** (or "notes" as the case may be) and lock the layer so that artwork cannot be added to this layer.

**TIP**

As a general rule, it's a good idea to keep layers containing labels at the top of your layer hierarchy so that the labels are easy to see.

**TIP**

To add a frame label that is specifically a note and is not to be used with ActionScript, you can add a double-slash (//) to the beginning of the label text (or select Comment from the Type menu). Frame notes will not be published with your movie.

You may need to add frames (F5) to be able to read your frame label on the Timeline.

**Navigating to a Frame Label Using ActionScript**

You may already be aware that the gotoAndStop and gotoAndPlay methods allow you to navigate to a specific frame number. For example, the following code will move your playhead to frame 15 and begin playing from there:

```
gotoAndPlay(15);
```

However, you can also navigate to a frame label by passing the label name rather than a frame number. The following code will move your playhead to the "start" label and begin playing from that keyframe:

```
gotoAndPlay("start");
```

3. Select frame 1 of the labels layer. In the Name field within the Properties panel, type in a word or a short description of what takes place at that point in your movie, such as **start** (**Figure 1.5**).

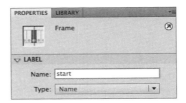

Figure 1.5 Type in a frame label using the Properties panel.

4. Each time you need an additional label, select the desired frame on the labels layer, add a blank keyframe (F7), and type a new label, description, or note into the Name field in the Properties panel (**Figure 1.6**).

Figure 1.6 The Timeline with frame labels added.

With the addition of frame labels, you can keep your Timeline organized and make it easier to jump to different sections, especially if you are sharing the file with others. The next two sections describe additional techniques to organize your Timeline.

## Timeline Customization

A number of lesser-known ways to customize the look of the Flash Timeline panel are available. For instance, click the menu button in the Timeline panel's upper-right corner. In the menu, you can choose the size of the frames by selecting Tiny, Small, Normal (default), Medium, Large, Preview, and Preview in Context (**Figure 1.7**).

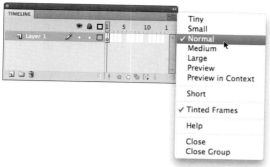

**Figure 1.7** Customize the look of the Timeline using the menu.

One option within the Timeline menu that can make a big difference is Short (located in the middle of the menu). This setting compresses the height of each layer, which is perfect for Timelines containing several layers. You can also use Small or Tiny to compress the width of the frames displayed in the Timeline (**Figure 1.8**). This can be effective when your document has a large number of frames and you find yourself scrolling horizontally in large jumps on the Timeline.

Choosing the Preview option provides you with a thumbnail of the contents of each frame within the Timeline (**Figure 1.9**).

**Figure 1.8** Setting your frames to Tiny (with Short also selected in this case) allows you to see more frames and layers in your Timeline panel.

Frame labels will not be visible in Preview or Preview in Context modes.

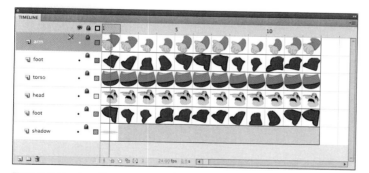

**Figure 1.9** Preview allows you to see thumbnails of any artwork on your frames within the Timeline.

Preview in Context is the same as Preview, but the thumbnails are shown as they appear on the Stage (rather than scaled to fit the thumbnail size).

*Layer properties*

In addition to altering the Timeline display using the Timeline's menu, you can alter the display of an individual layer by changing that layer's display properties. Most notably, you can change the height of a given layer within the Timeline.

To alter the height of a layer:

1. Ctrl-click/right-click on a layer name and choose Properties at the bottom of the context menu (**Figure 1.10**).

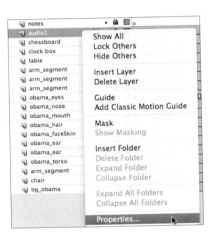

Figure 1.10 Access the Layer Properties from the context menu.

2. In the Layer Properties dialog box, change the Layer Height to 300% (**Figure 1.11**) and click OK.

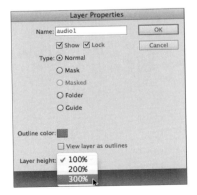

Figure 1.11 The Layer Properties dialog box allows you to adjust the Layer height.

Taller layers are especially useful when you want to see a waveform (the visual representation of the audio) more clearly on a layer that contains audio (**Figure 1.12**). See the "Incorporating Audio" section later in this chapter, as well as the "Lip Syncing" section in Chapter 2, for more information about working with audio on the Timeline.

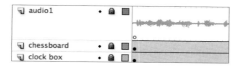

Figure 1.12  An audio layer with 300% height allows you to see changes in the audio waveform.

### Layer folders

Another great way to keep your Timeline tidy is to organize your layers into folders. You can expand and collapse the folders as needed to hide layers that you are not currently working on (**Figure 1.13**).

Figure 1.13  Layer folders are used in this file to group elements for different characters.

To add a new layer folder, click the New Folder button. The New Folder button is right next to the New Layer button in the Timeline (**Figure 1.14**).

Figure 1.14  The New Folder button allows you to add folders to your Timeline.

In addition to organizing a single Timeline in Flash, you can split your file into several timelines, each with its own content. These timelines are known as *scenes*.

### Scenes

Scenes are great to use for each different setting in your story. Scenes help segment your overall Timeline into smaller pieces, so that you don't have a single Timeline with thousands of frames that you have to scroll through. You can add as many scenes as you like to your Timeline. One important detail to remember about scenes, especially when exporting for the web, is that upon export, your movie will become one long Timeline. References to scenes are not included in the final output. For example, imagine you have two scenes that are 100 frames each. Upon export, frame 1 in scene 2 will become frame 101. This is important if you are using buttons and ActionScript to target different areas of the Timeline across several scenes. If you target a frame number in a different scene, the script may fail. It is always best practice to create a frame label and have your script point to that instead. We highly recommend using scenes just for Timeline organization and planning your story during the storyboard or animatic phase (storyboards and animatics will be covered later in this chapter). The main benefit of using scenes is to keep the number of layers and frames to a minimum, because each scene has its own Timeline when inside the Flash authoring environment.

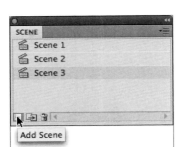

**Figure 1.15** Adding scenes using the Scene panel.

To add or remove a scene, use the Scene panel; choose Window > Other Panels > Scene (**Figure 1.15**).

In the Scene panel, you can click the Add Scene button to add new scenes to your movie. You can rename a scene by double-clicking on the scene name and typing in a new name. You can use the Duplicate Scene button (next to the Add Scene button) to generate an exact copy of an existing scene. If you want to rearrange scenes, simply drag them vertically to change their order. Flash will play them sequentially starting from the top to the bottom.

Now that you have your Timeline organized, let's look at organizing the assets in the Library.

**CLOSE-UP**

**Navigating to a Scene Using ActionScript**

You can also use the `gotoAndStop` and `gotoAndPlay` methods to navigate to a scene by passing a second argument. For example, the following code will move your playhead to frame 1 of a scene named "opening" and begin playing from that point:

```
gotoAndPlay(1, "opening");
```

### Library Organization

The Library serves as the repository for the artwork inside your Flash file. In addition to housing your graphic symbols, the Library stores all imported audio, imported bitmaps (JPEGs, GIFs, PNGs, PSDs), components used, component assets, font symbols, buttons, Movie Clips, and any Library folders (created by you or Flash). The Library can quickly become a very crowded place, which can be frustrating when you're looking for a specific item.

Every Flash document Library should apply these two basic principles:

▶ A naming convention

▶ A folder organization system

There are many different approaches to these two principles. No single approach is the "correct" approach. The important rule is to be consistent within each file so that your Library is both readable and navigable for you and anyone else who may need to use the file. When you share a file that has an organized Library, you exhibit your experience and professionalism to colleagues, and you'll likely make their job easier. It's a simple and subtle way to market yourself as "easy to work with." Additionally, even if you only ever work solo, you will at some point be reopening your own files, and then you'll be the one who is relieved to have an organized Library (**Figure 1.16**).

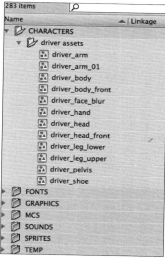

**Figure 1.16** A well-organized Library can make life a little easier.

Your folder system should be one in which each Library item has only one place to go. Items can then be located quickly. For example, if you separate your folders by item type (i.e., Movie Clips, Graphics, Sound, Bitmaps, and so on), each item will only be able to go into one folder. When you create a graphic symbol, it will go in the Graphics folder. Alternatively, you could organize your items by their purpose in the file. For instance, you could put all the assets that belong to a particular character in a single folder regardless of each item's type. You could also use subfolders to combine these two methods, item type subfolders within a character folder, or character folders within each type folder—as long as you can find what you want when you need it.

**TIP**

Expand and collapse folders (using the twirl arrow to the left of the folder icon) in the Library as needed. If you collapse folders that you're not currently using, it will make other Library items easier to locate.

In previous versions of Flash, saving your file would simply append changes to your document, but would not, for instance, remove the residual data from any Library items that had been deleted. To deal with this issue, previous versions of Flash had a *Save and Compact* option in the File menu. In CS5, the FLA format is no longer binary, so it is no longer necessary to Save and Compact your documents.

Consistency is the main goal when naming your Library items. Add relevant prefixes (e.g., "driver_") to your Library item names to ensure that they're listed together within the Library. You can also add suffixes to indicate other information such as symbol type (e.g., "_btn" for a Button symbol).

Now that you have your document, Timeline, layers, and Library in top shape, let's take a brief moment to discuss ActionScript.

## ActionScript

ActionScript is the language that allows you to add inter-activity to Flash. All ActionScript code in this book is ActionScript 3.0 (AS3). ActionScript techniques that utilize separate ActionScript files are covered in detail in Chapter 3. In this section, we want to mention a few best practices when adding ActionScript to your document.

ActionScript can be added to frames on the Timeline. Before adding any ActionScript to your Timeline, you should create a new layer, name the layer **actions** (or simi-lar), and lock the layer so that artwork cannot be added. This will keep your ActionScript separate and easy to find.

To begin adding actions to a frame, select the frame in the Timeline, and open the Actions panel (Window > Actions) (**Figure 1.17**).

Figure 1.17 The Actions panel allows you to add ActionScript to your frames.

Flash CS5 also has a brand-new Code Snippets panel. This panel contains common predefined actions (**Figure 1.18**). To implement one of the code snippets, double-click on it in the Code Snippets panel. Flash will add commented code to your actions layer and open the Actions panel (if it isn't open already). If you have not yet created an actions layer, Flash will create one for you when you apply the first snippet.

Figure 1.18 The Code Snippets panel facilitates adding commonly used code to your document.

**NOTES**

Certain snippets will require that you have a Movie Clip instance selected, and some may require that the instance have a name. In these cases, you may get a warning instructing you that Flash will automatically convert your artwork to a symbol and provide it with an instance name.

**TIP**

You can also create and save your own snippets. To learn more about the Code Snippets panel, visit www.adobe.com/devnet/flash/articles/code_snippets_panel.html.

Now every corner of your Flash document should be organized, right? Don't worry; nobody's coming to your house to check. Just keep in mind the techniques we've covered thus far. They can reduce unnecessary hassle and save you from undue stress.

Now let's dive into some animation-specific topics!

## Camera Techniques

We know what you're thinking: What camera? Flash doesn't have a camera per se; however, in Flash the Stage serves as the window through which viewers look into your story. You can create the illusion of a roving viewpoint by moving your scenery on Stage. Different shots, angles, and "camera" movements within a scene can provide unique visual effects.

Two of the most common camera effects are known as *panning* and *zooming*. To set up a scene for panning or zooming, you need to place the entire scene in a single symbol. Once this has been done, panning and zooming is achieved by applying a motion tween to the instance of the symbol containing the actual scene.

**TIP**

For projects that will be exported to a format that allows the inclusion of ActionScript, there are components that have been created to behave like cameras in Flash. You can move them, scale them, rotate them, and even change their color properties. When the movie is published, your camera manipulations are seen onscreen. Visit the following web page for a great ActionScript camera (with demos): http://bryanheisey.com/blog/?page_id=18.

### Panning

Panning is the technique of moving or rotating the camera horizontally to follow an object in motion or to reveal other objects within the scene. Panning in Flash generally refers to 2D movement.

A perfect example of (3D) panning occurs in the opening scene of the original *Star Wars* movie. The scene is deep space, and the audience sees the mother ship flying past in all its glory. The ship moving through space is very convincing to the eye. If you were to look behind the scenes, however, you'd find that the ship never actually moves. On the set where this scene was filmed, the ship was a stationary model. To create the illusion of the ship flying, the camera was moved in reverse, past the immobile ship. When the footage is played back, the ship appears to move forward through space past the camera.

You use the same basic principle to create a panning effect in Flash. To pan across a scene, you need to follow two guidelines. Make sure that

▶ The scene is wider than the stage, so when you shift the "camera," there is still something to see.

▶ The entire scene is inside the symbol that will be Motion Tweened.

Panning your scene is as simple as dragging an instance of your scene onto the Stage and tweening horizontally from one side to the other (**Figure 1.19**).

**Figure 1.19** Preparing the scene for a camera panning effect.

In Figure 1.19 a red outline has been added to indicate the viewable Stage area. The background was intentionally drawn much wider for the purpose of creating a panning effect and converted to a symbol. The steps that follow describe how to create a pan effect on a background that has been encapsulated in a symbol.

1. Insert frames (F5) in the Timeline and position the frame indicator (aka playhead) at the last frame (**Figure 1.20**).

**Figure 1.20**  The Timeline panel with frames inserted and ready for the Motion Tween to be applied.

2. Ctrl-click/right-click over the symbol and select Create Motion Tween (**Figure 1.21**).

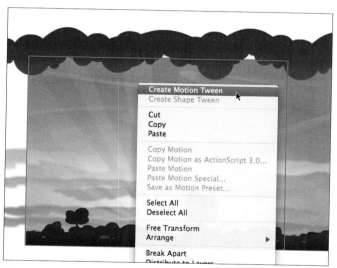

**Figure 1.21**  Applying the Motion Tween to the symbol instance.

3. Position the symbol containing the background to the opposite side of the Stage. The Motion Tween will automatically interpolate the symbol across the Stage between frame 1 and the last frame in the motion span.

There may be occasions when you realize that you want to add a pan to artwork that has already been drawn and animated on the main Timeline. The following steps describe how to convert an existing scene to a symbol.

1. Select all frames and layers by clicking and dragging across the Timeline (highlighting them in black).

2. Ctrl-click/right-click over the highlighted frames and select Copy Frames.

3. Create a new symbol in the Library, Ctrl-click/right-click over frame 1 of the new symbol's Timeline, and select Paste Frames.

4. Return to the main Timeline to delete the original animation.

5. Create a new layer, drag your scene onto the Stage from the Library, and reposition it accordingly.

Now you can move the symbol containing your scene around the Stage by using a Motion Tween (**Figure 1.22**).

Figure 1.22 The panning effect completed with the symbol repositioned to the opposite side of the Stage.

Upon playback, the illusion to the viewer is the camera being moved; when in actuality, it is the scene that is moving.

### Parallax scrolling

As a general rule, objects that are closer to you appear to move faster than objects in the distance (e.g., clouds or a mountain on the horizon). To add depth to your animations, you can simulate this natural phenomenon using a technique known as *parallax scrolling* to move your foreground objects greater distances than your background objects over an equal amount of time (i.e., number of frames).

Parallax scrolling grew out of the multiplane camera invented at Disney in the 1940s. The multiplane camera involved layering different pieces of artwork in front of the camera. As the camera moved, the layers of artwork moved differently based on their relative distance from the camera (**Figure 1.23**).

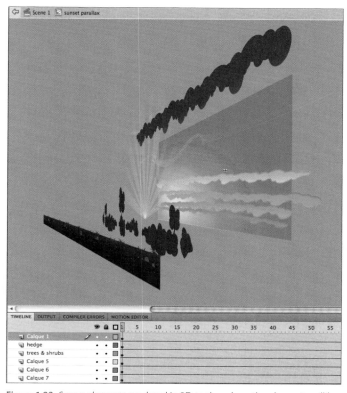

**Figure 1.23**  Scene elements rendered in 3D to show how the elements will be affected by their varied depths.

To simulate parallax scrolling within an existing (multi-layered) scene in Flash:

1. Make sure each piece of artwork in your scene has been converted to a symbol and each symbol has its own layer.

2. Add a Motion Tween to each layer by Ctrl-clicking/right-clicking on each symbol instance that will move, and choose Create Motion Tween.

3. Adjust each tween to the desired duration by dragging the right edge of the final keyframe in the tween (**Figure 1.24**).

4. On the last keyframe of each tween, move each object according to the desired camera movement. Adjust the foreground objects more than the background objects. Suppose, for example, you have three layers (e.g., background, character, and a foreground in front of the character) and you'd like to create a parallax pan effect. Sample last-frame adjustments might include moving the lowest layer horizontally by 100 pixels, the middle layer by 200 pixels, and the top layer by 400 pixels (**Figure 1.25**).

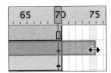

**Figure 1.24** You can adjust the duration of a Motion Tween by clicking and dragging.

You can also blur the more rapidly moving objects to add extra realism to your parallax effect (see Chapter 3 for a motion blur effect using ActionScript). These same parallax techniques can be applied to zoom effects as well.

### Zooming

Zooming is a method of decreasing the apparent view angle of an image so that the image appears closer to the viewer. Zooming effects in Flash are accomplished in a similar manner to panning except that the symbol is scaled instead of repositioned (or rotated).

1. To zoom into a scene, start with a symbol (containing your scene) at its default size so that the scenery fills the entire Stage area.

2. Insert any number of frames in the Timeline, Ctrl-click/right-click over the symbol, and select Create Motion Tween.

**TIP**

You can easily create a motion blur on the Timeline using the *MotionBlur* extension found in the Extensions folder on the CD.

**Figure 1.25** An example of horizontal parallax scrolling. Note how the tree has moved with respect to the relatively immobile sky in the background.

3. With the playhead at the last frame, use the Free Transform tool or the Transform panel (Window > Transform) to make the symbol larger.

4. Play back your animation to see the illusion of the "camera" zooming into the scene (**Figure 1.26**).

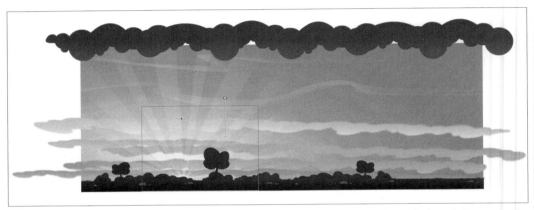

**Figure 1.26** The zooming effect is achieved in the same manner as panning except that the symbol is scaled as opposed to repositioned.

Camera effects go a long way toward pulling your audience into your animation. You can also engage your audience by including music, sound effects, and/or dialogue. In the next section you'll read about how to make your movie a "talkie."

## Incorporating Audio

Flash enables you to add sound to your movies with ease. Flash can import WAV, AIFF, and MP3 files. Generally, WAV files are preferred, because they are usually of higher quality and allow you to control the amount of compression (for online animations) for each audio file.

Flash doesn't allow you to alter many of the properties of an audio clip once it's been imported (only the endpoints and the volume). To make significant changes to your audio (effects, cuts, pitch, and so on), you'll need to use a digital audio-editing application such as Audacity, Audition, GarageBand, Pro Tools, or Soundbooth.

An audio track requires as much planning as any other aspect in animation. You should consider your production needs when processing your audio. For instance, if you have dialogue that spans multiple scenes, you'll want to cut your audio accordingly before importing it into Flash. Generally, smaller audio clips are more flexible because they can be played back to back on the Timeline, whereas one long clip cannot be easily separated across multiple Timelines in Flash.

To apply an audio clip to your Timeline:

1. Choose File > Import > Import to Library. Select the desired audio file. Once imported, your audio file becomes a Library item.

2. Create a new dedicated layer for your audio. Give the layer a clear name, such as **audio** (or be more specific when possible, e.g., "dialogue" or "music"). As a matter of best practice, audio should always be on a separate layer.

3. Lock your audio layer to avoid accidentally adding art-work to this layer.

4. Select the first keyframe in your audio layer, and then in the Properties panel, under Sound, select your imported sound from the Name menu (**Figure 1.27**).

5. Insert new frames (F5) to extend your Timeline so that it is long enough to accommodate your audio (use the waveform displayed on the Timeline as your guide).

6. Add new keyframes to your audio layer as necessary, and repeat the previous step to start an audio clip at a different location (**Figure 1.28**).

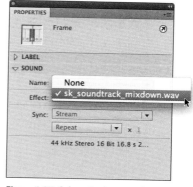

**Figure 1.27** Select the imported sound using the Sound menu in the Properties panel.

**Figure 1.28** Audio clips spanning multiple keyframes.

If you move the playhead back and forth, you won't hear anything at this point. This is because the default behavior is Event. The next section shows you how to adjust the sound properties.

### Sound Properties

In the Properties panel, when your sound is selected in the Timeline, you can choose the Sync menu to select from four behavior options: Event, Start, Stop, and Stream.

▶ **Event.** Synchronizes the sound to the occurrence of an event, such as when a user clicks a button. An event sound plays when its starting keyframe first appears (and plays in its entirety, independently of the Timeline, even if the SWF file stops playing). If an event sound is playing and the sound is instantiated again (for example, by the user clicking the button again), the first instance of the sound continues to play and another instance begins to play simultaneously.

▶ **Start.** The same as Event except that if the sound is already playing, no new instance of the sound plays.

▶ **Stop.** Silences the specified sound.

▶ **Stream.** Synchronizes the sound with the Timeline. Flash forces animation to keep pace with stream sounds. If Flash can't draw animation frames quickly enough, it skips frames. Unlike event sounds, stream sounds stop if the SWF file stops playing. Also, a stream sound can never play longer than the length of the frames it occupies.

As an animator, you'll want to use the Stream behavior almost exclusively so that you can time your music, effects, and dialogue with your visual elements. The other three behaviors are useful in games and when you need to play audio using ActionScript. To update your existing audio on the Timeline so that it will sync with your artwork:

1. Select the first keyframe (or whichever keyframe has an associated sound item) in your audio layer.

2. Switch the Sync behavior to Stream in the Properties panel (**Figure 1.29**).

3. Move the playhead around again. You should now hear the sound, assuming your speakers are on and Mute Sounds (Control > Mute Sounds) is deselected.

Figure 1.29 Set the sound behavior to Stream using the Sync menu in the Properties panel.

You can now see (and hear) how the Stream behavior enables you to sync your audio with your animation. You'll put the Stream behavior to good use in Chapter 2 when you sync a character's mouth to an audio clip.

Although Flash doesn't allow you to manipulate audio to any great extent, you can make some adjustments to how the sound plays by editing the sound *envelope*.

### Editing the Sound Envelope

A sound envelope effectively clips the volume of an audio file based on the shape of the envelope and the shape of the audio *waveform*. A waveform is a visual representation of the amplitude (basically volume) of an audio clip over time. Flash has a number of presets to quickly adjust the envelope of an audio clip, such as Fade in or Fade out, Fade to left or Fade to right, and so on. When you have a keyframe with audio selected, you can apply one of these presets via the Effect menu under the Sound heading within the Properties panel (**Figure 1.30**).

To edit the audio envelope more precisely, click the Edit sound envelope button (the pencil icon) next to the Effect menu (**Figure 1.31**). With the Edit Envelope window open, you can edit the envelope by hand (**Figure 1.32**). The two waveforms represent the left and right channels (for stereo audio).

**Figure 1.30** You can apply an Effect preset from the Properties panel.

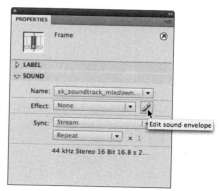

**Figure 1.31** Click the Edit Sound icon to open the Edit Envelope dialog box.

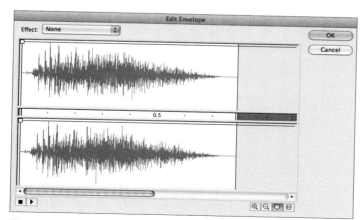

**Figure 1.32** The Edit Envelope dialog box lets you make custom edits to the audio's envelope.

To alter the sound envelope, drag the envelope handles to change levels at different points in the sound (**Figure 1.33**). To create additional envelope handles (up to eight total), click the envelope lines. To remove an envelope handle, drag it out of the window. Note how adding or removing a handle applies to both channels.

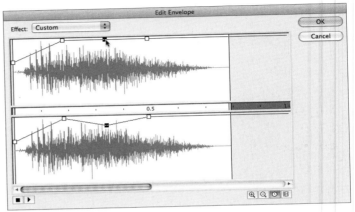

**Figure 1.33** Drag the handles to customize the envelope.

Effects such as fading from one channel to the other channel (essentially, one speaker to the other) can add realism to an action that takes place on one side of the Stage and ends on the opposite side. For example, a character running from offstage onto the Stage, across the Stage, and eventually off the Stage on the opposite side would be greatly enhanced by editing the sound effect files of his footsteps from one channel to the other.

Now that you can import and customize your sounds, let's briefly touch on how to apply sounds to animated projects that contain multiple scenes.

## Using Sounds Across Multiple Scenes

Using the same sound across more than one scene can be tricky. Why? Because within Flash you must manually add the sound into each scene you create. This is not a problem if your sound is composed of several small files that can be moved around on the Timeline. But this is a huge problem if your audio is one continuous soundtrack, like music (as we have discussed). You can't split an audio file in Flash between two scenes and expect an audibly seamless result. If the audio is a continuous sound and you add it to the Timeline in Scene 1 and then again in Scene 2, there will most likely be a noticeable glitch in the audio during playback. Within the Flash environment, there's really no way around this issue. Thus, if you have an audio track similar to a piece of music and there are no obvious breaks or moments of complete silence, we recommend keeping your movie as a single scene.

Conversely, you'll want to set up your Flash file so that it's easy to edit. Try to avoid having a 30,000-frame Timeline during the planning of your project, before even opening Flash. In some projects, a long Timeline will be unavoidable. Use the techniques from the "File Setup Tips" section earlier in this chapter to keep your Timeline as manageable as possible.

If you have several audio files containing effects and spoken lines from actors, it's much easier to implement the separate files across multiple scenes. Remember that scenes are only a function of the Flash authoring tool. Once you export your movie, your animation becomes one long Timeline.

One last topic, sound settings, needs to be addressed before we wrap up this section on incorporating audio into your animation.

### Sound Settings

When you've finished working on your animation and if you're exporting a SWF, you should ensure that you use appropriate compression settings for the type of audio in your movie. Dialogue and music will likely require a higher-quality compression setting than will sound effects. Because sound has a considerable effect on file size, you will have to balance quality against bandwidth on your animated web projects.

**NOTES**

In addition to adjusting global Publish Settings, you can individually adjust the quality of each sound item in the Library. Note that the Override sound settings check box in the Flash Publish Settings allows you to supersede those Library item settings if you so desire.

To alter your sound settings:

1. Choose File > Publish Settings and select the Flash heading (**Figure 1.34**).

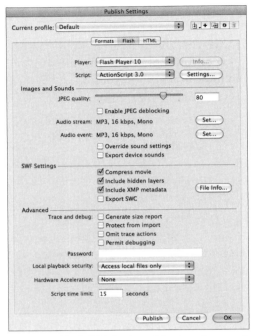

Figure 1.34 The Publish Settings dialog box allows you to access the sound export settings.

2. Click the Set button to the right of the Audio Stream label to open the Sound Settings for all audio with the Stream behavior (**Figure 1.35**).

Figure 1.35 The Sound Settings allow you to change the quality of the audio in your exported SWF.

In the Sound Settings dialog box, you can change the Compression, Bit rate, and Quality. Bit rate is generally the most effective setting to change. For publishing to the web, MP3 generally has the best compression-to-quality ratio.

3.  Once you've adjusted the Sound Settings to your liking, click OK in the Sound Settings dialog box, and then click OK to save your Publish Settings.

4.  Test your movie (Command+Return/Ctrl+Enter) and listen for the difference. Return to the Sound Settings as necessary to adjust the audio quality to your satisfaction. The new SWF History heading in the Properties panel keeps a log of your published SWF file size and will give you an indication of how your Sound Settings are affecting the file size of your output.

Now that we've covered the technical aspects of animating in Flash, let's consider the creative phases of animation.

## Narrative

The sequences of events that constitute your story are considered its *narrative*. The word "narrative" is often synonymous with story, but is more specifically used when referring to the structure of a story. Narrative defines how your story is told.

Before delving into the specifics of a project, you should have a rough idea of the story's narrative. This will help you develop a broad understanding of where your animation is going before you begin investing your time in implementation. Here are some questions to consider when assembling a narrative:

▶ Is the story driven by a character or a situation?

▶ What characters are present in the story?

▶ How do the characters' actions affect one another?

▶ From whose point of view is the story told?

▶ In what sequence are the story elements presented?

▶ What is the setting (time and place) of the story?

▶ What conflicts occur in the story?

▶ How are the conflicts resolved?

Answering the preceding questions will help flesh out your story. Take *Star Wars* as an example again, and answer these questions regarding its narrative. The answers tell you in broad strokes what makes *Star Wars* a compelling story. Answering these questions will also make it easier for you to explain your story to others, which is especially helpful if you are seeking funding or need additional help producing your animation. In addition, answering these questions can help you decide what type of narrative to employ.

## Types of Narrative

There are a few basic types of narratives. You can use a single narrative type, or you can exploit multiple narrative types in a single story. There are three broad types of narrative to consider: *linear, nonlinear,* and *branching*. These narrative types can be used on their own or combined with each other in various ways.

### Linear

A linear narrative occurs in a straight, cause-and-effect, chronological sequence. A sample linear narrative might proceed as follows:

- We, the audience, meet Boy (what a nice, troubled young man)
- We meet Girl (hey, she should meet this Boy we know)
- Boy meets Girl (and we realize they'd be perfect together)
- Conflict ensues and it appears that Boy and Girl cannot be together (and the suspense is unbearable…)
- Conflict is resolved, and Boy and Girl end up together in the end (phew!)

This may be a plain-vanilla narrative, but the truth is that many good stories utilize such a linear narrative. As with any other art form, execution is key. Plenty of fantastic events occur in the original *Wizard of Oz* movie, but it's essentially a linear travel narrative until the very end (when we learn that most of the story may have all just been a dream).

### Nonlinear

Nonlinear structure rejects the cause-and-effect, chronological sequence. Displaying a character's memory onscreen as a *flashback* is an example of a nonlinear narrative device. Many nonlinear narratives are meant to mimic human memory. Some of these narratives can be reconstructed (chronologically) in your head once you've seen the whole story (e.g., *Memento*), whereas others cannot. Some film theorists argue that these movies, which can be reconstructed into chronological order after the fact, are better described as *out of sequence*. Other narratives are designed precisely so that a chronological sequence cannot be reconstructed (e.g., David Lynch's *Lost Highway*). As you can imagine, there are several variations within the general category of nonlinear narrative.

### Branching

Interactive storytelling is especially well suited for a particular subtype of nonlinear narrative: branching. A branching narrative allows the path of the story to change as the story is being told (or shown), as in the context of a game. Shifts in the narrative can be based on user interaction, they can be based on environmental factors (e.g., time of day or location), or they can be entirely random.

With Flash's capabilities, all narrative options are on the table. It's up to you to determine what kind of structure best serves your story. Depending on the specific project and how you work, you may develop your narrative first and then begin sketching your characters, or you may sketch a character that sparks an idea for a narrative.

## Character Design

Your character's motives and mannerisms contribute greatly to your story. For this reason, it's important to have a good understanding of your character before you begin animating. Character design is the process of defining your character's physical and behavioral traits.

Character design is especially important in animation because you are creating your character from scratch; that is, there's no actor who already has a nose, eyes, shoulders, hair, and a certain way of speaking and moving. It's up to you to invent all of these characteristics. You should write up any relevant ideas while constructing your narrative. If you want to take your character description a bit further, you can write a *story bible*. Story bibles are reference documents written for comics and television shows that include detailed information on character, setting, and other story elements. Story bibles are especially helpful for maintaining consistency on projects that have multiple authors or writers.

In addition to creating a written description of your character, you'll want to design a *model sheet*.

## Model Sheets

A model sheet depicts a character in several different poses, often from different angles. These poses help to determine how a character will be rendered from various vantage points. Additionally, these poses help to establish the character's onscreen personality.

Model sheets serve two distinct purposes: exploration and communication. If it's early in a project and you're trying to "figure out" your character, your mode is one of exploration. If you're ready to begin production and you're working with a team of animators that need to render a character consistently in every scene, the model sheet serves as a means of communication between animators. A model sheet can be rendered as rough sketches (**Figure 1.36**) or as polished, full-color drawings (**Figure 1.37**), depending on the specific project (and its current stage).

**TIP**

For sample model sheets from famous animated television shows, visit http://animationmeat.com/modelsheets/modelsheets.html and http://www.animationarchive.org/2008/09/design-mice-and-duck-model-sheets.html.

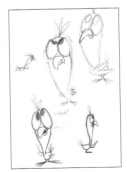

**Figure 1.36** A rough-sketch model sheet.

Front    3/4    Side    Back

CHICKEN **Model**

**Figure 1.37** A polished model sheet.

Once you've designed your characters, you can start rendering them into scenes within your narrative. Usually, rough sketches are drawn to determine shot composition and timing. The process of drawing a rough version of your story is known as *storyboarding*.

## Storyboarding

A *storyboard* is a sequence of drawings, as in a comic book or a graphic novel, that serves as a blueprint for your story. The act of "storyboarding" is the process of drawing (and/or laying out) each scene of your movie based on a script or a soundtrack. Think of the storyboard as a visual plan for your project or as a script with sketches instead of words.

When developing a game, storyboards are useful for mapping out the overall game play, action sequences, and scene breaks. If you're creating a game or other interactive experience, you may be employing a branching narrative (see the "Types of Narrative" section earlier). If this is the case, your storyboard may require a more complex layout that includes arrows to describe branching outcomes (similar to the look of a flowchart).

A successful animated project is the result of good preparation. Whether your project is a motion picture film, video, animated cartoon, or interactive game, a storyboard is often a necessary part of the production process. If you're working on your own, you might be able to keep everything in your head, but if you're working in a team, you'll want to use a storyboard to communicate your ideas. A storyboard ensures that all animators are on the same page. The storyboard also gives you a feel for how your movie will look and enables you to decide on changes before doing the full-fledged animation.

Now that you know what a storyboard entails, you might be curious to see what one looks like.

**NOTES**

In Chapter 2 you'll see how the rubber meets the road by translating a rough sketch into a polished, animated character.

**NOTES**

Like many other techniques in animation, storyboards were first created at Disney in the 1930s. Since then, the elements of storyboarding have remained essentially unchanged.

Many live-action movies are also storyboarded to help plan shots.

**TIP**

To learn more about storyboarding, see this interview with a storyboard artist at Pixar (www.pixar.com/artistscorner/joe/interview.html).

### Storyboard Format

Storyboards, like characters, come in all shapes and sizes. All storyboards contain an indication of *framing*. The frame (in film, not in Flash) denotes the edges of the screen that will display the image. All actions take place within the frame. Each frame of the storyboard translates to a frame in the finished animation. Usually, only frames with important actions are included in the storyboard (i.e., keyframes).

Storyboards can be rough hand-drawn images because their purpose is to save time, but the drawings should be clear enough to make the action evident to someone else. Each frame in the storyboard should include just enough detail to convey the setting, characters, and camera shots (collectively known as *blocking*).

Don't worry if your drawing skills are lacking, you do not have to be an artist to draw a storyboard. We've seen plenty of storyboards from nonillustrators that convey the story or gameplay just fine. Some of the best storyboards have even been drawn on restaurant napkins. It doesn't really matter how imperfect your storyboard is, as long as it communicates the story visually (**Figure 1.38**).

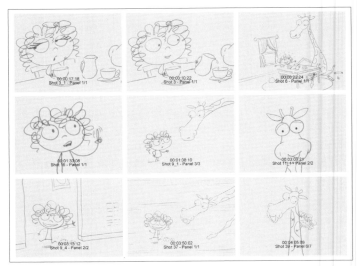

**Figure 1.38** Drafting a rough storyboard before the actual animation is started can prevent time-consuming revisions later.

Your storyboard page can contain 1, 2, 3, 4, 6, or 8 frames (or *panels*) of action. If you try to fit more than eight on a page, you'll end up with some pretty tiny drawings. You can download preformatted storyboard templates or create your own by drawing panels (on paper or in Flash). If you use Flash to create your storyboard and include one action per keyframe, the Stage will serve as your frame border.

Beyond including a frame border on your storyboard pages, you can also choose to include space for information about the production and/or company, a scene number, dialogue boxes for each frame, descriptions of the actions on each frame, and any other information that you deem relevant to the storyboard (**Figure 1.39**).

**TIP**

If you build your storyboard in Flash, don't forget that you can use frame labels to include notes.

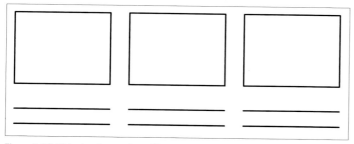

**Figure 1.39** This simple storyboard format contains three panels and a space for action, notes, and/or dialogue.

The tools that you use to create your storyboard may affect the particular format that you choose for your storyboard.

### Digital tools

Traditionally, storyboards are drawn with pencil on paper, and then each image is scanned and saved as a file. You may prefer to use this method, or you may prefer to remain completely paperless by drawing entirely on the computer. Drawing directly into Flash is certainly a fast and easy way to start your Flash animation project.

There are several digital alternatives to drawing in Flash: Adobe Photoshop, Adobe Illustrator, and Autodesk SketchBook Pro are our favorites, but you can use whatever you are most comfortable with. There is also a program from Toon Boom (http://toonboom.com) called

**TIP**

You can download preformatted storyboard templates for television and feature animation at http://animationmeat.com/templates/templates.html. You can print this template for a hard copy or import the PDF to Flash and work with it digitally.

Storyboard Pro that is designed specifically for the creation of storyboards and visual storytelling (**Figure 1.40**).

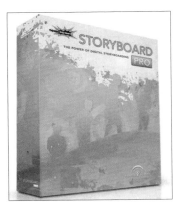

Figure 1.40  Toon Boom's Storyboard Pro software.

### Storyboarding on Tablet Devices

With new technology comes new ways of creating content. The iPad from Apple (http://www.apple.com/ipad) can be turned into a portable drawing tablet if you install the Brushes application (http://brushesapp.com), or you can use Autodesk's SketchBook Pro for mobile devices (http://autodesk.com/sketchbookmobile). These applications are designed so that your finger is the actual drawing tool. But for more precision, you can purchase a Pogo stylus from Ten One Design (http://tenonedesign.com).

If you will be drawing your storyboard in Flash or any other graphics program, we recommend setting the width and height of the Stage to the same dimensions as your final Flash file. You can locate the dimensions of your Flash file in the Document Settings dialog box (Modify > Document) (**Figure 1.41**).

Figure 1.41  The Document Settings dialog box; here you can retrieve (as well as set) the width, height, and frame rate of your project.

Consider your output format when deciding on your Flash dimensions. See Chapter 5 for more information.

Now that you're familiar with potential storyboard formats, let's address the less tangible elements that constitute a good storyboard.

### Storyboard Composition

One of the most important functions of the storyboard is to establish your framing (i.e., shot composition). This is essentially how the camera (and thus, the audience) will see your characters and the scenes they inhabit. Several elements combine to form successfully drawn storyboard images. The following subsections detail the primary elements that should be considered when drawing your storyboard frames.

### Setting

Setting determines where the action takes place: inside a building or outside, in a city, a jungle, or perhaps a desert. The setting may be very minimal, such as a simple background texture or color that doesn't play a large role in the story other than to help provide a specific look and feel to the project. On the other hand, the setting may play an integral part of your project, provided certain areas of the background interact with the character.

### Plot

Plot describes what happens to the character(s) in the story or the game. In a game, a plot can be as simple as getting the character from point A to point B, or something more complicated such as accumulating points by collecting various types of hidden objects on different levels. A character may have to traverse a particular terrain and overcome various obstacles before reaching the finish line. Obstacles can be physical obstructions, difficult path choices, trivia questions, or just other people who stand in the character's way. Conflicts develop as the protagonist attempts to battle the obstacles in a particular path. The conflict might consist of a sequence of events linked by cause and effect (in a linear narrative). The decisive event is the climax—a final conflict that determines whether or not the protagonist will reach the goal. In the event you are planning an interactive game, the climax could be as simple as time running out, or the user reaching the final and most difficult level.

### Action

Action determines how the story or game will play out from beginning to end. Actions are the events that drive the plot. When it comes to interactive narratives, the user contributes to those actions (which are generally controlled with ActionScript).

**Figure 1.42** A wide shot.

**Figure 1.43** A medium shot.

**Figure 1.44** A close-up shot.

**Figure 1.45** An extreme close-up shot.

*Camera shots*

Storyboards are quite useful for deciding on camera shots, as well as on any pans and zooms. Typically, Flash animated shorts and games do not have as many different camera shots as a traditionally animated cartoon, but a new camera angle here and there can be refreshing and can help convey emotions within a scene. There are several traditional camera shots that describe the camera's distance from the character. In a storyboard, these roughly translate to how much space a character consumes in a particular frame.

▶ **Wide shot (or long shot).** This is a shot that shows your entire scene or stage. It can also be called an *establishing* shot. You will usually see this as the very first shot of a film because it does a good job of setting the scene for your movie. When used in other parts of a story, the wide shot can be used to emphasize a character's isolation (**Figure 1.42**).

▶ **Medium shot.** This type of shot is "closer" to the subject than a wide shot. If the subject is a character, the medium shot would be from about the waist up. The medium shot can also serve as a transition from a wide shot to a close-up. If you don't transition using a medium shot, going from wide to close-up may be disorienting for the viewer (**Figure 1.43**).

▶ **Close-up shot.** This shot is very close to the subject and tends to show your character from the shoulders up. The Stage could potentially be filled with your character's head. It's a very useful shot for showing details of expression and emotion (**Figure 1.44**).

▶ **Extreme close-up shot**. Use the extreme close-up sparingly, especially in any animation. Since animation contains less detail than live-action photography, an animated character's face may be slightly less engaging than that of a real person (**Figure 1.45**).

▶ **Two-shot.** This is a shot in which the frame encompasses a view of two people (**Figure 1.46**).

▶ **Over-the-shoulder shot.** This is a great shot to use when two or more characters are interacting with each other. It gives the viewer a solid visual understanding of who is where in the scene. The over-the-shoulder shot is an effective way to transition from one shot to the next (**Figure 1.47**).

In addition to considering the camera's relative distance from your characters, you should also consider the camera's angle when viewing your characters.

### Perspective angle

The camera's perspective (or point of view) determines the angles at which objects are displayed within the frame and creates spatial depths for the scene. The simplest way to imply a camera angle is to add angle lines in the background. Angled lines can add depth to an otherwise flat scene (think railroad tracks trailing off into the distance). Angled lines also serve to draw a viewer's eye to specific points in your composition.

Different angles can alter the interpretation of a given shot or serve to reinforce a mood that is being conveyed with other elements (e.g., music, dialogue, and actions). The angle you choose can convey a certain relationship between two characters or between the character and the audience. One angle can make your character look powerful; yet another can make your character appear meek and helpless (**Figure 1.48**).

**Figure 1.46**  A two-shot.

**Figure 1.47**  An over-the-shoulder shot.

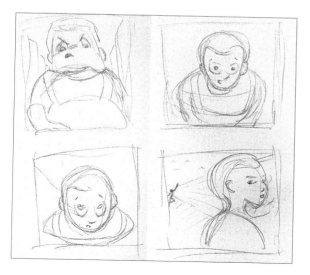

**Figure 1.48**  Note how the four different angles depicted invoke four different emotions.

It can be difficult to render characters at an angle if you're used to drawing them straight on. Rendering characters from various angles can also generate more work for the final animation because it entails creating more new drawings instead of reusing symbols. Even when rendering a character essentially flat, consider angling your background to add depth to your scene (**Figure 1.49**).

**Figure 1.49** Note how the background texture and angled lines lend depth in this frame.

For more tips on perspective and storyboarding in general, visit http://animationmeat.com/notes/televisionanimation/televisionanimation.html. This page contains notes from Brad Bird (director of *Iron Giant*, *The Incredibles*, and *Ratatouille*) on composition, notes on "Storyboarding *The Simpsons* Way" by Christian Roman (story artist on *The Simpsons* and *Toy Story 3*), as well as layout notes from Hanna-Barbera (producers of *Scooby-Doo*, *The Flintstones*, and several others) and Spumco (producers of *Ren & Stimpy*).

Now that we've covered the aesthetics of a storyboard, let's look at an example!

## Sausage Kong Storyboard Example

Sausage Kong is a game developed by Thibault Imbert (Adobe Systems Flash Player Product Manager) and Chris. This game started as a simple way to showcase the peer-to-peer capabilities of Flash Player 10.1 by controlling a single character running across the screen on Android mobile devices. What started off as a very simple example quickly grew into a fully interactive Flash game that includes various characters, animation, and a scoring system. Sausage Kong is the result of several fun ideas tossed back and forth by Thibault and Chris via email. At the time, Thibault was living in Paris, France, and Chris lives in Boston, Massachusetts, so it was helpful to construct a storyboard to ensure that both parties were on the same page when it came to determining how the game would work and what assets were necessary to create and program the game. This is a situation in which a rough storyboard came in handy.

### The Concept

Within Sausage Kong, the user presses the arrow keys on the keyboard to control the direction of a character (left and right). To start the game, the user presses the spacebar, and a boy jumps in the air. Pigs with parachutes begin floating down from the sky, and the boy has to run back and forth to "catch" them. Once caught, the boy must run toward a grinder machine, and the user presses the spacebar to make the boy throw the pig into the grinder. The grinder cranks out sausages made from the pig. The more sausages made within a predetermined amount of time, the more points earned.

Working from this concept, Chris began creating storyboards.

### Storyboard Panels

The first frame of the storyboard shows what the preloader screen will look like. Since the pigs are parachuting from a high elevation, the background environment is an exterior shot with grass, trees, and sky. The preloader includes a percentage load bar as well as a fun animation of sausages dancing in a circle (**Figure 1.50**).

**Figure 1.50** Panel 1 of the Sausage Kong storyboard shows the preloader screen.

The second frame of the storyboard roughly shows how the introductory splash page will look. The preloader disappears, and the game logo drops down from outside the viewable area, as indicated by the red arrow. When creating a storyboard in Flash, it can be useful to dedicate an additional layer just for drawing arrows and notes to specify how various elements will move (**Figure 1.51**).

**Figure 1.51** Panel 2 of the Sausage Kong storyboard shows the splash screen.

If the user selects New Game (with the arrow keys), the logo will disappear and the game begins. The third drawing in the storyboard shows the character entering from a hole that appears in the ground. The boy jumps up from the hole, the hole disappears, and the boy lands safely on the ground (**Figure 1.52**).

**Figure 1.52** Panel 3 of the Sausage Kong storyboard shows the boy entering.

Immediately, the game starts as the pigs begin falling, and the timer (in the upper-left corner) appears and starts counting from 0 to 60 seconds (**Figure 1.53**).

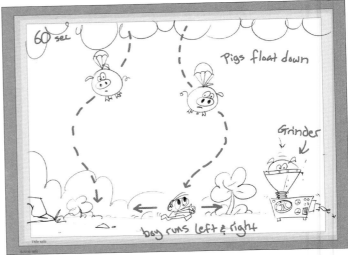

**Figure 1.53** Panel 4 of the Sausage Kong storyboard shows the game play.

The fifth frame simply shows how the boy will run toward the grinder and throw the pig into it; the resulting sausages made from the pig are also shown (**Figure 1.54**).

**Figure 1.54** Panel 5 of the Sausage Kong storyboard shows the boy throwing a pig into the grinder.

When time has elapsed, the game will end and the entire screen will pan to the left (**Figure 1.55**).

**Figure 1.55** Panel 6 of the Sausage Kong storyboard shows the screen panning to the left.

In this screen, a meat truck will drive in from the right in reverse (**Figure 1.56**).

**Figure 1.56** Panel 7 of the Sausage Kong storyboard shows the meat truck entering from right to left.

Next, the driver exits the truck and walks to the sausage pile (**Figure 1.57**).

**Figure 1.57** Panel 8 of the Sausage Kong storyboard shows the driver exiting the truck and walking toward the sausages.

The high score and the player's score will appear while the driver throws the sausages into the back of his truck (**Figure 1.58**).

**Figure 1.58** Panel 9 of the Sausage Kong storyboard shows the driver loading the truck with sausages.

The last frame shows a button to play the game again while the driver drives off the screen to the right (**Figure 1.59**).

**Figure 1.59** Panel 10 of the Sausage Kong storyboard shows the "play again" screen.

In storyboard format, the visual plan could be shared between everyone involved in the project. A concise storyboard makes for a great starting point for projects of all scopes and sizes.

For more storyboard examples, visit:

▶ http://animationarchive.org/2006/03/media-john-ks-storyboard-for-stimpys.html

▶ http://johnkstuff.blogspot.com/2009/10/storyboard-slug-stimpys-invention.html

▶ http://characterdesign.blogspot.com/2009/05/pixars-up-storyboards.html

When you've completed your storyboard, you can jump right into production, or you can first create an *animatic*.

**TIP**

If you're interested in learning more about storyboarding, be sure to check out *Prepare to Board! Creating Story and Characters for Animated Features and Shorts* by Nancy Beiman (Focal Press, 2007).

## Animatics

An animatic is an animated (or timed) version of your storyboard. The purpose of an animatic is to work out the timing of each shot, as well as the timing of specific animated sequences and key poses of the characters. An animatic often includes rough dialogue, music, or narration, so that the shots can be timed with the soundtrack. An animatic can give you a good idea of how your shots will play as a sequence and provide a better feel for the overall pacing of the animation. Think of the animatic as the rough draft for your animation.

Building an animatic in Flash is a rather straightforward process, since Flash is time-based and allows you to incorporate audio. When building an animatic in Flash, it's recommended that your file dimensions match your final project dimensions (which means planning ahead), and you only include one panel (shot) per keyframe. Having your animatic shots fill the Stage will make your animatic file useful as a template when you begin building your final animation.

The rhythm of your animation is critical. Every story has a certain tempo, much like a musical composition. You are the songwriter, and you decide how fast or how slow your song will be. Unfortunately, this is often not as easy as it sounds. The animatic phase allows you to make last-minute adjustments to the storyboard and soundtrack before starting production. This process can save money and ensure that larger projects have fewer scenes that later hit the cutting room floor. It is much more difficult to make timing changes after the animation is complete.

Chris often creates a character animatic using a sequence of key poses. This helps him adjust the overall timing of the action he wants his character to perform. To make his MudBubble character perform a forward body roll and then leap high in the air and land standing up, he drew a series of key poses (**Figure 1.60**).

**Figure 1.60** Chris's character's key poses roughly drawn in Flash using the Brush tool.

Chris then placed each key pose in its own keyframe and inserted frames between each keyframe to work out the timing of the overall action sequence. Quick actions include fewer frames (such as the roll); in contrast, the jumping is slower and therefore more frames are included between the key poses (**Figure 1.61**).

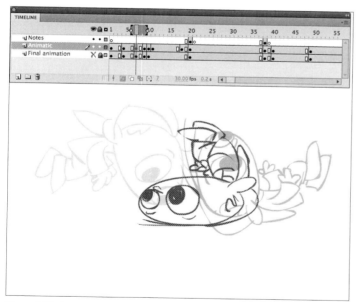

**Figure 1.61** An animatic sequence created by inserting frames between key poses.

**TIP**

To find more examples of animatics, check the DVD special features of your favorite animated television show or feature film. Many of them include scenes from the animatic.

When you've completed your storyboard or animatic in Flash, you can go back to frame 1 and play back your Timeline (Return/Enter). You can then get a feel for the timing of your animation sequence. It is very important to make sure the timing is perfect before proceeding to the final animation stage. Some sequences may feel too long or short as you watch them. Insert and/or remove frames to adjust the timing. You may even decide additional sequences are needed, or in some cases, that some existing sequences should be eliminated. Ultimately, knowing how long or short a specific sequence should be is often based on your intuition as an animator (**Figure 1.62**).

**Figure 1.62** The final animated sequence.

Now you're ready to start creating the actual animation and writing some code. Chapter 2 will focus on building an animated character. Chapter 3 will show you how to make your characters interactive.

# 2

# Character Animation

Creating the illusion of life is at the very heart of character animation. Successful animators are able to infuse their renderings with characteristics that allow their audience to empathize with a series of illustrations, even if the characters in those illustrations are inanimate objects like toys, cars, or even flour sacks (**Figure 2.1** on the next page).

This chapter demonstrates how to create your characters in Flash so they can be easily animated on the Timeline or with ActionScript. In this chapter you'll use the Timeline to animate the "driver" character from the Sausage Kong game described in Chapter 1. Then, you'll use ActionScript in Chapters 3 and 5 to animate the driver dynamically.

The goals for this chapter include:

- ► Learn about character animation techniques
- ► Build a character rigged for animation in Flash that can be used in later chapters
- ► Create a "run cycle" for your animated character
- ► Explore inverse kinematics (IK) in Flash
- ► Learn the basics of syncing a character's lips to an audio track

Before diving in, let's discuss some existing animation techniques and decide which technique will best suit the project at hand.

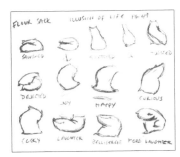

**Figure 2.1** A collection of flour sack sketches from Justin's notebook.

The flour sack exercise is a famous animation test. The goal of the exercise is to breathe life into an inanimate object by generating various expressive "portraits" of that object. To learn more, see *The Illusion of Life: Disney Animation* by Ollie Johnston and Frank Thomas (Disney Editions, 1981).

*The Animator's Survival Kit* by Richard Williams (Faber and Faber, 2001) is the undisputed bible of character animation. If you're interested in learning more about animation of any kind—especially traditional animation—you should own a copy of this book.

## Animation Techniques

Several basic animation techniques have been invented over the last century or so; each one, when properly executed, enables you to capture a viewer's imagination. As a tool, Flash is capable of accommodating any number of styles. The extent to which Flash animation can be pushed depends on the combination of creativity and craft that you bring to your projects. Knowledge of well-established styles will help provide a framework for designing your characters. Let's go over some existing techniques before constructing your animated character.

### Hand-drawn (Traditional) Animation

Hand-drawn animation prior to computer software was also known as *cel* animation because the frames were drawn on transparent celluloid such that images of different objects could be overlaid (e.g., a character on top of the background). Cel animation is also referred to as *traditional* animation. Prior to cel animation, every frame had to be redrawn in its entirety, including the contents of the backgrounds (think flipbook).

Several cels would then be superimposed in a single frame, similar to how layers function in Flash. Each cel could then be manipulated separately so that stationary objects (e.g., backgrounds, static characters, or character parts) did not have to be redrawn. The independent functioning of each cel and the ability to only move what's necessary are both approaches similar to how you can use symbols in Flash. Finally, a camera would photograph each frame.

Characters originally animated via this method include Mickey Mouse, the Roadrunner, Bugs Bunny, Porky Pig, Betty Boop, Popeye, and many, many more. Although traditional animation has become less common as large studios have favored 3D computer animation, many of the techniques and terminology from traditional animation have been applied to digital animation. In addition, a number of the skills and terms developed for traditional animation remain relevant in Flash. For example, the concept of onion skinning in Flash (addressed later in this chapter) is derived from the original use of translucent "onionskin" paper over a light source in order to visualize adjacent images (frames) when the animator was drawing by hand.

### Frame rate

A certain number of frames per second (fps) are necessary to successfully create the illusion of movement. Traditional animation generally employed a frame rate of 24 fps. At a length of 90 minutes, that frame rate requires the generation of 129,600 frames of drawings, which is no small task. The frame rate for most live-action films has customarily been 29.97 fps. At 24 fps, well-executed traditional animation can simulate motion as convincingly as live-action film.

The technique of creating a new drawing for every frame (at 24 fps) is known as drawing on *ones*. For certain scenes, it is only necessary to create a new drawing for every other frame. This latter technique is known as drawing on *twos*. For reasons related to budget and expediency, some animations are done entirely on twos (12 fps). *Ren & Stimpy*, for example, was drawn entirely on twos. While 24 fps is considered the gold standard, great animation can still be created at 12 fps. However, at rates less than 12 fps, an animation will usually look pretty choppy.

### Tweening

Even when cels were used in traditional animation, it was necessary to create new drawings for nearly every frame (at least for the objects that were moving). Generally, a master animator would draw key poses (known as keyframes) for important moments of action, and junior artists would complete the somewhat less important *in between* images (or *tweens*). When inbetweeners were tasked with transforming a drawing from point A to point C, it was their job to figure out where to place point B. In other words, the job of the inbetweener was to *interpolate* what should happen to the image between the master animator's drawings. *Tweening* then took on additional meaning with the advent of computers.

With the birth of digital animation, tweening has come to refer to interpolation performed by software. When a

**TIP**

Generally, any rate between 12 and 24 fps will work; 15 or 18 fps will offer smoother motion than 12 fps but not require nearly as many drawings as 24 fps. Experiment with different frame rates and see what works for you.

**CLOSE-UP**

**Rotoscoping**

Rotoscoping is a technique in which animators trace movement (using video footage), frame by frame. Rotoscoping has been employed on many films, including *Snow White and the Seven Dwarfs*, *Waking Life*, and even the original *Star Wars* Trilogy for the light-saber sequences. A handful of cartoons on *Adult Swim* were originally animated by rotoscoping old Hanna-Barbera series.

computer tweens, it evaluates the distance between point A and point C, and then divides that distance in half, thereby producing point B. In this regard, a computer's notion of an inbetween is somewhat more literal than that of a human artist. A trained human artist will also consider concepts like anticipation and exaggeration while animating an object (**Figure 2.2**).

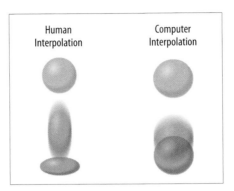

**Figure 2.2** The human interpolation on the left applies a concept called "squash and stretch" to exaggerate the bouncing motion.

The inverse kinematic (IK) armature system also allows for tweening. IK is discussed later in this chapter.

**TIP**

In Chapter 3 you'll learn how to add Shape Hints to make a Shape tween do your bidding.

The Spring feature added to Flash CS5 is an example of a slightly "smarter" tween that moves more like a real object. To learn more about the Spring feature, see Chris's article at *www.adobe.com/devnet/flash/articles/spring_tool.html*.

Flash CS5 includes three types of tweens: Motion, Shape, and Classic. Classic is the old (pre-CS4) version of the Motion tween. Both Motion and Classic tweens interpolate frames based on the properties of a symbol instance (such as the instance's position on Stage). A Shape tween interpolates based on the points and curves of two vector shapes.

Tweens can be very useful, especially for moving objects around on Stage. However, tweens can sometimes appear mechanical and unnatural. There are circumstances in which point B should not reside immediately in between points A and C. For example, objects in real life have inertia, and they sometimes overshoot their destination before settling into position. If you get tween-happy, your audience may notice it. To avoid overapplication of any such effect, first precisely envision what you want your animation to look like, and then figure out how to realize the image in your head. This approach will prevent the software's tools from dictating your style.

Whereas tweening interpolates between poses, there is another method that requires the adjustment of poses on every frame. This technique is known as *stop motion*.

## Stop Motion

Stop-motion animation is roughly as old as (or slightly older than) hand-drawn animation. Stop-motion animation consists of arranging objects in front of a camera, snapping a photo, moving the objects slightly, and then snapping another photo. Each photo corresponds to a single frame in the animated sequence.

Stop motion most frequently involves clay (Claymation), puppets, felt, or construction paper. As basic as this technique is, it affords the animator endless conceptual creative license as well as an almost limitless choice of materials to use. The manipulation of actual physical objects often gives stop-motion animation a very tactile feel. Examples of stop-motion animation include *Robot Chicken*, *Gumby*, *Fantastic Mr. Fox*, and *Wallace and Gromit*.

The frame rate of stop-motion animation varies depending on the project. Stop motion can be extremely labor intensive, but it can also be a way to create animation on the cheap. By repositioning physical objects, you can avoid having to draw thousands of frames of action. Inexpensive animation is generally shot at 12 fps. Several popular stop-motion animations have been made on minimal budgets simply by the arrangement of cutout pieces of paper.

### Cutout animation

Animation produced by arranging cutout pieces of paper or fabric (or any flat object for that matter) is known as *cutout* animation. Since the rise of computer animation, cutout animation can now incorporate digital as well as physical objects. When executed correctly, cutout animation can be a very efficient way to bring your character to life.

In 1992, the pop culture phenomenon *South Park* was first conceived using cutout animation. The prototype incorporated real paper cutouts for a University of Colorado project by Matt Stone and Trey Parker. Since then,

**NOTES**

Terry Gilliam's animated sequences from the *Monty Python* series and films were made using cutout animation.

*South Park* has become a wildly popular television series with 14 seasons currently under its belt. Although *South Park* is now produced digitally (using Photoshop, Illustrator, and Maya), it maintains the simple cutout style of its roots. The success of shows like *South Park* has led to a proliferation of simply produced, cutout-style animation.

Cutout animation is an efficient and popular Flash animation technique. The use of symbols in Flash facilitates easy manipulation of discrete pieces of artwork. Symbols can easily be moved and scaled to quickly render new frames.

### Choosing a Technique

Now that you know the animation techniques available, let's consider how best to design your character in Flash. Your animation can be as simple or as complex as you want it to be. You can borrow from one style to simplify your animation and borrow from another to add an extra bit of nuance. Given Flash's great capacity for creating cutout-style animation using symbols, you'll focus on creating a character using this approach. However, you will also utilize tweening, as well as techniques from traditional animation, to create an entertaining but not overly labor-intensive character.

So, without further delay, let's dive in to the deep end of the Flash pool and examine how to conceptualize a character and bring it to life.

## Designing a Character

Years of creating visual content across a variety of media will teach any animator that successful design doesn't always follow a set of rules. This book focuses on designing characters for interactivity, and therefore some rules are necessary, but these rules should not become strict limitations. Keep your options open when you're starting to design your character. You can always narrow your focus later.

**CLOSE-UP**

**The Flash Animation Boom**

In the late 1990s, the Internet became the "wild west" for animators (cutout and traditional) thanks to a simple vector-based animation program called Flash. The first Flash-based animated series on the Internet was *The Goddamn George Liquor Program* by John Kricfalusi (creator of *Ren & Stimpy*). More Flash animation began to sprout across the Internet, such as the popular series *WhirlGirl*, which was also simultaneously televised on the cable network Showtime. The popularity of Flash on the Internet grew exponentially with *Happy Tree Friends*, *The Critic*, Joe Cartoon's *Frog in a Blender*, *Queer Duck*, and a handful of clever shorts by JibJab and the Brothers Chaps (*homestarrunner.com*).

Since then, Flash has continued to spread throughout the Internet and continues to expand its imprint on television. Some of the more noteworthy series to utilize Flash are *Home Movies*, *Mucha Lucha!*, *Xiao Xaio*, *Foster's Home for Imaginary Friends*, *Atomic Betty*, *Little Einsteins*, *Yin Yang Yo*, *Total Drama Island*, *Growing Up Creepy*, and *El Tigre*, to name just a few.

## Conceptualizing

Before putting pencil to paper, the first step is to decide the basic type of character you want to design. Is this character human, animal, insect, alien, or a hybrid of any combination of these categories? If this is a personal project, the sky is the limit. However, you may be creating a project for a client who has already provided a description. It is then up to you to translate that typically verbal information into a unique and tangible visual design.

The difference between good and bad character design can often be a simple matter of starting with a solid plan, even if it's just a mental plan. A good initial plan can prevent you from aimlessly sketching lines and shapes. In most cases, unplanned drawings result in a failure to create anything visually worthwhile.

On the other hand, the practice of drawing randomly (doodling) is the best way to hone your craft, even if it doesn't always end up producing something worthwhile or appealing. Good designers are always drawing, whenever time permits, and they always have a drawing pad and pencil nearby in the event there's two minutes or two hours to kill (**Figure 2.3**). When Chris worked for an animation production house, he used to always bring his pad and pencil into meetings, because doodling was usually a better use of time than taking notes. As is the case with athletes, artists must exercise their skills frequently to reach their full potential.

**Figure 2.3** Doodling is a great way to practice your craft.

Not all designers make good character artists. Additionally, the qualities that combine to generate a great character design can be very subjective. The most important aspect to any character should be its appeal. Good character design is a subtle balance between lines and shapes that are thoughtfully integrated to form a cohesive image. Some happy medium between random doodling and planned sketches will probably produce the best results. The act of doodling can take away the anxiety of a blank page and lead to a more planned and purposeful drawing. Continue to think and sketch until you have a solid character design.

*Cleaning up your sketches*

After your character design is solidified, you'll want to clear away any unnecessary lines or artifacts (either with an eraser or an application like Photoshop) that will not be part of your final version. You can then use this cleaned-up character design when you begin drawing in Flash. If your character is drawn on paper, you may want to convert it to a digital format before you begin working in Flash.

*Choosing a file format*

There's no best practice when it comes to the format to use when conceptualizing your characters. Some people prefer pencil and paper, whereas others like to remain entirely paperless and draw in programs such as Photoshop, Illustrator, or SketchBook Pro. You can also sketch directly in Flash using any of the drawing tools Flash has to offer. If you have drawings on paper that you'd like to use as the basis for a Flash character, you'll need a scanner to import your image as a digital file. Most scanners are paired with software that will make this process easy. Some of the more widely used graphic formats that Flash can import are PNG, GIF, JPEG, and TIFF.

When your cleaned-up character sketch is ready in digital format, you can begin constructing your character in Flash.

## Building a Character in Flash

Before rendering your character in Flash, consider how your character will need to move. Will your character be walking, running, flying, or falling at any point throughout the project? Optimization and efficiency are key elements for a web project that needs to load quickly and play smoothly. The more times an object can be reused, the more efficient the file will be.

After you import your sketch into Flash, you should consider how the character's features could best work as individual objects. This process depends ultimately on your style of animation and the style of your character. Efficient use of symbols will facilitate the production of cutout-style animation in Flash.

## Working with Symbols

Symbols are the building blocks of Flash. You can convert anything you draw or import into a symbol, and there's a good reason to do so: When an object is converted into a symbol, it automatically becomes an item in the Flash document's Library. Every Flash document has its own Library from which you can drag a symbol onto the Stage. When you do so, the object on the Stage is referred to as an *instance*. No matter how many instances of a symbol reside on the Stage, Flash only needs to load the source symbol once. This is how Flash delivers smoothly streaming animations while maintaining small file sizes. It's extremely efficient to reuse symbols as many times as possible. You can also apply effects such as Scale, Tint, Alpha, and Brightness to instances and apply Motion Tweens in combination with one or more effects without increasing file size.

When you convert artwork to a symbol, you have a choice of three possible symbol behaviors:

▶ **Movie Clip.** Movie Clips are dynamic, which means they can be targeted with ActionScript, the Flash programming language. They can have any number of layers and frames, but their Timelines are independent of all other Timelines. Movie Clips can have Blend Modes and Filters applied to them to achieve sophisticated effects. You will utilize Movie Clips in Chapters 3 and 5 to create custom effects and behaviors. Movie Clips can also be created dynamically at runtime and can also act as a container for other objects, such as external images.

▶ **Button.** Buttons have four states: Over, Up, Down, and Hit. These are represented as keyframes in a button symbol's Timeline. You can place graphics in any of these states and then apply ActionScript to the instance of a button to add interactivity to your Flash movie.

▶ **Graphic.** Graphic symbols are similar to Movie Clips except that they are not dynamic and cannot be targeted with ActionScript. Like Movie Clips, Graphic symbols can have any number of frames and layers. Graphics are useful, because their Timelines can be

**TIP**

If you are authoring content for video output, see the "Publishing for Broadcast" section in Chapter 5 for more details.

The act of manually moving the playhead back and forth on the Timeline is called *scrubbing*.

manipulated via the Properties panel. The most important feature of Graphic symbols is that they will always be in sync with parent (Graphic) Timelines and the main Timeline. This feature becomes crucial when you are creating frame-based animations, which is why most animators use Graphic symbols for fixed-frame output formats (such as video). Unlike animation within Movie Clip Timelines, animation nested inside Graphic symbols can be seen when the playhead is moved back and forth along the Timeline within the Flash authoring environment. The only drawback to Graphic symbols is that they do not support Blend Modes or Filters.

In this chapter, you will focus primarily on building a character using Graphic symbols. You will apply a technique known as *nesting* to easily manipulate the character on the Timeline.

### Nesting

The process of nesting involves placing a symbol instance inside another symbol's Timeline. This allows you to manipulate a symbol and all of its nested objects, or *children*, as a single object.

Flash animators and developers of all stripes lean heavily on the concept of nesting; thus, nesting will play a large role in the techniques covered in this chapter.

Here's a simple example of a character designed for cutout animation (**Figure 2.4**).

**Figure 2.4** This diagram shows a character with nested parts designed for cutout animation.

In Figure 2.4, image A shows the monster character as he will appear when the movie is rendered. Image B illustrates how the monster is broken into component parts. Image C shows how the component parts can be animated individually. Because all the parts are stored within a single symbol, the monster can be animated as a whole as well. The next section demonstrates the process of creating a character with nested parts.

### Building the Driver Character

The driver character pictured in **Figure 2.5** plays a small role in the Sausage Kong game introduced in Chapter 1. The driver appears after time has elapsed in the game, and he is only seen from the side while he is driving his truck and then when he is running across the Stage. Due to the character's limited movement, we only need to design a single view of the character.

**NOTES**

SketchBook Pro was used to create the initial sketches.

**CLOSE-UP**

#### Graphics Tablets

A graphics tablet is an input device that allows you to hand-draw images in a manner similar to that of using a pencil and paper. A graphics tablet has a flat surface on which to draw or trace an image using a stylus (a pen-like tool). Some tablets (the Wacom Cintiq, for example) have a built-in screen with which you can directly interact using the stylus. Tablets range from $50 to thousands of dollars (depending on the features) and are a worthwhile investment for any digital artist.

Figure 2.5 Concept sketches of the driver character.

### *Working with the imported sketch*

You'll use the sketch of the driver as a guide for your Flash artwork.

1. Choose File > New, (under the General heading) select ActionScript 3.0 at the left, and click OK to create a new document (**Figure 2.6** on the next page).

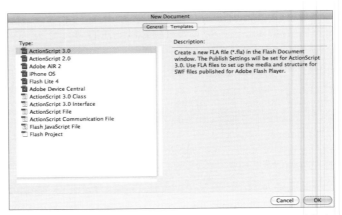

Figure 2.6  The New Document dialog box allows you to create a new blank document.

2. Save the file as **driver.fla**.

3. Choose File > Import > Import to Stage, locate the Chapter 2/assets/driver_sketch.tiff file on the accompanying CD, and click Open.

4. With the imported sketch selected, press the F8 key to convert the sketch to a Graphic symbol. Name the symbol **sketch**, and click OK.

Figure 2.7  Ensure that the height and width values are locked as you scale the sketch instance.

5. In the Position and Size area of the Properties panel, ensure that the chain link icon is unbroken so that width and height will be scaled proportionally, and change the W value to **550** (**Figure 2.7**).

6. Center the sketch on the Stage (**Figure 2.8**).

Figure 2.8  The sketch is now centered on Stage.

7. In the Color Effect area of the Properties panel, select Alpha from the Style menu and set the Alpha value to **30%** (**Figure 2.9**).

**Figure 2.9** The Alpha value settings will render the sketch partially transparent.

8. Rename the current layer **sketch**, lock the layer, and covert it to a guide by Ctrl-clicking/right-clicking and choosing Guide.

9. Create a new layer named **head** above the sketch layer.

10. Switch to the Brush tool and ensure that object drawing mode is turned off at the bottom of the toolbar. Using a black fill color, trace the outline of just the head shape. Make sure you overlap your drawing where the head meets the neckline of the body to avoid a gap appearing between them when you start animating later (**Figure 2.10**).

**Figure 2.10** The top of the head is outlined to match the rough sketch underneath.

**11.** Use the Selection tool and Properties panel to soften the black outline to a dark brownish tone (#BE984C), and use the Brush tool to close the neckline gap at the bottom with a line drawn using a lighter yellowish tone (#FFCC66) (**Figure 2.11**).

**Figure 2.11** The neck and head graphic outline drawn using Flash's Brush tool.

**12.** Use the Paint Bucket tool to fill in the head with the lighter tone (**Figure 2.12**).

**Figure 2.12** The completed head artwork.

**13.** Select the entire head artwork and press F8 to bring up the Convert to Symbol dialog box. Name your Graphic symbol **driver_head** and click OK (**Figure 2.13**).

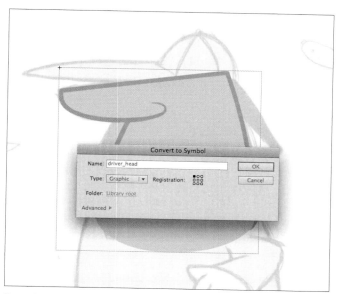

**Figure 2.13** Convert the head to a Graphic symbol.

**14.** Save your document.

The next step is to add the eye graphics.

### Drawing the driver's eye

You'll create three different objects: the shadow of the eye socket, the white of the eye, and the pupil.

**1.** In your driver.fla file, lock and hide your head layer, and create a new layer named **eye**.

**2.** Switch to the Oval tool, select the darker fill color (#BE984C) with no stroke, and draw a circle (**Figure 2.14**).

**Figure 2.14** The circle that will become the completed eye.

3. Because the top half of the driver's eye is designed in a way that it can't be seen, you'll cut the circle in half horizontally. Using the Selection tool, drag a marquee over the top half of the circle (**Figure 2.15**).

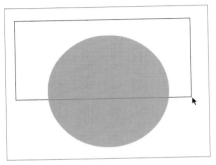

**Figure 2.15** Use the Selection tool to select the top half of the circle.

When you release the Selection tool, the upper half of the circle will be selected (**Figure 2.16**).

**Figure 2.16** The partially selected circle will appear with small dots to indicate the selected area.

4. Press the Delete key to remove the top half of the circle (**Figure 2.17**).

**Figure 2.17** The resulting semicircle.

5. Switch to the Free Transform tool, and rotate and scale the semicircle to fit the eye shape on the sketch (**Figure 2.18**).

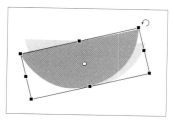

Figure 2.18 Use the Free Transform tool to rotate the semicircle.

TIP

For several of the steps in this section, if you require precision when adjusting shapes using the Selection or Free Transform tools, turn off snapping in the toolbar while making adjustments.

6. For the eyeball, copy the semicircle (Command+C/Ctrl+C) and paste a copy in place (Command+Shift+V/Ctrl+Shift+V). Scale down the new shape and replace the fill color with white (**Figure 2.19**).

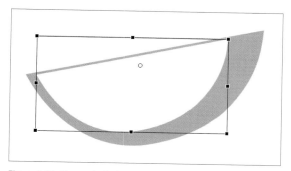

Figure 2.19 The eyeball shape is now in place.

7. Use the Brush tool (or the Oval tool) with a black fill to add a pupil (**Figure 2.20**).

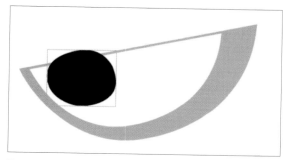

Figure 2.20 A pupil is added to the eye.

8. Turn the head layer visibility on. Select the eye layer and group the eye parts together (Command+G/Ctrl+G). Use the Free Transform tool to position and rotate the eye to fit on the head (**Figure 2.21**).

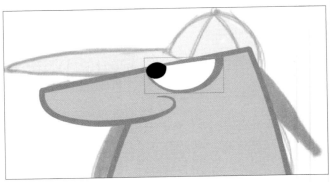

Figure 2.21 The completed eye is now in place.

Save your file, and let's get a cap on this fella!

### Drawing the driver's hat

The hat is drawn in a manner similar to the eye. You'll start with basic shapes and then manipulate them into something more complex.

1. Lock and hide all of your existing layers and create a new layer named **hat**.

2. Use the Oval tool to draw a circle with a light blue fill (#58A3ED) and no stroke (**Figure 2.22**).

Figure 2.22 The initial circle created with the Oval tool for the character's hat.

3. Use the Transform tool to squash the circle to a very thin oval (**Figure 2.23**).

**Figure 2.23** The squashed shape will form the brim of the hat.

4. Using the Selection tool, draw a marquee over the right half of the thin oval and press the Delete key (**Figure 2.24**).

**Figure 2.24** The hat now has a flat right edge.

5. Create a larger light blue circle, but this time select and delete the bottom half of the circle (**Figure 2.25**).

**Figure 2.25** The second shape with a flat bottom edge.

6. Use the Free Transform tool to stretch the current shape vertically (**Figure 2.26**).

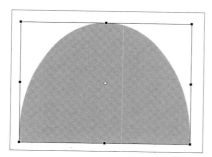

**Figure 2.26** The semicircle stretched vertically using the Free Transform tool.

7. Use the Selection tool to align the bottom edges and merge the two light blue shapes together. The end result should look like a hat with a brim (**Figure 2.27**).

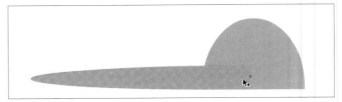

Figure 2.27 The driver's hat with a brim.

8. To add a two-tone color design to the hat, use the Rectangle tool to create a dark blue (#0066CC) rectangle inside the hat (**Figure 2.28**).

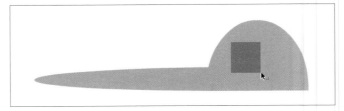

Figure 2.28 The first step in applying a two-tone color to the hat.

9. Switch to the Selection tool and make sure the Snap feature is on in the toolbar (**Figure 2.29**).

Figure 2.29 The Snap feature in the toolbar must be turned on.

10. Using the Selection tool, drag each corner so that the bottom edges (**Figure 2.30**) and the top edges (**Figure 2.31**) of the shape snap to the edges of the hat.

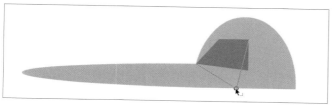

**Figure 2.30**  Use the Selection tool to snap the color patch to the bottom and left edges of the hat.

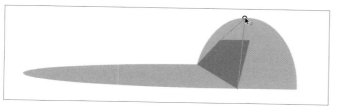

**Figure 2.31**  Use the Selection tool to snap the top of the shape to the edge of the hat.

**11.** Use the Paint Bucket tool to fill in the left edge (**Figure 2.32**).

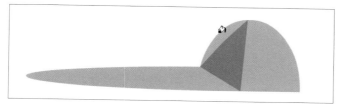

**TIP**

You may need to adjust the Gap Size of the Paint Bucket tool in the toolbar to avoid filling in the entire hat.

**Figure 2.32**  You can use the Paint Bucket tool to fill in the final piece of the dark blue shape.

**12.** Use the Selection tool to curve the right edge of the dark blue shape as if the hat were three-dimensional (**Figure 2.33**).

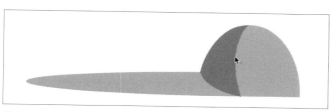

**Figure 2.33**  Use the Selection tool to curve the darker shape toward the edge of the hat.

**13.** Repeat the last several steps (8–12) to create a second dark blue area at the right side of the hat (**Figure 2.34**).

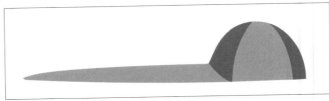

Figure 2.34  A second dark blue area is added to the hat.

**14.** To be consistent with the rest of the character's design style, use the Ink Bottle tool to add an extra dark blue (#004D9B) stroke to outline the entire hat (**Figure 2.35**).

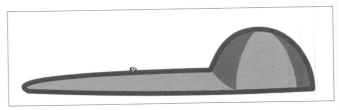

Figure 2.35  The completed hat artwork.

**TIP**

Hold the Shift key to constrain proportions when using the Free Transform tool.

**15.** Select the entire hat, group it together (Command+G/ Ctrl+G), unhide the sketch layer, and use the Free Transform tool to position and scale the hat so that it fits on the driver's head (**Figure 2.36**).

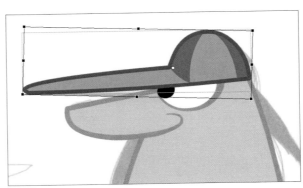

Figure 2.36  Use the Free Transform tool to make the hat appear as though it fits on the driver's head.

Looking good so far! It's time to add some facial hair.

### Drawing the driver's mustache and hair

The mustache, like the previous parts of the character, is initially drawn as a basic shape and then can be manipulated into more complex artwork.

1. Lock and hide your previous layers so that you can see only the sketch layer underneath. Create a new layer named **hair**.

2. Switch to the Rectangle tool with a black fill color and no stroke. Draw a rectangle in the area of the mustache (**Figure 2.37**).

**Figure 2.37** A simple rectangle is all that is needed to begin the mustache shape.

3. Use the Selection tool to pull the corners of the shape into the basic shape of the mustache in the original sketch (**Figure 2.38**).

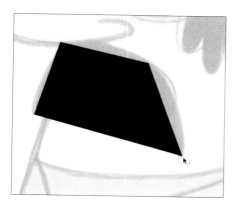

**Figure 2.38** The Selection tool is used to pull the mustache into its general shape.

4. Use the Selection tool to alter the edges of the shape to create rounded corners and curves (**Figure 2.39**).

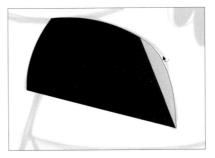

**Figure 2.39** The Selection tool is used to curve the edges of the shape.

5. Use the Selection tool to drag a selection at the bottom edge of the mustache shape (hint: Start your selection below the mustache and drag up) (**Figure 2.40**).

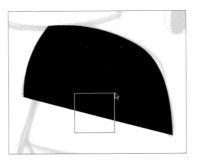

**Figure 2.40** The Selection tool is used to select a portion of the shape.

6. With this small section selected, press the Delete key (**Figure 2.41**).

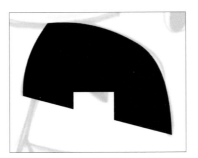

**Figure 2.41** A piece is now removed from the shape.

7. Use the Selection tool to pull the corners of the cutout piece to create the suggestion of points on the mustache.

8. Repeat the last few steps (5–7) to create as many individual points as you desire (**Figure 2.42**).

Figure 2.42  The mustache now contains a couple of points.

9. Use the Ink Bottle tool to add a dark grey (#333333) outline color to the mustache. You can then use the Brush tool (with the dark gray fill) to extend the outline in some areas to suggest a slight amount of depth (**Figure 2.43**).

Figure 2.43  The outlined mustache.

10. Select the entire mustache and choose Modify > Shape > Optimize. In the Optimize Curves dialog box, adjust the Optimization Strength to achieve as much optimization possible while retaining the integrity of the original drawing (**Figure 2.44**).

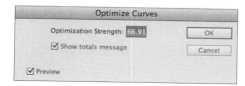

Figure 2.44  The Optimize Curves dialog box allows you to reduce the number of vector points needed to render the mustache.

11. Use the Selection tool to select the entire mustache shape and group it together (Command+G/Ctrl+G). Show your other layers and use the Free Transform tool to position and scale the mustache (**Figure 2.45**).

Figure 2.45  Place the mustache into position on the face.

12. Hide all layers except the hair and sketch layers. Use the Brush tool with a dark grey fill (#333333) to draw the outline of the driver's hair (**Figure 2.46**).

**Figure 2.46**  The outline of the driver's hair.

13. Use the Paint Bucket tool to fill the outline of the hair with black (**Figure 2.47**), and then select the entire shape and group it together.

**Figure 2.47** Fill in the hair outline with black.

**14.** Move the hat layer above the hair layer so that the hair appears underneath the hat.

**15.** Show all of your layers. Create a new layer named **grit**. On this layer, use the Brush tool to add some darker-colored (#BE984C) grit to this hard-working driver's face (**Figure 2.48**).

**Figure 2.48** The driver's face is completed with a little bit of grit.

**16.** Now that the facial features are complete, let's move all the elements into the driver_head symbol for easy manipulation later. Unlock all layers except the sketch layer. Select the frames in the grit, hat, hair, and eye layers that you created. Ctrl-click/right-click on the selected frames and choose Cut Frames.

**17.** Switch to the Selection tool, and double-click on the driver_head instance to edit the symbol.

18. Create a new layer, Ctrl-click/right-click on that layer's first frame, and choose Paste Frames.

19. With the artwork still selected, drag the set of features into place within the symbol. Note that your driver_head Timeline has retained the grit, hat, hair, and eye layers.

20. Return to the main Timeline by clicking Scene 1 at the top-left, and delete the empty layers. Your main Timeline should now have only a head layer and a sketch layer (**Figure 2.49**).

21. Save your document.

**Figure 2.49** The driver's head is now in one symbol, and the main Timeline is nice and clean.

Now that the driver's head is complete, you can start working on the rest of the body.

*Drawing the driver's torso*

The creation of the torso will begin in the same fashion as the previous elements.

1. Hide your head layer, and create a new layer above it named **body**.

2. Use the Rectangle tool to draw a shape with a blue fill (#0066CC) and no stroke that approximates the driver's body (**Figure 2.50**).

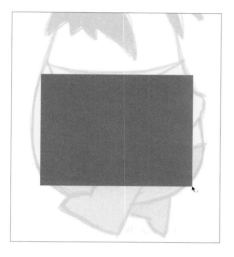

**Figure 2.50**  This rectangle will form the driver's body.

3. Use the Selection tool to pull each corner so that the rectangle more accurately resembles the size and shape of the body in the sketch (**Figure 2.51**).

**Figure 2.51**  The adjusted body shape.

4. Pull the sides to create curves that resemble the body in the sketch (**Figures 2.52** and **2.53**).

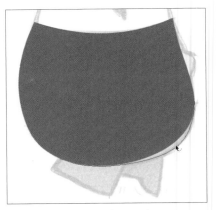

**Figure 2.52** Adjust the curves one at a time.

**Figure 2.53** Continue adjusting the curves until the shape matches the original sketch.

5. Draw a second rectangle with a light blue fill color (#58A3ED) inside the body shape. This will be the shirt collar (**Figure 2.54**).

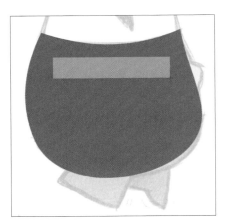

**Figure 2.54** The light blue rectangle will form the shirt collar.

6. With the Snap feature selected, use the Selection tool to snap the corner points of the collar shape to the corner points of the shirt shape. Bending the top edge of the collar shape will help make this easier (**Figure 2.55**).

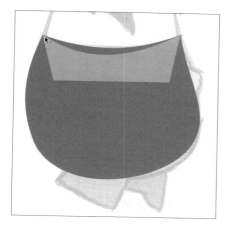

**Figure 2.55** Use the Selection tool to reshape the collar.

7. Continue bending edges, and use the Paint Bucket tool, if necessary, to fill in the top of the collar (**Figure 2.56**).

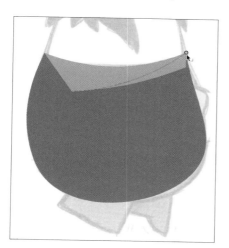

**Figure 2.56** The collar is flush with the top of the torso.

8. Bend the left edge of the collar shape inward so that it appears as though the collar is sitting on top of the shirt (**Figure 2.57**).

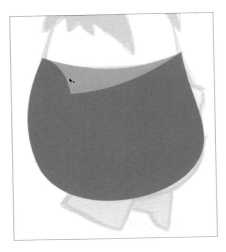

**Figure 2.57** The completed collar.

9. To create the pants, use the Selection tool to select the bottom third of the body shape (**Figure 2.58**).

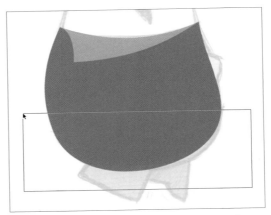

**Figure 2.58** Use the Selection tool to drag a rectangular selection at the bottom third of the torso.

**10.** With this area still selected, select a dark gray (**#333333**) fill color from the Properties panel (**Figure 2.59**).

**Figure 2.59** The driver's pants now sport a separate color.

**11.** Deselect all (Command+Shift+A/Ctrl+Shift+A), and then use the Selection tool to bend the shape where the two colors meet at the waist. This will suggest some volume to his torso (**Figure 2.60**).

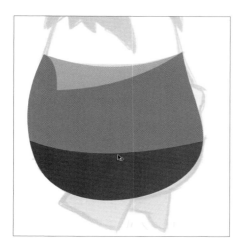

**Figure 2.60** The adjusted waistline.

**12.** Use the Ink Bottle tool to apply a dark blue (#004D9B) stroke to the shirt and a black (#000000) stroke to the pants. If necessary, select your stroke with the Selection tool and use the Properties panel to adjust its thickness (**Figure 2.61**).

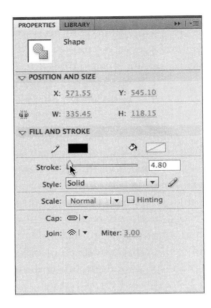

**Figure 2.61** You can adjust the width of the stroke in the Properties panel.

**13.** Add a dark blue stroke around the collar as well (**Figure 2.62**).

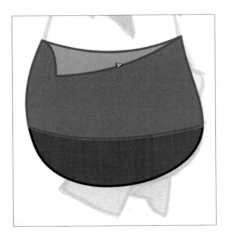

**Figure 2.62** The driver's torso and pants outlines are now complete.

**14.** Select the contents of the body layer and convert them to a single Graphic symbol (F8) named **driver_body**.

**15.** Show your head layer and reposition the body and head as necessary. The collar should be slightly wider than the head symbol to ensure that when the head moves, it remains behind the body symbol (**Figure 2.63**).

**Figure 2.63** The driver's collar is slightly wider than his face.

**16.** Save your document.

Now that you have the head and the body, only the extremities remain.

### Drawing the driver's limbs

A character's arms and legs are essential to creating the illusion that the character is walking or running. Thus, the corresponding artwork will require a bit of extra detail.

**1.** Hide the head and body layers to reveal the sketch underneath. Create a new layer named **arm**.

**2.** Use the Brush tool with a dark blue fill (#004D9B) to draw the outline of the sleeve (**Figure 2.64**).

**Figure 2.64** The outline of the sleeve drawn with the Brush tool.

3. Use the Brush tool with a dark skin fill (#BE984C) to draw the outline of the hand (**Figure 2.65**).

**Figure 2.65** The outline of the hand drawn with the Brush tool.

4. Switch to the light blue fill color (#0066CC) and draw a shoulder to close the sleeve (**Figure 2.66**).

**Figure 2.66** Gaps are removed along the outline of the shape in order to add the fill.

TIP

Normally, when designing a character, you might draw the arms in a relatively relaxed position. However, because this driver will be running, the character has been designed to be in a running pose from the start.

5. Use the Paint Bucket tool with the same blue color to fill the sleeve. Then use the Paint Bucket tool with the lighter skin color (#FFCC66) to fill the hand. (**Figure 2.67**).

**Figure 2.67** The completed arm.

6. Select the entire arm and convert it to a symbol named **driver_arm**.

You'll now create the two legs using a single symbol. The driver's leg and foot will be drawn as one object. In many cases the leg and foot are broken down into three parts: upper leg, lower leg, and foot (or shoe). This character is somewhat simple because his only tasks are to stand still and run.

1. Lock and hide the arm layer, and create a new layer above it named **front leg**.

2. Draw a rectangle with a dark gray fill (#333333) and no stroke to begin the leg shape (**Figure 2.68**).

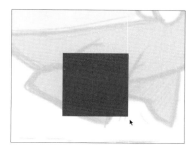

**Figure 2.68** The leg starts with a simple rectangle.

3. Using the Selection tool, pull the corners of the shape until it roughly resembles the shape in the sketch (**Figure 2.69**).

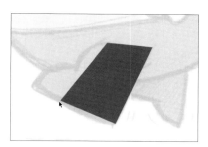

**Figure 2.69** Adjust the shape using the Selection tool.

4. Continue using the Selection tool to pull the edges of the shape to create contours that closely match the leg in the sketch (**Figure 2.70**).

**Figure 2.70** The contoured leg shape.

5. Draw a second, smaller rectangle for the foot (**Figure 2.71**).

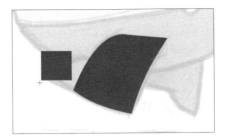

**Figure 2.71** The smaller rectangle will form the foot.

6. With the Snap feature on, use the Selection tool to snap the corner points to the leg and bend the edges to create the contours and curves that resemble the sketch (**Figure 2.72**).

**Figure 2.72** Use the Selection tool to reshape the foot.

7. Use the Ink Bottle tool to add a black stroke to the completed shape (**Figure 2.73**).

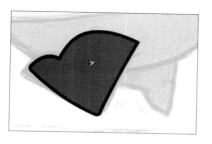

**Figure 2.73** The completed leg artwork.

8. Convert the entire leg to a Graphic symbol (F8) named **driver_leg**. Instead of drawing a second leg, you'll reuse the symbol you just created.

9. Copy your leg instance (Command+C/Ctrl+C), and create a new layer named **back leg** below the body layer. Paste (Command+V/Ctrl+V) the leg into your new layer and lock the front leg layer.

10. Use the Free Transform tool to rotate and position the back leg; you may want to make it slightly smaller to suggest perspective (**Figure 2.74**).

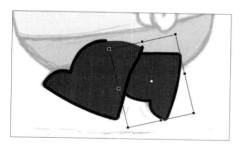

**Figure 2.74** The back leg in position.

11. In the Properties panel, in the Style menu under Color Effect, select Tint. Apply black as the tint color with a Tint value of about **33%** (**Figure 2.75**). This will darken the second leg slightly, pushing it back as if in shadow (**Figure 2.76**).

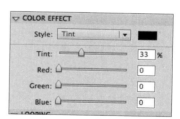

**Figure 2.75** Apply a tint via the Properties panel.

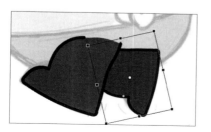

**Figure 2.76** The back leg with the tint applied.

Now you want to encapsulate your entire character (head, hat, eyes, mustache, hair, etc.) into a single symbol that can be moved and scaled as one object.

1. Select all of your frames (including the one on the sketch layer), Ctrl-click/right-click, and choose Cut Frames.

2. Choose Insert > New Symbol, and create a new Movie Clip symbol named **driver**.

3. Inside your new symbol, Ctrl-click/right-click on the first frame, and choose Paste Frames. All your layers should be intact (**Figure 2.77**).

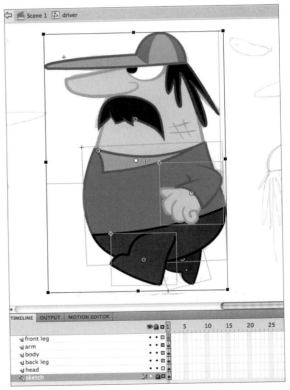

**Figure 2.77** All the driver's layers are now inside the driver symbol.

4. Create a new layer just above the sketch layer named **shadow**.

5. Use the Oval tool with a black fill (no stroke) mixed with about **20%** Alpha transparency to draw flattened oval.

6. Select the oval and convert it to a symbol named **driver_shadow** (**Figure 2.78**).

7. You can now hide your sketch layer, because you no longer need it, and return to the main Timeline by clicking Scene 1 at the top-left corner of your screen.

8. Create a new layer named **driver**, and drag an instance of the driver symbol from the Library onto the Stage. Delete all layers on your main Timeline except for the driver layer.

9. Save your document.

Congratulations! The driver character is complete and ready for animation (**Figure 2.79**).

**Figure 2.78** The shadow adds an extra bit of realism to the character.

**Figure 2.79** The final character, composed of individual symbols, is ready for animation.

Now that you're almost rolling, let's get that character prepped for animation.

## Animating a Character

Traditional cartoon characters typically share a common design thread: They have eyes, a nose, ears, hair, a mouth, a torso, arms, hands, legs, and feet. As much as all of these objects augment the visual appeal of a character, they also complicate the roles of the designer and animator. The animation workflow grows exponentially because of all these elements, and the animator can quickly feel overwhelmed before even having started. Character designs vary infinitely, which leads to an unlimited number of ways in which they can be *rigged* for animation.

The term *rigging* is used to describe the process of preparing and assembling assets for character animation into a virtual skeleton of sorts. There are a couple of different techniques that can be employed to rig a character in Flash. This section begins by showing you how to rig your character manually, which will facilitate small adjustments. Later in the chapter, you'll look at rigging objects with Flash's built-in skeleton system, the IK Bone tool. However you rig your character, the limbs should have joints that allow the character to move in an anatomically feasible manner.

Let's begin by rigging the driver character that you created in the previous section.

### Animating the Driver Character

The driver character's main task in the game is to run from his truck to a pile of sausages, pick them up, and throw them into the back of his truck. Then he runs back into his truck and drives away. Let's prep his joints for running.

### Creating joints

The first step is to hinge each body part so that it rotates appropriately. Using the Free Transform tool, you'll select each symbol and adjust the small white circle to the appropriate area.

1. Double-click on your driver symbol to enter symbol edit mode, and use the Free Transform tool to adjust the point of rotation for each leg symbol so that it will

hinge where the top of each leg meets the body. This center point becomes the character's hip (**Figure 2.80**).

Figure 2.80  The hip joint for the front leg.

2. Use the Free Transform tool to adjust the point of rotation for the arm. The arm symbol should hinge where it meets the body. This center point becomes the character's shoulder (**Figure 2.81**).

Figure 2.81  The shoulder joint for the arm.

3. Use the Free Transform tool to adjust the point of rotation for the head so that the head symbol hinges

where it meets the body. This center point becomes the character's neck (**Figure 2.82**).

Figure 2.82 The neck joint.

Now that your character is rigged, you can easily alter your character's poses.

### Creating the driver's run cycle

A run cycle (or walk cycle) is a loop of a stationary character performing running (or walking) movements. That cycle can then be played while the character is in motion. In Chapter 3 you'll learn how to make your character run at varying speeds using ActionScript.

The first step is to create a rough animatic sketch of the run cycle to use as a guide. You can draw your own animatic sketch or use the one provided in the Chapter 2/assets folder on the CD (**Figure 2.83**).

Figure 2.83 Frames from the sample animatic of the run cycle.

To create the animatic in Flash:

1. Open your driver.fla document and save it as **driver_run_cycle.fla**.

2. Double-click your driver instance on the Stage to edit the symbol.

3. Select frame 12 on every layer and extend the frames (F5) on those layers. You're aiming for a 12-frame run cycle.

4. Create a new layer at the top to house your animatic and name it **rough**.

5. Turn on the Onion Skin feature in the Timeline so that you'll be able to see the adjacent frames for reference as you draw. You can adjust the bracket-like Onion Skin handles at the top of the Timeline to control how many forward or backward frames appear.

6. Use the Brush tool to sketch how you imagine the driver might run frame by frame. Add a keyframe (F6 or F7 for a blank keyframe) for each frame as you go.

7. After using the first frame as a reference for position, you may want to hide all layers except the rough layer, so you can focus on the animatic.

8. As you keyframe each pose, play back the animation (Return/Enter) to make sure the drawings move the way you want them to. Continue to make any adjustments necessary. The key here is to animate the character running in place as if it is on a treadmill. This way you can place all the keyframes in a symbol and control the speed and direction of the character using either a Motion Tween or ActionScript.

**TIP**

You can use the Chapter 2/ assets/rough_animatic.fla file as a guide, or you can copy the frames and paste them into your driver_run_cycle.fla file.

When you're satisfied with how your animatic moves, you can apply the corresponding adjustments to the driver character.

1. Show the layers containing the driver's body parts. Double-click on the little color swatch to the right of the layer name ("rough") to open the Layer Properties panel (**Figure 2.84**).

Figure 2.84 Double-click on the outline toggle to open the Layer Properties panel.

Set the Outline color to red and make sure the "View layer as outlines" check box is selected (**Figure 2.85**).

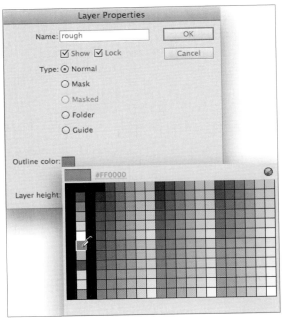

Figure 2.85 The Layer Properties panel allows you to change the outline color of a layer.

2. Ensure that your animatic overlaps the character on all 12 frames, and then hide all layers except for the rough and arm layers.

**3.** Using the outline of the rough animatic as a guide, rotate and position the arm symbol on each frame, adding all 12 keyframes (F6) as you progress (**Figure 2.86**).

**4.** If you want to go the extra mile on this character, you'll need to draw a few different arms as needed. There will be some frames where the arm might need to be slightly more bent at the elbow, and in other frames you may need a new arm that is in a slightly different perspective (**Figure 2.87**).

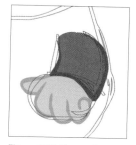

**Figure 2.86** Rotate the arm to match the rough animatic.

**Figure 2.87** A new, slimmer drawing of the arm was created to match the animatic.

You can also simply use the single arm symbol and then rely on the Free Transform tool to skew the perspective, but often it doesn't accomplish the same level of realism. In most cases, each drawing you make of the arm can be reused in other frames and will only require some rotation and repositioning.

You may have to draw new arms on some frames that have a slight bend to them and a little more foreshortening (**Figure 2.88**).

On other frames, the arm will need to be bent even more and positioned further back on the body (**Figure 2.89**).

**Figure 2.88** A more bent and foreshortened arm.

**Figure 2.89** An arm that is bent and pulled back.

When you've completed keyframing the arm layer and you're happy with the resulting motion, you can begin animating the legs.

1. The leg is animated in much the same way as the arm. Hide the arm layer, and unhide the front leg layer.

2. Use the rough animatic as a guide to position and draw (when necessary) each new keyframe so that the front leg is rendered appropriately (**Figure 2.90**).

**Figure 2.90** The front leg is rotated to match the animatic.

3. Similar to the arms, you may want to redraw some of the frames to match the animatic more accurately. The leg in this frame is descending downward toward the ground (**Figure 2.91**).

**Figure 2.91** A redrawn front leg.

4. When the leg is fully against the ground, you may want to redraw its bottom edge flat and wide to suggest weight (**Figure 2.92**).

**Figure 2.92** The flattened bottom of the foot suggests weight.

5. When the leg is starting to come up off the ground, you can emphasize this by drawing a bend so that the toe is still in contact with the ground while the heel is curved upward (**Figure 2.93**).

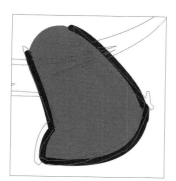

**Figure 2.93** The foot drawn as though the heel were lifting off the ground.

6. When the foot is completely off the ground, you can reuse the original leg shape (**Figure 2.94**).

**Figure 2.94** The leg returns appropriately to its original shape as the foot leaves the ground.

7. Bend the knee as the foot starts to move forward (**Figure 2.95**).

Figure 2.95 The knee is bent as the leg begins to move forward.

8. You can curve the arch of the heel as the leg is still moving forward to emphasize an upward direction (**Figure 2.96**).

Figure 2.96 The shape of the foot can indicate the direction in which the leg is traveling.

9. As the leg continues to move forward, you may want to rotate it so that the toe is pointing more forward in the direction of the run cycle (**Figure 2.97**).

Figure 2.97 The toe begins to point forward in the direction of the motion.

10. Straighten the leg out just before it begins its descent toward the ground again (**Figure 2.98**).

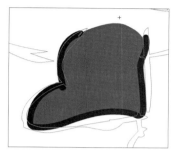

Figure 2.98 The leg is straightening out to touch the ground again.

Continue to hone the front leg until you're satisfied with the resulting animation.

In the following steps, you will nest your arm and leg animations in new symbols. Nesting these animated parts can allow for the layering of animations inside other animations to produce very sophisticated results. Once you nest the arm and leg animations in new symbols, you will easily be able to animate both symbols as single objects.

1. Select all the frames in the front leg layer, Ctrl-click/ right-click, and select Cut Frames (**Figure 2.99**).

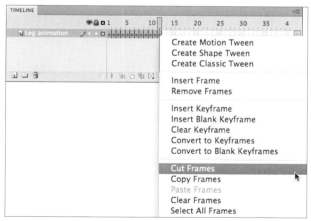

Figure 2.99 Cut all the frames of your animated leg.

**2.** In the Library panel, select New Symbol from the menu in the top-right corner (**Figure 2.100**).

Figure 2.100 Create a new symbol from the Library panel.

**3.** In the Create New Symbol panel, enter a descriptive name (e.g., **leg_ani**) and select Graphic from the Type menu (**Figure 2.101**).

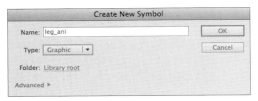

Figure 2.101 The Create New Symbol dialog box.

**4.** Ctrl-click/right-click on frame 1 of this new symbol and select Paste Frames (**Figure 2.102**).

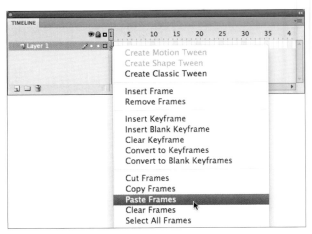

Figure 2.102 Select Paste Frames from the context menu.

**5.** Repeat steps 1–4 for the arm animation.

6. With both the arm and leg animations nested in their own symbols, drag the new animated symbols back into the original (arm and front leg) layers within the driver symbol and position them appropriately on the character's body. As individual symbols, the arm and leg animations are now much easier to animate (**Figure 2.103**).

**Figure 2.103** Position the nested animations to match the rough outlines.

7. Ctrl-click/right-click on the back leg symbol and select Swap Symbol. In the Swap Symbol dialog box, select the animated leg symbol and click OK. The updated instance should retain the rotation, scaling, and tint that you added previously.

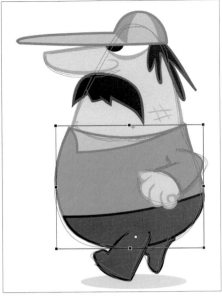

Figure 2.104 Scale, rotate, and position the body to match the animatic.

8. Set the First (frame) value in the Properties panel to **7** (and the Options to Loop) so that the back leg motion complements the front leg (i.e., they are six frames apart in a 12-frame loop).

9. Using the rough animatic as your guide, animate the driver's body by positioning and rotating his symbols on new keyframes to match the poses, just as you did with the arm and leg (**Figure 2.104**).

10. Match the head to the animatic positions as well, adding keyframes when needed (**Figure 2.105**).

11. Continue to make further adjustments as needed. When you adjust one piece, it may force you to adjust another piece to match (**Figure 2.106**).

12. Once you've finished animating the driver's component parts, return to the main Timeline and save your document. This document will be used later to animate the driver dynamically.

Figure 2.105 Scale, rotate, and position the head to match the animatic.

Figure 2.106 Continue to make adjustments using the Free Transform tool.

You'll now animate your driver's run using a Motion Tween.

1. Save a new copy of your document as **driver_animation.fla**.

2. Move the driver instance to the right edge of the Stage, Ctrl-click/right-click on the instance, and choose Create Motion Tween.

3. With the playhead on the last frame of the tween, move the driver to the left edge of the Stage.

4. In the Properties panel, change the Instance behavior to Graphic and press Return/Enter to preview your animation to see the driver run across the Stage (**Figure 2.107**).

**TIP**

If you want your character to run left to right, turn your character around by choosing Modify > Transform > Flip Horizontally before adding a tween.

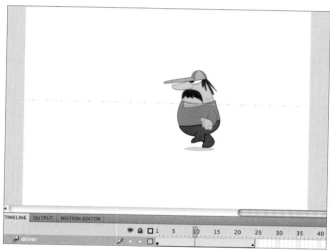

Figure 2.107 The driver runs across the main Timeline using a Motion Tween.

Adjust the frame duration of the driver layer as needed to match the tween speed with the driver's run cycle.

Congratulations! You have a fully animated character! Now that you know how to rig and animate your character by hand, let's look at *inverse kinematics.*

## Animating a Character with Inverse Kinematics

*Inverse kinematics* (IK) is a method for animating an object or set of objects in relation to each other using an articulated structure of *bones*. Bones allow symbol instances and shape objects to move in complex and naturalistic ways with a minimum of design effort. A system of bones created with IK in Flash is known as an *armature*. You can create armatures using several symbols or using a single shape. When you move a single bone, the connected bones move as if connected by joints. You'll use the Bone tool in the following exercises to create two different types of armatures.

### Creating an armature using symbols

Let's start by building a basic armature using symbols.

1. Choose File > New, (under the General heading) select ActionScript 3.0 at the left, and click OK.

2. Use the Rectangle tool to draw a rectangle on Stage with a solid fill (**Figure 2.108**).

Figure 2.108  A rectangle drawn on the Stage.

3. Convert the rectangle to a Graphic symbol (F8) named **segment**.

**4.** Drag four copies of your rectangle on Stage so that you have a line of five segments in a row (**Figure 2.109**).

Figure 2.109  The five instances of the segment symbol will be used to connect the "bones" of the armature you are about to create.

**5.** Switch to the Bone tool (**Figure 2.110**).

**6.** Click on the center of the leftmost segment instance, drag to the next segment, and release (**Figure 2.111**).

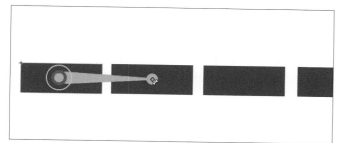

Figure 2.111  The first bone is drawn from the leftmost segment to its neighbor.

This creates the first bone in your armature.

**TIP**

Press the Option/Alt key to simultaneously drag and duplicate an element on the Stage.

Figure 2.110  The Bone tool can be found in the toolbar.

**NOTES**

When you apply the first bone to the first symbol in an armature, that symbol becomes the parent bone by default. All subsequent bones will be children of the parent bone.

7. Now drag from the second segment to the third and repeat until all the segments are joined (**Figure 2.112**).

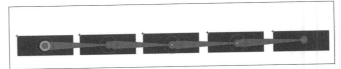

Figure 2.112 The completed armature.

You now have a complete armature.

8. Switch to the Selection tool and try dragging the right-most segment. Notice how the segments are linked like joints (**Figure 2.113**).

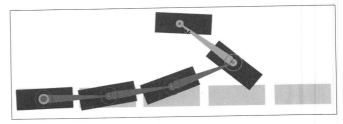

Figure 2.113 The manipulation of one segment can affect the entire armature.

You can quickly see how an armature could be useful in quickly rigging an animated character.

9. When you begin applying bones to your symbols, Flash will automatically move your artwork to a new Armature layer. Drag out the first frame of your Armature layer to frame 40 (**Figure 2.114**).

Figure 2.114 Drag the frame to extend the Armature layer's Timeline.

**10.** Reposition your Armature layer using the Selection tool (**Figure 2.115**).

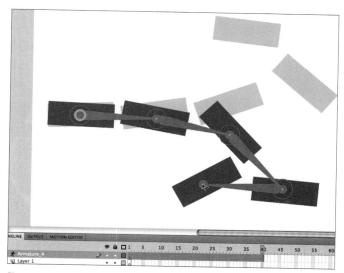

**Figure 2.115** Reposition the armature on frame 40.

**11.** Press Return/Enter to preview your animation on Stage.

Congratulations! You've just animated an armature! To apply this technique to a character, you would simply need to use your character's body parts rather than rectangles. In some cases, you may be able to rig a character's entire body as an armature. This will depend heavily on your character design. In most situations, you will exert more control over your character's poses if you rig your character's limbs separately (**Figure 2.116** on the next page). It's important to note that each piece of your armature serves as a joint, so in many cases, you'll need to create a dummy symbol to use as a handle at the end of your armature (as illustrated in Figure 2.116).

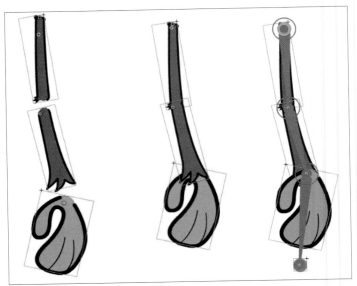

**Figure 2.116** An illustration of a monkey character's arm rigged using IK. The red circle symbol acts as a handle so that the hand can be manipulated.

Now that you can create an armature using symbols as segments, let's look at how to create a more fluid armature using a shape.

### Creating an armature using a shape

The Bone tool can also be used to create an armature entirely within a vector shape. This is a great way to animate and "morph" shapes. In this exercise, you'll create the beginning of a flexible limb from a plain rectangle.

1.  Choose File > New, select ActionScript 3.0 at the left, and click OK.

2.  Use the Rectangle tool to draw a long rectangle on Stage with a solid fill (**Figure 2.117**). Instead of converting your shape to a symbol, you'll jump right to creating an armature.

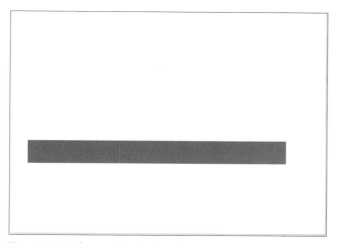

**Figure 2.117** A shape ready to be rigged.

**3.** Select the Bone tool. Start at the left side of your rectangle and draw several bones until you reach the right
side of your rectangle (**Figure 2.118**).

**Figure 2.118** A shape rigged as an armature.

**4.** Switch to the Selection tool and drag the right side of
your armature around the Stage. Notice how the shape
bends and deforms (**Figure 2.119**).

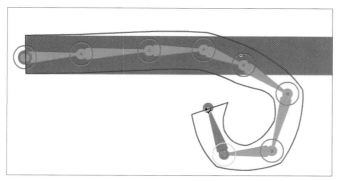

**Figure 2.119** You can deform and animate a shape using an armature.

You can now animate your shape armature just as you did with the segmented armature in the previous section.

Both IK rigging and the standard rigging demonstrated earlier in this chapter have their strengths. The speed at which an armature can be created makes IK great for prototypes and rough mockups. If you want absolute control of your character, you will likely want to rig your character and adjust each body part manually.

Now that you know how to get a character walking, let's get one talking, too!

## Adding Dialogue

Animation genres can vary as much as or more than live-action genres. Some animated projects focus entirely on depicting beautiful movement; others are driven almost entirely by dialogue. If you work on enough animated projects, chances are you'll need to work with dialogue at some point. The task of matching a character's dialogue to his/her/its mouth to create the illusion of speech is known as *lip syncing*.

### Lip Syncing

Lip syncing can be an extremely laborious process. Having dialogue in your scene almost guarantees you'll need to make adjustments on nearly every frame. On many projects, lip syncing consumes more time than any other task. Seeing the final result of your labor can be very rewarding, but while you're in the thick of it, you may feel like there's no end in sight.

The goal of the following exercises is to show you how to make lip syncing as painless as possible. Flash offers three common lip syncing methods. The first involves drawing a new mouth for your character on every frame to match (or sync) with your character's dialogue. This *frame-by-frame* method is arduous and pretty much self-explanatory. The second method involves creating several different mouth symbols and swapping an instance on Stage as needed to match the character's dialogue. This *swapping* method

**TIP**

See more examples of Flash IK armatures at www.cartoonsmart. com/inverse_kinematics.php5.

**TIP**

There are also tricks to minimize the amount of lip syncing needed—such as covering a character's mouth with a mask or drawing your character from behind. But use these tricks sparingly, or your audience will notice that you're taking shortcuts.

is a vast improvement over drawing each frame by hand (**Figure 2.120**). The third method employs different mouth shapes nested within a Graphic symbol. You'll focus your efforts on this *nesting* method.

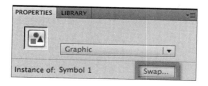

Figure 2.120 You can swap a selected instance to another symbol using the Properties panel.

A few years ago, when Chris worked at an animation studio, his team would often have two days to complete all the lip syncing for an entire 22-minute show. After having swapped symbols for thousands of frames, he sought a way to reduce the number of mouse clicks required to sync each frame. As a result of this search, the nesting method was born.

The nesting method is made possible by the attributes of a Graphic symbol (discussed previously in this chapter). By manipulating the First (frame) value in the Properties panel, you can control which frame of a Graphic symbol's Timeline is displayed. Thus, you can use a Graphic symbol as a repository for a certain category of artwork, and you can then access and display that artwork as you see fit from outside the symbol (usually on the main Timeline or whichever Timeline in which your symbol is nested). In this exercise, you'll create a symbol to hold all the different mouth shapes that you might apply to your character.

### Creating the mouth symbol

You'll create a simple character and sync the character's mouth to the words in an audio file. Even when your animation is extremely simple, good lip syncing (and good timing in general) can make for a convincing and compelling animation.

1. Choose File > New. In the New Document dialog box, switch to the Templates heading, choose Media Playback > Title Safe Area NTSC D1 (**Figure 2.121** on the next page), and click OK.

**TIP**

If you want to see simple characters animated masterfully, do a search for videos by Don Hertzfeldt.

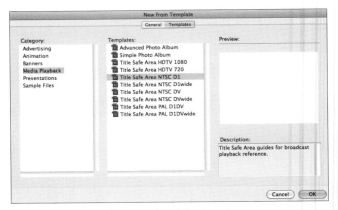

**Figure 2.121** The New from Template dialog box allows you to create a new document with a title safe area.

Your new document will already contain a title/action safe guide layer.

2. Save your document as **lipsync1.fla**.

3. In the Properties panel, set the FPS to **24**. The audio clip that you will import is short (~ 1 sec) and fast, so you'll use a high frame rate to more effectively sync the audio.

4. Select the first frame on the content layer and switch to the Brush tool.

5. Ensure that object drawing mode is turned on within the toolbar (**Figure 2.122**).

Object drawing mode converts your brush strokes into a distinct object. Object drawing mode is discussed at length in Chapter 4.

**Figure 2.122** Object drawing mode has been toggled on in the toolbar.

6. Choose a solid black fill in the Properties panel.

7. Draw a simple shape for your character's face (**Figure 2.123**).

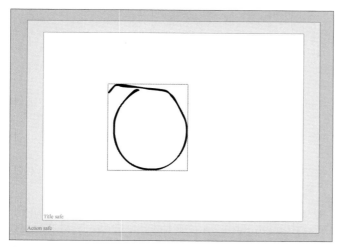

**Figure 2.123**  A simple oval for the character's face with a little wisp of hair at the top.

8. With the Brush tool still selected, draw two simple shapes for the character's eyes (**Figure 2.124**).

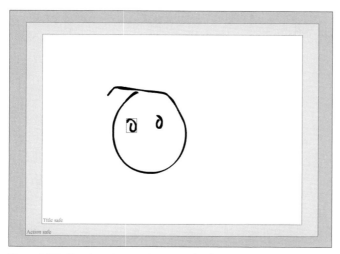

**Figure 2.124**  The character now has a couple of eyes.

9. Draw an open mouth for the character in the shape of a backwards "C" (**Figure 2.125**).

Figure 2.125 The character's mouth is now in place.

This shape will serve as the character's default mouth for now, but you'll create several more mouth shapes in a moment.

10. Switch to the Selection tool, click on the mouth (Shift-click if you need to select multiple parts), and convert the mouth into a symbol (F8).

11. In the Convert to Symbol dialog box, name the symbol **mouth**, choose Graphic from the Type menu, and make sure the registration point is in the center (**Figure 2.126**).

Figure 2.126 Convert your mouth shape to a Graphic symbol.

The center registration will serve as a guide so that each of the mouth shapes you create in the next section will be positioned appropriately on the face.

12. Save your document (File > Save).

Now that you have your file set up and your mouth in place, let's prep the mouth for some incoming audio.

### Populating the mouth shapes

A basic unit of sound is referred to as a *phoneme*. The mouth shape and facial contortions that correspond with vocalizing phonemes are known as *visemes*. Animators generally refer to phonemes and visemes interchangeably (even though they are technically different concepts).

There is a standard set of about six or seven phonemes/visemes (i.e., mouth shapes) that are sufficient to create the illusion of speech on an animated character. The basic shapes correspond to the following spoken sounds (**Figure 2.127**):

▶ *A* as in "cat" and "say," and *I* as in "kite" (same shape)

▶ *E* as in "street" or "trek"

▶ *O* as in "boat" and *U* as in "clue" (these two are sometimes separated)

▶ *F* and *V* as in "favor"

▶ *M* as in "might," *B* as in "back," and *P* as in "pass"

▶ *L* as in "laundry"

You can include more mouth shapes for specific sounds, but at some point, you will find that you reach a point of diminishing returns when you expend a lot of effort for small improvements. Ideally, you'll be able to find a balance where minimal effort meets maximal reward. On that note, it should be mentioned that simpler mouth shapes tend to work well because they're only onscreen for a fraction of a second. Simple shapes are also easier for the brain to process in the time available (1/24th of a second, in this case).

Now you'll draw the basic mouth shapes onto the mouth symbol's Timeline.

**1.** Double-click on your mouth symbol to edit its contents.

**2.** Select frame 2 and insert a blank keyframe (F7).

**3.** Switch on the Onion Skin feature at the bottom of the Timeline (**Figure 2.128**).

You should now see a light version of the content from the previous frame.

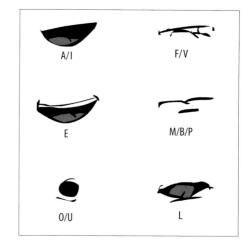

**Figure 2.127** Six mouth shapes that correspond to the most common phonemes.

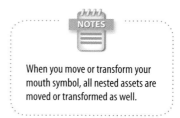

When you move or transform your mouth symbol, all nested assets are moved or transformed as well.

You may find it helpful to act out and exaggerate the different sounds as you're drawing them. Most animators have a mirror handy as well.

**Figure 2.128** The Onion Skin feature allows you to see faded versions of content on adjacent frames.

4. Switch to the Brush tool. Using the registration point (the crosshairs) and the onion skin as a guide, draw and position a mouth for an "ah" sound on frame 2 (**Figure 2.129**).

**Figure 2.129** The "ah" mouth shape on frame 2.

5. Insert a blank keyframe (F7) at frame 3 and draw a mouth shape to match an "eh" sound (**Figure 2.130**).

**Figure 2.130** The "eh" mouth shape on frame 3.

6. Insert a blank keyframe at frame 4 and draw a shape to match an "oh" sound (**Figure 2.131**).

**Figure 2.131** The "oh" mouth shape on frame 4.

This frame will double as "oh" and "ooh" since they are reasonably similar.

**7.** Insert a blank keyframe at frame 5 and draw a mouth that looks like your character is biting his/her lip for an f/v sound (**Figure 2.132**).

**Figure 2.132** The f/v mouth shape on frame 5.

**8.** Insert a blank keyframe at frame 6 and draw a mouth that looks like the character is forming an "m," "b," or "p" sound (**Figure 2.133**).

**Figure 2.133** The m/b/p mouth shape on frame 6.

**9.** Insert a blank keyframe on frame 7 and draw a closed mouth (**Figure 2.134**).

**Figure 2.134** The closed (neutral) mouth shape on frame 7.

The closed mouth will be useful for separating words when syncing your mouth shapes to the audio.

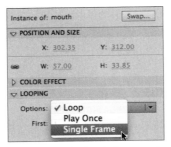

**Figure 2.135** The Single Frame option ensures that the Graphic symbol remains on a single frame.

**10.** Turn off the Onion Skin feature, and then return to the main Timeline by clicking the Scene 1 button at the top-left corner of the Stage.

**11.** Select only the mouth symbol instance on Stage. In the Looping section of the Properties panel, click the Options menu and choose Single Frame (**Figure 2.135**).

The Single Frame option instructs your symbol's Timeline to stay put rather than Play Once or Loop (play multiple times). You'll want your mouth symbol to stay on the frame you've assigned until you create a new keyframe for a different mouth shape.

**12.** Ctrl-click/right-click on the mouth symbol and choose Distribute to Layers (**Figure 2.136**). This will move the mouth symbol to its own named layer (**Figure 2.137**).

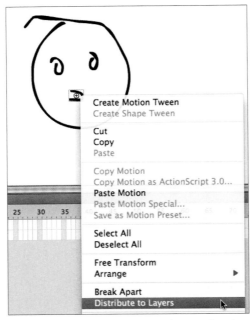

**Figure 2.136** The Distribute to Layers feature is found in the context menu.

**Figure 2.137** The mouth now has its own named layer.

**13.** Save your document.

Now that your mouth symbol is ready to go, it's time to bring in some audio.

*Importing the audio*

You'll import a short audio clip to whet your lip syncing appetite. This short clip, voiced by John Smick (talented writer, voice actor, and all-around funny guy), will give you a good sense of just how much effort can go into a single second of lip syncing.

1. In your lipsync1.fla document, choose File > Import > Import to Library (**Figure 2.138**).

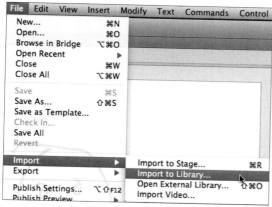

Figure 2.138  The Import to Library option lets you bring in external assets like audio files.

2. Using the Import to Library window, navigate to the Chapter 2/assets folder on the CD, select the Are you kidding me.wav file, and click Open.

3. Create a new layer. Double-click on the layer name and change it to **audio**.

4. Lock all the layers except the mouth layer.

5. Select frame 30 on all four layers and press F5 to extend each layer to frame 30. This will make room for the audio track on the Timeline.

6. Select frame 5 of your audio layer and add a new keyframe (F6). You'll start the audio on this frame to provide a lead-in before the character begins speaking.

Recall from Chapter 1 that you can adjust the height of your audio layer to get a better look at the waveform as you're lip syncing.

7. With frame 5 selected, in the Sound section of the Properties panel, click the Name menu and choose the Are you kidding me.wav sound (**Figure 2.139**).

Figure 2.139 The Properties panel allows you to assign a sound item to a keyframe.

8. Still in the Properties panel, set the Sync to Stream (**Figure 2.140**).

Figure 2.140 The Stream setting allows you to sync your mouth shapes to the audio.

Now that your sound is configured to Stream, you'll be able to match the audio to the mouth shapes you've created. You should now see your audio's waveform on the Timeline (**Figure 2.141**).

Figure 2.141 The waveform is displayed on the audio layer.

9. Add a keyframe (F6) to frame 5 of your mouth layer. You will begin syncing on this frame in the next exercise.

10. Save your current document (File > Save As) as **lipsync2.fla**.

With your audio in place and your mouth symbol ready to go, your character is ready to start jabbering.

*Using the nesting method*

Lip syncing is an art form. The process of matching sounds to shapes can be somewhat subjective. In the end, two things matter: the successful illusion of speech and the toll that it took on the animator. In the steps that follow, you'll get a taste of both.

As mentioned earlier, the method described here involves nesting mouth shapes inside a single symbol and then adjusting the shape that the symbol displays on a given frame.

**1.** Save your current document (File > Save As) as **lipsync3.fla**. This will keep lipsync2.fla clean so that you can apply another lip syncing technique in a moment.

**2.** Turn on your computer speakers and ensure that Muted Sounds (Control > Muted Sounds) is not selected (so that you can hear the audio on the Timeline).

**3.** Move the playhead to frame 5. Drag (*scrub*) the playhead from frame 5 to frame 6. You should barely hear the beginning of the word "are." This means that you'll want to use the "ah" mouth shape for frame 5.

**4.** Move the playhead to frame 5 and use the Selection tool to select the mouth instance on the Stage.

**5.** Recall that the "ah" mouth shape was on frame 2 of your mouth symbol. In the Properties panel, under Looping, update the First (as in first frame shown) field to a value of **2** and press Return/Enter (**Figure 2.142**).

**TIP**

Due to the short length of each phoneme, it can be difficult to identify individual sounds using a single frame. You may want to scrub multiple frames or preview the entire Timeline (Return/Enter) to put the sound in context. This process gets easier with practice.

**Figure 2.142** You can change the frame that is currently being displayed in the Properties panel.

Your symbol should now be displaying the "ah" shape on Stage (**Figure 2.143**).

**6.** Scrub from frame 6 to frame 7. It sounds a bit like the word "are" is already ending. You can press

**Figure 2.143** The mouth shape has been updated on Stage.

Return/Enter to preview the entire sound in context. The word "you" seems to already be starting on frame 7. So, move the playhead to frame 6, select the mouth on the Stage, and update the First value in the Properties panel to **7** (the closed mouth). This frame will separate the words "are" and "you."

7. Because you already know frame 7 is the start of "you," select the closed mouth on frame 7 and update the First value to **4** (the "oh" and "ooh" shape).

8. Continue scrubbing each frame and updating the First value until you run out of audio to sync.

9. Preview what you've done by pressing Return/Enter. If something doesn't look right, try to locate the keyframe that appears out of sync and try a different mouth shape. Lip syncing is a skill that takes practice.

10. Close Flash entirely before continuing to the next section.

Now that you've done the lip syncing manually using this technique, let's add an extension to make this technique even better.

### Using the FrameSync extension

FrameSync is a free Flash extension developed by Justin to speed up the lip sync workflow. It is largely based on Chris's lip sync technique covered in the previous section.

1. Locate the FrameSync.mxp file in the Extensions folder on the CD included with this book, or download the file from http://ajarproductions.com/blog/?p=45.

2. Install the extension by double-clicking on the FrameSync.mxp file, and follow the Extension Manager CS5 install instructions.

3. When you've completed the install, reopen Flash.

4. Open the lipsync2.fla file that you saved earlier and save a new copy as **lipsync4.fla**. The mouth layer in this file should only have a keyframe on frame 1.

TIP

To see video of Chris lip syncing using the nesting method, check out www.adobe.com/devnet/flash/articles/lipsync_macrochat.html.

NOTES

Finished lip sync files are on the included CD for reference.

TIP

You'll learn how to build your own Flash extensions in Chapter 4.

5. Open the FrameSync panel by choosing Window >
   Other Panels > FrameSync (**Figure 2.144**).

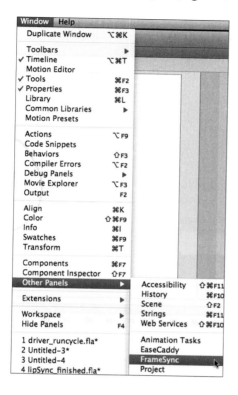

Figure 2.144 The
FrameSync exten-
sion is found within
the Window > Other
Panels menu.

The FrameSync panel should now be displayed within
Flash (**Figure 2.145**).

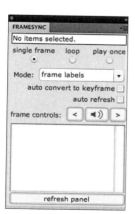

Figure 2.145 The FrameSync panel is
now open for business.

**TIP**

If you want to refresh the panel manually, you can click the Refresh Panel button at the bottom of the FrameSync panel.

**TIP**

You can expand the FrameSync panel as needed to display all your mouth symbol frames without scrolling.

Figure 2.148 The mouth shape has been updated on the FrameSync panel.

6. Select the "auto refresh" check box within the Frame-Sync panel (**Figure 2.146**).

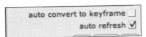

Figure 2.146 Turn on the auto refresh option.

The auto refresh setting automatically checks to see if your selection on Stage has changed. You can deselect this check box when you're not using the FrameSync panel.

7. Update the Mode in the FrameSync panel to keyframes and select your symbol. You should now see all the frame numbers from within your mouth symbol listed in the FrameSync panel (**Figure 2.147**).

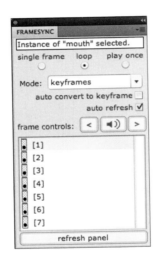

Figure 2.147 The FrameSync panel lists the mouth keyframe numbers.

8. Add a keyframe (F6) on frame 5 of the mouth layer to begin lip syncing.

9. Click on the [5] item in the FrameSync panel and notice that your mouth symbol is now displaying the f/v mouth shape from frame 5 (**Figure 2.148**).

This feature prevents you from having to highlight the frame number in the Properties panel, type a new number, and press Return/Enter. You can accomplish the same task with a single click.

**10.** Normally, you'd have to scrub the Timeline to hear the audio. Click the button that looks like a speaker in the frame controls section of the FrameSync panel (**Figure 2.149**).

You should hear the audio from the current frame, just as if you'd scrubbed the playhead.

**11.** Select [2] in the FrameSync panel to set frame 5 to the "ah" mouth shape. Use the next frame (>) button in the FrameSync panel to navigate to the next frame.

**12.** Select the "auto convert to keyframe" check box to have FrameSync automatically create new keyframes for you when you change mouth shapes (within the FrameSync panel) on a new frame (**Figure 2.150**).

**13.** Click the Play Audio button to hear the audio on frame 6. Remember that this is the frame between "are" and "you" in the audio. Select [7] to set this frame to a new mouth position. Note that a new keyframe has automatically been created on frame 7.

**14.** Now that you're getting an idea of how much time FrameSync can save you, save your current document and close it. There's one more important FrameSync feature to try out.

**Figure 2.149** The Play Audio button in the frame controls allows you to play the current frame's audio from the FrameSync panel.

**Figure 2.150** The "auto convert to keyframe" setting automatically creates new keyframes for you.

So far, FrameSync has reduced the number of clicks needed to lip sync to a bare minimum. But it's still up to you to keep track of which mouth shapes correspond to which frame numbers (which gets slower as you get more tired after hours of lip syncing). Remembering the frame numbers gets easier if you do a lot of lip syncing, and if you use the same frame numbers across all of your characters' mouths. But FrameSync can relieve you of the need to memorize frame numbers entirely.

**1.** Reopen lipsync2.fla (the clean file) and save it as **lipsync_labels.fla**.

**2.** Double-click the mouth symbol on Stage to edit it.

**3.** Within the mouth symbol's Timeline, create a new layer named **labels**.

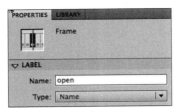

Figure 2.151 Add a frame label using the Properties panel.

4. Lock the labels layer.

5. Select the first keyframe of the labels layer. In the Properties panel, add a label Name of **open** (**Figure 2.151**).

6. Select the second frame in the labels layer and create a blank keyframe (F7). Give this keyframe a label of **ai**, since this frame's shape can be used for "ah" and "ai" sounds.

7. Repeat the previous step so that frames 3, 4, 5, 6, and 7 have values of **eh**, **oh**, **fv**, **mbp**, and **closed**, respectively (**Figure 2.152**).

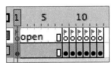

Figure 2.152 Each mouth shape now has a corresponding label (as indicated by the red flags on the frames).

8. Optionally, you can select a frame on both the label and artwork ("Layer 1") layers (**Figure 2.153**) and add frames (F5) until the label is readable on the Timeline.

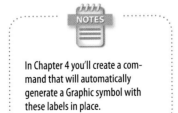

Figure 2.153 Be sure to select the frame on both the artwork and label layers before adding frames; otherwise, the label and the mouth shape will end up on different frames.

Repeat this step with each label/shape so that you can read every label on the Timeline (**Figure 2.154**).

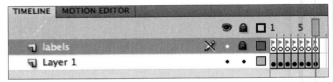

Figure 2.154 Every label is now readable on the Timeline.

9. Return to the main Timeline by clicking Scene 1 in the top-left corner.

**NOTES**

In Chapter 4 you'll create a command that will automatically generate a Graphic symbol with these labels in place.

**10.** In the FrameSync panel, switch the Mode to frame labels. You should now see your labels in the FrameSync panel (**Figure 2.155**).

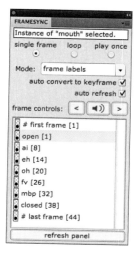

Figure 2.155 FrameSync displays the mouth symbol's frame labels so you don't have to memorize the frame numbers.

**TIP**

Warren Fuller, aka Animonger, also has a great extension for lip syncing called *AnimSlider*. A free version of AnimSlider and a couple of commercial versions are available at www.animonger.com/flashtools.html.

No more need to memorize frame numbers!

**CLOSE-UP**

### SmartMouth Extension

Justin also has a new lip syncing extension in the works called *SmartMouth* (**Figure 2.156**). In the SmartMouth dialog box, you can input your mouth shapes (as symbols, frame numbers, or frame labels) for the common phonemes, and SmartMouth will analyze your audio and place your mouth shapes right on the Timeline! SmartMouth is not meant to replace the animator. You'll still have to make some adjustments by hand, but it should be a huge time-saver. The extension will probably cost about $45 for a single license. Check http://blog.ajarproductions.com for details on when SmartMouth will be released.

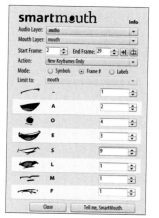

Figure 2.156 A preview of the SmartMouth extension interface.

The lip sync techniques demonstrated can also be used to animate other facial features and body parts. They can be particularly useful for animating eyes (**Figure 2.157**).

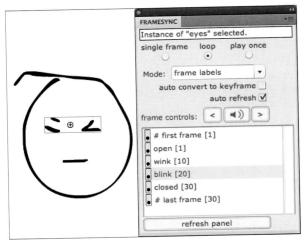

**Figure 2.157** The FrameSync extension can be used to sync other parts (like eyes).

Now that you have a solid foundation in animating your character on the Timeline, Chapter 3 will illustrate how to animate your character with ActionScript. You'll also learn how to create some powerful effects for the world that your character might inhabit.

# 3

# Introduction to ActionScript Classes

**F**lash is a powerful tool for Timeline animation. Over the last several product releases, Flash has also become a powerful application development tool. ActionScript is the scripting language that has allowed Flash users to add interactivity to their Flash movies. With the introduction of ActionScript 3.0, a world of possibilities has opened up for Flash users, bu t as the ActionScript language has matured, the barrier to entry has jumped significantly for users who are new to coding.

This chapter is not a comprehensive guide to using ActionScript. We assume that you have some basic familiarity with ActionScript. If you're entirely new to ActionScript, you may also want to read *Adobe Flash Professional CS5 Classroom in a Book* (Peachpit, 2010) or *ActionScript 3.0 for Adobe Flash Professional CS5 Classroom in a Book* (Peachpit, 2010). You'll only delve into the world of programming as far as is useful for an animator. Learning about complex data structures and number crunching is not generally useful to an animator, but knowing just enough ActionScript to create a fantastic visual effect or to move your character around the Stage is fair game for an animator's toolbox. Because an animator isn't likely to open the Code Editor and just start typing, this chapter will focus on augmenting Timeline elements with ActionScript.

The goals for this chapter include:

► Demystify ActionScript classes

► Take advantage of tools and techniques normally reserved for programmers

► Write code that can be reused in multiple projects

► Balance best programming practices with what's useful for an animator

► Create powerful visual effects by combining Action-Script with Timeline animation

Before diving into any ActionScript code, let's first examine when you might want to use ActionScript.

## Reasons to Use ActionScript

Flash is a tool. Much like a hammer, Flash can be used in different ways and for various purposes. If your job is to drive nails, the blunt end of the hammer may be all you require. On the other hand, if you find it necessary to remove a nail from time to time, you may want to learn how to use the other end of the hammer.

The distinction between the two ends of Flash (Action-Script and Timeline animation) is less clearly defined than the two ends of a hammer. Visual elements and code elements can live happily together inside Flash, and from the point of view of the person interacting with your Flash movie, it may not be clear which is which.

Deciding when you need ActionScript for your animation can be tricky and should be considered early in the planning stage of your project (see the next section). Here are a few reasons to use ActionScript instead of Timeline animation alone:

► The intended effect cannot be accomplished with Timeline animation.

► It takes less time to accomplish the effect with ActionScript.

► The ActionScript effect is easier to reuse.

► The ActionScript effect has already been developed.

▶ The ActionScript effect is more flexible in the event that there are changes.

▶ User interactivity is required.

ActionScript might seem complex at first. But after you endure the initial complexity at the core of ActionScript concepts, you will have extraordinary power at your fingertips. The more you learn, the more you can put to use. This chapter introduces you to one of the fundamental building blocks of ActionScript 3.0, *classes.* Before getting into the specifics of ActionScript classes, let's go over factors to consider prior to starting your project.

## The Importance of Planning

*The mere formulation of a problem is far more often essential than its solution, which may be merely a matter of mathematical or experimental skill.*

—Albert Einstein

*By failing to prepare, you are preparing to fail.*

—Benjamin Franklin

Good planning is an important part of a successful Action-Script project. Further, good planning is important for any successful Flash project. One measure of success is the quality of the final product. But success can also be measured by the ease of the process that led to the final product. Was the project a last-minute scramble? Could the stress of the project have been lessened? Changes happen in all projects, so it is the savvy Flash user who builds flexibility into a project.

You can't plan for every possible scenario. So, part of the planning process is to determine which aspects of the project are likely to change. If you're planning a character's walk cycle, one predictable change will be the character's position in space. Therefore, it makes sense to have all the appendages and moving parts of the character nested into one symbol so the entire character can be moved to simulate walking. If you animated your character's moving parts on the main Timeline and then realized that you needed to move everything into a symbol, it could be a bit of a headache trying to copy everything and move it into a new symbol.

Here are some factors to consider before even opening Flash:

▶ What does the movie need to achieve? Will it require user interaction?

▶ What are the likely output formats? Web? Broadcast? Mobile? How will these affect the color palette?

▶ Is file size an issue?

▶ For larger projects, can the project be broken into smaller, more manageable pieces?

▶ Is this project likely to require future updates? What's feasible to build now versus over the lifetime of the project?

▶ What can be reused from this project for future projects?

▶ What can be reused from past projects for this project?

If you spend the proper time and energy during the planning stage of a project, the beginning of your project will be the slowest part. Ideally, after this initially slow start to your project, your work will get progressively smoother as you approach the end of the project, because you have thought through likely changes and problem areas, and planned accordingly.

The planning process also helps to reveal any areas of the project that require more attention. These are areas where you may not be sure if such a task is even possible in Flash or if it is possible to implement without someone else's assistance. Once you have identified these areas, you can build specific tests.

Consider this situation: Suppose a client has asked you to design a simple Flash application that includes an accurate stopwatch. You've never built a stopwatch before, but it's a relatively small part of the application and you feel quite comfortable with everything else that the client has requested of you. Rather than building everything else first and waiting until the night before the project is due (when you may find out you need to contact a more experienced Flash developer for help), try building a prototype of the stopwatch before you start any other part of the project. If you find that you need help, you'll have plenty of time to locate a resource. If you find that the stopwatch is no problem for you to build, you can proceed with confidence knowing that the hardest part of your project is done. Also, since you built the stopwatch independently from the rest of your project, it will likely be easier to apply to future projects, because it doesn't rely on anything specific about the current project to function.

The more independent the working parts of your Flash project are, the more they are considered to be *modular*. Modularity allows the parts of your movie to be easily reused and recombined to serve different purposes. Modular design is the first step toward reusability. When deciding which pieces of your project should be modular, you will have to weigh the costs and benefits. Modular parts generally take a little longer to develop. However, when you need to make a change to a part of your project that you've built to be flexible, the change will be so painless that the extra initial development time will have been well worth it.

A solid building requires a solid foundation. The planning process described in this section is about designing the foundation for your Flash project, even when what will go on top of that foundation is somewhat uncertain. Consider this scenario: You're laying the foundation for a house, and you don't know if the room on the east side will be a study or a garage, but you have a deadline nonetheless. To move forward with your task, you wire the room so that it could become a study or a garage. In your Flash project, it will be up to you to decide which components need to be flexible. Think about how these choices will affect the project's foundation and what can potentially be built on top of that foundation.

Now, on to the nuts and bolts! Let's starting talking about ActionScript.

## ActionScript Basics

The basic unit of ActionScript is an *object*. The process of creating a new object is called *instantiation* because it involves creating a new *instance* of an object. Flash objects can be visible entities like symbol instances on the Stage, or they can be abstract containers for data. Instantiating a new object in ActionScript is not unlike dragging a new instance of a symbol from the Library to the Flash Stage (**Figure 3.1**).

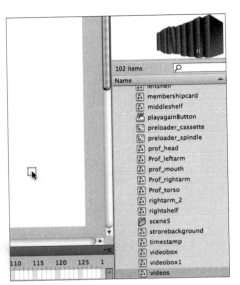

Classes, like symbols, provide reusable material for objects that can be made into as many instances as you need.

**Figure 3.1** Dragging a symbol from the Library to the Stage will create a new instance of the symbol.

### What Is a Class?

Every object instance in Flash has an associated class. A class is a description of methods and properties that serves as a blueprint for how instances should behave. All Action-Script instances are tied to their class the way all symbol instances on the Flash Stage are tied to their Library item. When a change is applied to a class, it affects all instances of that class.

The purpose of a class is determined by its methods and properties. The methods found in a class describe what the class does. Methods are generally associated with actions, such as go, find, hide, jump, and so on. The properties of a class describe characteristics that the class possesses. Properties are generally associated with attributes or features, such as visible, height, position, color, and so on. Some properties can have new values assigned to them, and some properties cannot be changed. Properties that cannot be changed are referred to as *read-only*.

The *Object* class is actually the most basic class in Action-Script. All classes *inherit* their basic methods and properties from the generic Object class. Inheritance is the mechanism that allows for the reuse of behaviors and traits (methods and properties) without writing new code.

You may remember a chart from Biology class that showed single-celled organisms (like protozoa) from billions of years ago at one end and complex multicellular organisms (like humans) of our contemporary age at the other. The progression from simple to complex occurred because nature tended to (and needed to) solve basic problems of survival and reproduction before tackling something as complex as the human eye. At the same time, complex organisms still benefit from the early mechanisms developed in protozoa. The Object class is much like the protozoa—simple, basic, and tackles the most essential problems only.

On the other end of the complexity spectrum, the MovieClip class is responsible for much of what is seen in Flash. The MovieClip class is much more complex than the Object class because it is the result of a much longer chain of inheritance—MovieClip > Sprite > DisplayObjectContainer > InteractiveObject > DisplayObject > EventDispatcher > Object.

Observe the trend from general to specific within the MovieClip's inheritance chain. Inheriting directly from the Object class, an EventDispatcher is an object that is capable of sending and receiving events (we'll cover events later in the chapter), but it doesn't do much more than that. Sending and receiving information is important to a number of other classes, so the EventDispatcher class is rightfully low in the inheritance chain. At any point in the chain, new limbs can branch out in different directions, leading to a Microphone class or a URLLoader class, but in the case of the MovieClip chain, it branches toward a limb for displaying objects onscreen.

The MovieClip class is built into the core functionality of Flash, but you can also write classes of your own that have brand-new functionality. New classes that you write are stored externally as ActionScript (.as) files. Your classes can inherit from built-in classes like MovieClip, they can inherit from other classes that you've written, or they can be written entirely from scratch (and by default, they will then inherit from the Object class). The process of inheriting from another class is also referred to as *extending* a class, because you are extending the functionality of an existing class. The extending class is considered a *subclass* of the class that it extends.

**TIP**

You can locate the inheritance chain for a class in the Flash Help documentation. Choose Flash > Help > Flash Help. In the Adobe Help application, select **Action-Script 3.0 and Components** under the *Adobe Reference* heading. On the next page, select *Action-Script 3.0 Reference for the Adobe Flash Platform*. Select a class from the bottom-left side of the window. The top of each class page lists a class's package and inheritance.

Understanding the trend from general functionality to very specific functionality is the basis for designing useful ActionScript classes. Writing a reusable class begins with considering how the desired functionality can be made more general or *abstract*. Later in the chapter you'll learn how to write a class that controls an animated character's walk cycle. To make your character walk, you could start by writing very specific code for the task, or you could take a moment and consider how this behavior could be made more abstract. You can start by asking the following questions: What's more primitive than walking? How about just moving? Moving also applies to fish, birds, and snakes as well as to walking characters. By writing a Mover class first, you'll be able to use your code for any type of moving object, be it a Pac-Man-style character, a side-scrolling Super Mario-style character for an adventure game, or a paddle for a simple Pong-style game. Once written, your Mover class never has to be rewritten. When you need new functionality, you can simply extend the Mover class.

Reusability is only one of many organizational benefits to writing code in classes with clearly defined behaviors. Consider this situation: You've been given a project that was designed by someone else. You've been tasked with updating some of the graphics and functionality. Which of the following would you rather see when you open the files: A) One 600-line ActionScript file with a list of directions for vaguely named instances on the stage, or B) four short ActionScript files named Paddle, Ball, Background, and Controller? In B, you have a pretty good idea of what the project entails just by looking at the names of the files. Every object has its own behaviors, and since the objects are clearly named, it's easy to intuit what those behaviors might entail. This kind of organization also pays off when you need to work on your own files that you haven't opened in a long while.

In addition to understanding how classes work, there are also some basic programming terms that you need to know to write ActionScript code. We'll define new terms as they appear in the examples, but you can refer to **Table 3.1** and **Table 3.2** as guides for the basic definitions and syntax of common programming terms.

**TABLE 3.1** Definitions for basic programming terms

| TERM | DEFINITION |
|---|---|
| Variable | A named object with an associated value that can be changed |
| Function | A portion of code that performs a specific task |
| Method | A function associated with a particular object |
| Parameter | A piece of data that can be used within a function |
| Argument | A parameter that is sent to a function |
| Loop | A piece of code that is repeatedly executed |
| Array | A collection of objects |

**TABLE 3.2** Syntax examples for basic programming terms

| TERM | EXAMPLE |
|---|---|
| Variable | `var myNumber = 10;` |
| Function | `function myFunction(){}` |
| Method | `function myMethod(){}` |
| Parameter | `function myMethod(myParam){}` |
| Argument | `myMethod(myArg);` |
| Loop | `for(var i = startNumber; i <= endNumber; i++){}` |
| Array | `myArray = [myVarA, myVarB, myVarC];` |

The best way to learn the terms in the preceding tables is to start using them. Before you put them into action, let's go over some words and symbols that ActionScript has reserved for special use.

## Keywords and Statements

One difficulty that arises for nearly everyone when they begin coding is discerning which words in a piece of code have special meanings and which words are simply created by the person writing the code. The words that have special meaning fall into a couple of categories; the largest two categories are *keywords* and *statements*. The words contained in these categories are reserved by Flash for specific purposes.

Keywords are used either to define entities like variables, functions, and classes, or to alter the meaning of certain definitions. Keywords include *class, extends, function, var, get, set,* and so forth.

Statements are language elements that perform or specify an action at runtime (when your movie is playing). For example, the *if* statement evaluates a condition to determine the next action that should be taken. Statements include *if, break, case, while, for, return,* and so forth.

You will naturally integrate keywords and statements into your vocabulary over time. As you go through the examples in this chapter, notice which words are used most often and how (or if) the Flash Code Editor highlights them. Generally, words that are reserved by ActionScript appear in dark blue by default in the Code Editor (**Figure 3.2**).

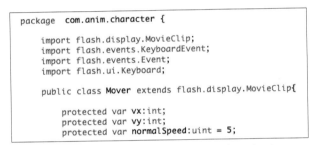

```
package  com.anim.character {

    import flash.display.MovieClip;
    import flash.events.KeyboardEvent;
    import flash.events.Event;
    import flash.ui.Keyboard;

    public class Mover extends flash.display.MovieClip{

        protected var vx:int;
        protected var vy:int;
        protected var normalSpeed:uint = 5;
```

**Figure 3.2** The Flash Code Editor indicates reserved words using different colors.

For a complete list of keywords and statements see http://help.adobe.com/en_US/FlashPlatform/reference/actionscript/3/statements.html.

## Operators

Operators, just like keywords and statements, are a built-in part of ActionScript. Operators are characters that have symbolic value. Operators allow you to combine, compare, or modify values inside ActionScript. Many of the operators function the same way you would expect them to on a calculator. Common operators include addition (+), subtraction (-), division (/), multiplication (*), increment (++), equality (==), less than (<), and so on.

### Changing Code Coloring

You can change the colors used in the Code Editor. To customize ActionScript highlight colors, choose Edit > Preferences (or Flash > Preferences on a Mac) and select the ActionScript category at the left. In addition to changing the highlight color for keywords, identifiers, strings, and comments, you can change the foreground and background colors of the Code Editor (**Figure 3.3**). If you find black text on a white screen hard on your eyes, you can try a light gray foreground on dark gray background.

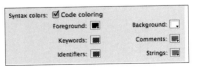

**Figure 3.3** ActionScript Code Editor coloring in the ActionScript settings inside the Flash preferences.

Also, logical operators help you evaluate the truth value of statements. Common logical operators include and (&&), or (||), and not (!). It's not important to memorize all the operators before continuing with the chapter, just be aware of their usage in the examples that follow.

There are also operators that help you organize your code. Four such operators that you will find in every example within this chapter are curly braces ({}), square brackets ([]), parentheses (()), and the semicolon (;). Let's examine each of these in detail.

### Curly braces

Curly braces are used to designate the start and the end of a code block. A *code block* can be defined as any discrete piece of code, be it a function, a package, a class, or a loop. A keyword or a statement always precedes curly braces and determines the nature of the code block. In the following example, the keyword *function* is used to define a function that is enclosed by curly braces.

```
function doSomething() {
    //function contents go here
}
```

### Square brackets

Square brackets are most often used to assign or access values within arrays. In the following example, the first line assigns values to a new array using brackets, and the second line uses brackets as array access notation to retrieve a value from the new array:

```
var animals = ["dog", "cat", "frog", "bear"];
var firstAnimal = animals[0]; //will have a value of
➥"dog"
```

### Parentheses

Parentheses serve a couple of different purposes in Action-Script. They are essential to both the definition and execution of functions (aka methods). The parentheses enclose the parameters within a function definition, and they enclose the arguments that are sent when the function is

NOTES

You can add comments to clarify aspects of your code. A single line can be converted to a comment by adding two slashes (//) to the beginning of the line. You can also write multiline comments by preceding them with a slash-asterisk (/*) and closing them with an asterisk-slash (*/). Code within a comment will not be executed when your Flash movie is run.

NOTES

The first item in an array is always at position 0. Therefore, the last item in the array will always be at a position one less than the length of the array.

executed. For example, the first set of parentheses in the following code serves as part of the function definition, and the set of parentheses after the closing curly brace serves to execute, or *call*, the function and pass on any necessary arguments:

```
function start(delay) {
    //function contents go here
}


start(100); //passes a delay with a value of 100
```

Parentheses are required to both define and call a function, even when the function has no parameters:

```
run; //simply references a function, but does not
➥initiate any action
run(); //calls the function into action, sends no
➥arguments
```

Parentheses are also used with conditional statements to enclose any conditions:

```
if(isReady){
    //actions go here
}
```

Additionally, parentheses can be used in the way that you are probably most familiar with, as a means of grouping to determine the order of operations:

```
var newWidth = (storedWidth + 10) / 2;
```

The parentheses in the preceding example ensure that the addition will be executed before the division, even though division would otherwise take place before addition.

### Semicolon

The semicolon is a simple but important piece of syntax. The semicolon tells the *compiler*, the mechanism that converts your human-readable ActionScript into byte code that the Flash Player can read, where to end a line. The semicolon in ActionScript operates much the way a period does in written English. The Flash compiler is pretty forgiving if you forget to add a semicolon; it will assume any line break is the end of a statement and will add a semicolon while compiling.

As a matter of best practice, all your discrete statements (lines of code) should end with a semicolon:

```
var myNumber = 10;
var myString = "hello"; myString = "goodbye";
```

The second line in the preceding example would be treated as two lines by the compiler because of the semicolon.

For a full list of ActionScript operators, see http://help.adobe.com/en_US/FlashPlatform/reference/actionscript/3/operators.html.

Enough talk about syntax. Let's write an ActionScript class already!

## The Document Class

There are two basic ways to add ActionScript to your Flash file: directly on a frame or attached as a class. As noted earlier in the chapter, organizing your ActionScript into classes makes the purpose of your code clearer. Additionally, classes are easier to locate than actions attached to frames, because each class is stored in its own ActionScript file. Once you have your class in its own ActionScript file, there are three ways to instantiate a class in Flash:

▶ Attached as a document class

▶ Attached to a Library symbol

▶ Using the *new* keyword within ActionScript

In this section, you'll attach your code as a document class. When your Flash movie is loaded, a single instance of your document class will be generated. Your entire Flash movie will then be an instance of your document class.

### Creating a Document Class

Before writing any code, you need a Flash document to which you can attach your code.

**141**

1. Create a new ActionScript 3.0 document by choosing File > New and selecting ActionScript 3.0 (**Figure 3.4**).

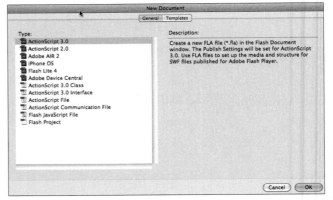

**Figure 3.4** The New Document dialog box allows you to choose what type of document to create.

2. For your document to locate your class, you'll want to make sure that both your Flash file and your Action-Script file are saved. Choose File > Save As to save your document, create and navigate to a new folder called **examples**, name the document **DocumentExample.fla**, and click OK.

3. Now you'll create the class file. Choose File > New and select ActionScript 3.0 Class. This generates a prompt asking you to name your class. Name the class **DocumentExample** (**Figure 3.5**). Click OK.

This opens the ActionScript in the Flash Code Editor.

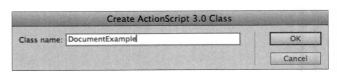

**Figure 3.5** The prompt to name your new class. Once you provide a name, Flash sets up the basic structure of the class for you.

4. Choose File > Save As and save the file as **DocumentExample.as** in the examples directory that you created in step 2.

5. Return to DocumentExample.fla, and attach the class to the document by typing the class name **DocumentExample** into the Class field in the Properties panel (**Figure 3.6**).

Figure 3.6 The Class field in the Properties panel allows you to assign a document class.

6. Make sure that Control > Test Movie > in Flash Professional (rather than in Device Central) is chosen and press Command+Return/Ctrl+Enter to test the movie. You'll receive the following error in the Compiler Errors panel:

```
5000: The class 'DocumentExample' must subclass
➥'flash.display.MovieClip' since it is linked to a
➥library symbol of that type.
```

This error occurs because the Flash document relies on the methods and properties found in the MovieClip class. Although you can write all kinds of new methods and properties for your document class, you need to start by extending the MovieClip class using the *extends* keyword.

7. Add the following highlighted code to the class statement:

```
class DocumentExample extends flash.display.
➥MovieClip {
```

As you type, the Code Editor will display a list of packages or classes available. You can navigate the list of choices with your keyboard or mouse. Press the Return/Enter key when the correct item is selected in

**TIP**

Be sure to save your class before you start adding any code. Many of the bells and whistles added to the Code Editor in CS5 depend on your file being saved first.

**CLOSE-UP**

**Basic Class Structure**

After you've provided a name for your class, Flash sets up the necessary structure of the class file for you (**Figure 3.7**). This structure includes the package block (starting with the keyword package), the class block (starting with public class), and the constructor method (starting with public function and a function name that matches your class name).

Every class must be in a package. The package gives the class context (you'll do more with packages later in this chapter). The class block defines the start and end of the class code. The constructor method is called when an instance of the class is created. Any code within the constructor will run when the method is called. The name of the constructor method must match the class name *exactly*.

```
package  {
    public class DocumentClass {
        public function DocumentClass() {
            // constructor code
        }
    }
}
```

Figure 3.7 The basic class structure created automatically by Flash.

the list to save yourself some typing. The Code Editor will automatically add an import statement above the line you just added (you'll learn about import statements in a moment).

8. Save your class and test your movie again (press Command+Return/Ctrl+Enter). You can test your movie from the Code Editor if you like. You should now have 0 errors listed in your Compiler panel. Although you don't have any errors, you also don't yet have much confirmation that your class has been instantiated (your movie is empty).

9. Replace the comment inside the constructor method block (// constructor code) with this trace statement:

```
trace("hello");
```

10. Save your class and test your movie again. You should now see the word "hello" in the Output panel (**Figure 3.8**), proving that your class has successfully been instantiated.

| TIMELINE | OUTPUT | COMPILER ERRORS |
| --- | --- | --- |
| hello | | |

Figure 3.8 The Output panel shows any messages passed using the trace method.

The methods and properties for document classes vary depending on the nature of each specific project. In general, the document class is not one that will be reused from project to project. You'll find that a document class is not necessary for every animation project.

To determine whether you require a document class, think about what information each object requires in your project. Place all your objects on a need-to-know basis (as if they were government spies under your supervision). If the objects within your project can act independently without your document acting as supervisor, by all means omit the document class. Conversely, if you find that there is information that must be present at the document level, use a document class (for example, the web project in Chapter 5 utilizes a document class). Sometimes a document class will be the simplest way to implement the desired functionality. Most of the examples later in this chapter focus on a different kind of class, but keep the document class in mind when planning your Flash projects.

To reference any other classes within your ActionScript file, as you did when DocumentExample extended the MovieClip class, you need a way to point to other classes. Enter *classpaths*.

## Classpaths

A classpath is a filepath separated by dots (.) that tells the compiler where to locate the corresponding ActionScript class file. The path serves as both a file location and an organizational system. For instance, in `flash.display.MovieClip`, the MovieClip.as class file is located in a folder named *display*, which is located within a folder named *flash*.

Folders (and folder paths) within classpaths are referred to as *packages*. The package root, *flash*, is pretty generic, as you might expect the outermost folder to be, but the subfolder, *display*, tells you a bit about how the MovieClip class behaves. The MovieClip class is a display class, meaning that MovieClip instances are meant to be shown onscreen. In contrast, even though a class such as `flash.geom.Rectangle` appears to refer to something visual, the class instead refers to the geometric concept of a rectangle (four points, four sides), so the Rectangle class is in the *geom* package.

Classpaths also allow you to differentiate between two classes with the same name. Within one ActionScript file you could refer to two classes named MathUtil by referencing each one using its entire (and unique) classpath. For example:

```
var random1 = com.ajarproductions.utils.MathUtil.
➥random(0,10);
var random2 = net.yoursite.utils.MathUtil.random();
```

Classpaths are often used to denote the author of the classes (most frequently, in the form of an inverted web address). For example, the web address *http://ajarproductions.com* becomes the *com.ajarproductions* package. Using a web address keeps your classpath unique. Within the *com* directory of your Flash project, you may have several subfolders, all referring to packages created by developers with .com websites. Named packages are generally used with classes that are designed for reuse. For project-specific classes, like the DocumentExample class, there is no need to create a named package. Project-specific classes can simply reside in the project folder with your Flash document.

To create your own classpath, you can invert your web address as described. If you do not have a web address, you can make up a unique package name of your choosing. Many developers use the *com* convention followed by their full name, for example, com.johnsmith. Within the base package, subfolders can be created to reflect the different purposes of classes housed inside, for example, core, ui, display, fx, animation, and so on.

Package paths should be all lowercase. Only the class name should contain capital letters. When you place your class into a package, the package statement at the top of your ActionScript class file must match the file's folder structure. For example, the package statement and class statement within the class file at com/johnsmith/fx/WarpEffect.as must read:

```
package com.johnsmith.fx {
    public class WarpEffect {
```

If your package statement does not match the class's folder structure, the Compiler panel produces an error (if not several).

For the examples later in this chapter, you will use a base package named *com.anim*.

**NOTES**

The Flash CS5 Code Editor now supports code hinting for custom classes. When you reference one of your classes and start typing a method within that class, Flash shows auto-completion options for your classes, just as it does with Flash's built-in classes. The Code Editor is even smart enough to help complete your package name if you've already saved your class in the proper folder.

**ActionScript Settings**

By default, Flash looks for any custom classes at compile time in your document directory. If you want Flash to search for classes in other locations, you'll need to tell Flash where to look. To add a directory, choose File > ActionScript Settings (**Figure 3.9**).

You can use absolute paths (paths that refer to an exact location on your machine) or relative paths (paths based on the location of your document). If you want to point your file to a standard class archive that you keep on your machine, use an absolute path by clicking the browse to path button (the folder icon) to browse to a folder on your machine.

More commonly, you may just want to organize all your ActionScript files for a single project into one folder. In that case, use a relative path. For relative paths, a dot (.) refers to the document folder, and two dots (..) refer to one level above the document folder. So to point to a folder named *actionscript* that is one folder up from your document, you'd click the button with the plus (+) sign, type **../actionscript** into the new path, and click OK to save the settings.

**Figure 3.9** The ActionScript Settings dialog box allows you to direct Flash to other locations that contain class packages.

## Importing Classes

When you insert ActionScript on a frame along the Timeline, Flash assumes you will be using some common classes like MovieClip and MouseEvent. When coding a class file, you must explicitly state all the classes you plan to reference using *import* statements. Inside the new Flash CS5 Code Editor, in most cases, when you reference a class that you've not yet imported, Flash automatically adds the necessary code for you. In the case of the MovieClip class, the import statement containing the classpath appears as follows:

```
import flash.display.MovieClip;
```

The import statement is necessary if you want to reference your class by name only (e.g., MovieClip). If you don't use an import statement, you must reference your class using the entire classpath (e.g., flash.display.MovieClip). It's always preferable to import your classes rather than referencing the entire classpath. Import statements go at the top of the ActionScript file, just within the package block and outside the class block:

```
package {
    import flash.display.MovieClip;
    import flash.events.MouseEvent;

    public class MyClass extends MovieClip{
```

By placing all the import statements at the top of a class, you further organize your class and keep the purpose of the class clear at a glance. Bear this in mind as your classes become more complex.

### Interacting with Objects on the Stage

Thus far, you've successfully attached a document class and confirmed that the class has been instantiated. Now you'll take it one step further and update the class to manipulate an object on Stage.

**Figure 3.10** Make your symbol big enough to click, but leave plenty of room for it to expand.

1. Return to DocumentExample.fla. Draw a square on Stage by selecting the Rectangle tool and holding down the Shift key to constrain the proportions while you draw. Make your square large enough to click on but significantly smaller than the Stage (**Figure 3.10**).

2. Select the square (Command+A/Ctrl+A to select all) and press F8 to convert the square to a symbol. When the Convert to Symbol dialog box appears, name the symbol **square**, make sure that MovieClip is selected in the Type menu, and click OK (**Figure 3.11**).

**Figure 3.11** The Convert to Symbol dialog box allows you to make your artwork available to ActionScript.

**3.** With the symbol still selected, name the instance **square_mc** using the Properties panel (**Figure 3.12**).

Figure 3.12 The Properties panel allows you to add a name to your symbol instance to access it with ActionScript.

**4.** Return to the ActionScript file and replace the trace statement with the following line:

```
square_mc.width *= 2;
```

**5.** Save your document (Command+S/Ctrl+S) and then test your movie (Command+Return/Ctrl+Enter).

Note that step 4 uses the multiplication assignment operator (*=). This operator is shorthand for `square_mc.width = square_mc.width * 2`. The result is a doubling of the square's width every time it's clicked with the mouse (**Figure 3.13**).

**TIP**

It is considered best practice to use clearly named functions to ensure that your code is easy to read. Ideally, each function will serve a single purpose. For example, a function named `doubleWidth` should double an object's width and do little else.

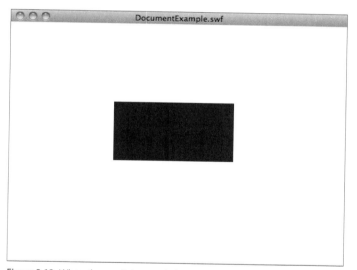

Figure 3.13 When the movie is tested, the instance should appear twice as wide as the (square) instance on Stage.

For more examples using a document class, see Chapter 5. For the rest of this chapter you'll be writing a different type of class.

**CLOSE-UP**

**Case Sensitivity**

ActionScript is case sensitive. If you create a variable named `myVar` and attempt to reference it using `myvar`, ActionScript will fail to find the variable.

It is considered best practice in ActionScript to use camel case, meaning that the first letter of your variable or function name is lowercase and any subsequent words within the name start with capital letters rather than spaces, for example, `camelCase`.

## Object-oriented Programming

Writing code in classes is generally referred to as object-oriented programming (OOP), because the objects that inhabit the code govern its behavior. Prior to OOP, most programming was *procedural* in nature, meaning it followed a sequence (e.g., execute step A, then execute step B, then step C, etc.). One benefit of writing object-oriented code is that it allows several different processes to run simultaneously because all the objects operate independently of each other. Each object is in charge of its own behavior.

Objects in your object-oriented Flash project have the potential to move around like ants in ant farms. You can pluck an ant from one farm and drop it into another and the ant will still function. The ant doesn't need directions from a leader or a central command to operate. The ant just does what it's supposed to do. The logic that powers the ant is considered *decentralized*.

As the designer of the ant farm, this takes a huge burden off your shoulders. It's not necessary to conceive of a farmer smart enough to direct all the workings of the ant farm. You can simply design a reasonably "dumb" ant that knows how to complete a few tasks and possibly how to interact with other ants, and then instantiate as many copies of the ant as you need.

The remaining examples in this chapter will all be decentralized in the manner just described. Instead of attaching your classes to a document, you will attach new classes to Library items. Once the class has been written, you will never have to look at it again (if you don't want to). Your symbols won't require any directions from your document; they will simply go about their business. After you've attached a class to a Library item, you can instantiate the class by dragging your Library item onto the Stage. Although you will be treading into the domain of a programmer, you will maintain the graphical workflow of an animator—the best of both worlds!

**Object-oriented Design Patterns**

Advanced programmers also use *design patterns* as part of their OOP projects. Design patterns are solutions to commonly occurring problems. These patterns have names like Builder, Factory, and Singleton. As an animator, you're not likely to be developing projects that require the use of design patterns, so they won't be covered in depth in this book, but it's good to be aware that they exist.

## Attaching Classes to Library Items

You'll start by reconceiving the functionality from the DocumentExample files as a class that could be attached to a Library item.

1. Open DocumentExample.fla and choose File > Save As. Then save the document as **LibraryClassExample.fla** in the examples folder created previously.

2. Under the Publish options in the Properties panel, highlight and delete the previously added document class, DocumentExample.

3. Create a new class (choose File > New and select ActionScript 3.0 Class). When prompted, name the class **ClickSquare**.

4. Save the ActionScript file as **ClickSquare.as** in the examples folder.

5. This class should also extend the MovieClip class since you'll be attaching it to a MovieClip in the Library. Add the following highlighted code:

```
public class ClickSquare extends flash.display.
➥MovieClip{
```

6. Replace the comment inside the constructor method (`// constructor code`) with the following code:

```
this.addEventListener(MouseEvent.CLICK, onClick);
```

7. Add the following code after the closing curly brace of the constructor method:

```
private function onClick(e:MouseEvent):void{
    this.width *= 2;
}
```

8. Be sure to add the following import statement below the existing import statement (`import flash.display.MovieClip;`) if the Code Editor doesn't automatically add it:

```
import flash.events.MouseEvent;
```

9. Save your class (Command+S/Ctrl+S).

Your ClickSquare.as file should now read:

```
package   {
       import flash.display.MovieClip;
       import flash.events.MouseEvent;

       public class ClickSquare extends flash.display.
➥MovieClip{

            public function ClickSquare(){
                   this.addEventListener(MouseEvent.CLICK,
➥onClick);
            }

            private function onClick(e:MouseEvent):void{
                   this.width *= 2;
            }

       }
}
```

Let's review the code so far. Your ClickSquare class resides in an unnamed package (because it's in the same folder as the document that will instantiate it). ClickSquare imports two native (built into Flash) classes: MovieClip and MouseEvent. ClickSquare extends the functionality of the MovieClip class. When the ClickSquare class is instantiated, the constructor adds an event listener that listens for a mouse click. When a mouse click occurs, the listener executes the onClick method of the ClickSquare class and passes a MouseEvent object to the method. When the onClick method is executed, the ClickSquare instance will be referenced using the keyword *this*, and the current width (an inherited property) of the ClickSquare will be doubled.

After the parentheses containing the parameter in the onClick method definition, there is a colon followed by the keyword *void*. Colons in ActionScript are most often used for *typing*, also known as *strong typing*, *strict typing*, or *strict data typing*. Strict typing informs the ActionScript compiler as to which type of object you expect to be used. In the case of the `onClick` function, the strict typing *void* (all lowercase in ActionScript 3.0) informs the compiler that the `onClick` method will not be returning a value. If the `onClick` method attempts to return a value using the *return* keyword, the compiler generates an error.

Now you'll associate your ClickSquare class with the square Library item.

1. Ctrl-click/right-click on the square symbol in the Library panel and select Properties to bring up the Symbol Properties dialog box.

2. Click Advanced (if necessary) to show the Linkage properties.

3. Select the Export for ActionScript check box. This allows you to add a class name.

4. Type the class name **ClickSquare** into the Class field. You can click the button with the check mark icon to the right of the field to verify that Flash can locate your class file (**Figure 3.15**).

### Reasons to Use Strict Typing

Here are three very good reasons to use strict typing in your code:

▶ Clarifies the intention of your code

▶ Helps the compiler catch potential errors

▶ Enables additional code hinting in the Flash Code Editor (**Figure 3.14**)

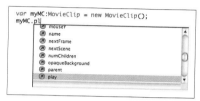

**Figure 3.14** The Code Editor shows the methods and properties available for a variable that has been strictly typed.

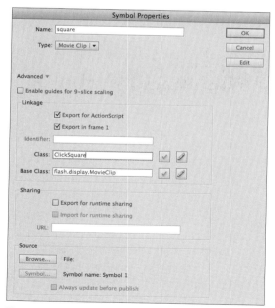

**Figure 3.15** The Linkage properties within the Symbol Properties dialog box allow you to add a class to a Library item.

**TIP**

You can also type your custom class name into the Base Class field within the Symbol Properties dialog box. This will leave the Class field open if you want to provide a unique class name for the symbol. You can then instantiate your Library item from ActionScript using the unique name from the Class field. Your instantiated symbol will still inherit the methods and properties of the custom class that you typed into the Base Class field.

5. Save your document (Command+S/Ctrl+S) and test your movie (Command+Return/Ctrl+Enter).

6. Click your square in the test window to ensure that the width doubles each time you click.

7. Close the test window and return to your document. Drag two more copies of the square symbol onto the Stage and test your movie again (**Figure 3.16**).

**Figure 3.16** Each square already has ClickSquare functionality, which eliminates the need to write new code.

When you click on any one of the squares, that particular square should double its width. All the square instances employ the functionality from the ClickSquare class. It's that easy to reuse the class!

## Events

The examples thus far have employed a click MouseEvent as a means of interaction. Since your object-oriented code allows objects to operate independently, sending and receiving events is a great way to allow your objects to communicate with the world around them. ActionScript 3.0 is loaded with built-in events. Using the techniques covered in this chapter, you can also create your own event classes.

An object that is notified when a particular event occurs is said to *listen* for that event. Conversely, an object that sends an event is said to *broadcast* that event, because the object is not sending the message anywhere in particular. Events are communicated in a manner similar to the broadcast of an FM radio station. The radio station is not sending its programs to anyone in particular. Instead, the station's signal is broadcast into the air for anyone to receive. If you have a stereo that can tune into the station's broadcast frequency, you can receive its programs. Additionally, the fact that you are tuned into that frequency does not prevent anyone else from listening to that station. The same is true for Action-Script 3.0 events. An object can broadcast an event for any interested party to receive. For these reasons, using events to communicate helps to keep your code modular.

The moment of triggering an event for broadcast is known as *dispatching* an event. When an event is dispatched, the event also carries information about the occurrence of the event. The information carried by the event varies depending on the type of event that was dispatched. For instance, a KeyboardEvent carries information about the key that was pressed.

You'll put events to good use in the examples that follow.

## Creating Reusable Classes For Animation

So far, you've written a class that takes advantage of the *extends* keyword to reuse the methods and properties found in the MovieClip class and applied that class to a Library symbol. There are also several other ways that classes can be reused. When extending a class, the class being extended is referred to as the *base class* or *superclass*. Any class that extends another class is referred to as a *subclass* of its superclass. After extending a class, you can rewrite certain methods from the superclass to fit the needs of the subclass. The ability to use a single method name for a method that behaves differently in different subclasses is known as *polymorphism* (*poly* for many, *morph* for shape).

Let's return to the animal kingdom to better understand polymorphism. Suppose you need to write a Cat class and a Dog class in your project. Following good object-oriented etiquette, you begin by writing a more abstract superclass called *Animal*. Because vocalization is a behavior common to most animals, you endow your Animal class with a speak method. Depending on your needs, you may decide to include a Mammal class to extend your Animal class, or you may write your Cat and Dog classes as direct subclasses to the Animal class. At this point, the behavior in your classes begins to diverge. In the Dog class, you redefine the speak method to act as a bark. In the Cat class, the speak method elicits a meow. Any object that can interact with the Dog class can use the same methods to interact with the Cat class, although when asked to speak, the Cat will meow instead of bark.

In addition to altering methods to suit the needs of your subclasses, you can override methods from a superclass entirely. Even though altering the functionality inherited from your superclass can seem like rewriting, this is generally still preferable to rewriting a base class that has been tested and may have other classes depending on it. Now that you're aware of polymorphism, you can plan your base classes accordingly. The examples that follow use polymorphism to generate various visual effects.

### Class Examples: Visual Effects

Before you start on effects, let's lay the groundwork for testing your effects. Let's first establish a classpath for the rest of the classes you will write in this chapter and then create some artwork to show off your effects classes.

1. Create a new folder called **com** inside your examples folder.

2. Create a subfolder within com named **anim** (short for *Animation with Scripting for Adobe Flash CS5 Professional Studio Techniques*).

3. Create a subfolder within anim named **fx**. The fx folder will store your effects classes.

4. Create a new ActionScript 3.0 document named **EffectsBase.fla** and save it in your examples folder.

5. In the EffectsBase.fla document, create a symbol to be the target of the visual effects you create. The more complex your artwork, the more it will demonstrate the performance of the effects you are about to create.

   The figures in this section use a depiction of a rocket, but you can use any piece of artwork that you'd like (**Figure 3.17**).

6. To see the full power of your effect, create a background as well. Make sure your background is on a separate layer. The examples in this section use a night sky as a background (**Figure 3.18**).

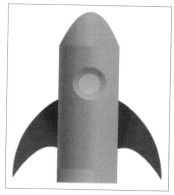

Figure 3.17 The rocket symbol made with simple shapes and gradients that will appear for the effects in this section.

Figure 3.18 The rocket against the night sky background rendered using a simple gradient and some blurred white circles.

7. Move your symbol instance to the bottom-left corner of the Stage.

8. Ctrl-click/right-click on your symbol and choose Create Motion Tween. When your tween is created, the playhead automatically moves to the last frame. Move your symbol to the top-right corner of the Stage. You should

now see the tween object depicting the path of your tweened symbol (**Figure 3.19**).

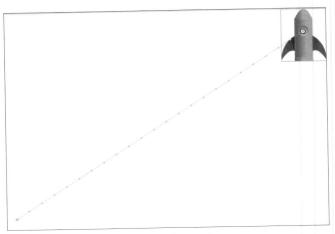

Figure 3.19 The tween object depicted as a path.

9. Hover over the middle of the tween path with the Selection tool. You should see a curved line appear next to your cursor. Click and drag the middle of the path toward the upper-left corner of the Stage to make a curved tween path (**Figure 3.20**).

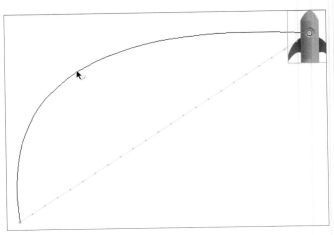

Figure 3.20 Curving the tween path using the Selection tool.

Now that your path is a curve, click on the path to select it. You can (optionally) select "Orient to path" under the Rotation heading in the Properties panel. This causes your instance to rotate as the path curves.

10. Add a frame (F5) to the end of your background layer so it's visible for the entire length of the tween.

11. Save your document.

Now it's time to create your first effect.

The symbol you create for this section can also contain nested animation. Try using the Deco tool to add a particle, smoke, or fire effect within your symbol.

### The MotionBrush class

You'll start your effects classes by tackling a common animation task: hand-written text. Crafting the illusion of text being hand-written in real time onscreen can be time-consuming. You'll create an easier-to-apply, reusable class that accomplishes a write-on effect. Not only that, but any graphic content can be employed as the "brush," and the application of the class will not be limited to write-on effects. Your MotionBrush class will also serve as a base class for effects that you will create later in this section.

To render your MotionBrush class, you'll need to employ the powerful Bitmap class. Nearly all visual effects in Flash exploit the Bitmap class. For instance, when you add a blur filter to a symbol instance on Stage using the Properties panel, Flash renders the instance as a bitmap to generate the blur effect. Most artwork generated using the Flash drawing tools is composed of vectors. Vectors are made up of lines and curves. Bitmaps are generally less complex to render for effects because they are simply composed of pixels rather than complicated vector data. Since you're rendering the bitmaps using artwork from the Flash file, your effect will not increase the file size.

The MotionBrush class will use a Bitmap object as a canvas and draw copies of a symbol instance onto the canvas. For programming simplicity and rendering performance, these symbol copies will simply be superficial pixel-based snapshots. Every so often, you'll take a snapshot of the "brush" symbol at its current position and display state. For other complex effects, you may even want to use your canvas as a mask, so let's be sure to build that into your MotionBrush class.

Start by making an inventory of what the MotionBrush class should accomplish:

- Start rendering the effect when the symbol is added to the Stage.
- Rerender the effect regularly.
- Stop rendering the effect when the symbol is removed from the Stage.
- Allow the retrieval of the bitmap used to render the effects so that it can be manipulated by code outside of the MotionBrush class.

This inventory will become the basis for the methods of the MotionBrush class. Additionally, you need to think about which parts of your class will be open to the outside world (i.e., other ActionScript classes or code). As a matter of practice, you should make no more than necessary available outside of the class. The practice of restricting the internal workings of a class is known as *encapsulation*. You will encapsulate parts of your class, both to protect parts of the class and to make it simpler for the outside world to interact with the class.

Since you will extend your class, and other classes will depend on this class working properly, you'll want to make sure that your class is relatively tamper-proof. Also, your class should do its job with as little outside instruction as possible. Imagine sitting down at a restaurant to order French fries. You don't have to tell the cook how to wash and cut the potatoes, what temperature to heat the oil to, how to store the salt, and so on because it is the cook's job to perform these duties. In fact, the cook's kitchen is so encapsulated that you probably will never even *see* the cook. You will be interacting with members of the wait staff, because that is part of their duties. If the instruction necessary for ordering French fries was too complicated, you'd be much more likely to stay home and cook for yourself. The instructions that you give to the MotionBrush class should be as simple as (or simpler than) ordering French fries.

Instead of starting by writing a heavily abstracted Effect class (as you will with the Mover class later in this chapter), you'll create a helper class to manage the interactions with the Bitmap object. This helper class will operate in a manner similar to a cook's kitchen: The code that interacts with MotionBrush will not have access to this helper class. The technique of utilizing a class within another class, instead of subclassing, is known as *composition*.

To protect access to your class, you will use access keywords. There are four keywords that determine the availability of a method or property within a class: *public*, *private*, *internal*, and *protected*. See **Table 3.3** for more details on each access keyword.

**TABLE 3.3** Access control attributes

| Keyword | Provides Access to |
|---------|--------------------|
| public | everyone |
| private | the class |
| internal | the package where the class resides |
| protected | the class and subclasses |

You will draw heavily on the *protected* keyword for your MotionBrush class. The *protected* keyword allows classes that extend the MotionBrush class to rewrite methods (and properties) but shields the methods from other ActionScript classes, even within your `com.anim.fx` package.

To reshape the MotionBrush class in subclasses, you'll use the *override* keyword to rewrite functions inherited from the MotionBrush class.

1. Save a copy of EffectsBase.fla (File > Save As) as **MotionBrushExample.fla** into your examples folder.

2. Create a new class named **MotionBrush**.

3. Save the file as **MotionBrush.as** in the examples/com/anim/fx directory. This will place the class into the `com.anim.fx` package.

4. Update the first line in the script to reflect the proper package:

```
package com.anim.fx {
```

5. You will attach MotionBrush to the Library symbol you created earlier. Update the class declaration so that your class extends MovieClip:

```
public class MotionBrush extends MovieClip {
```

6. Add the following method blocks after the Motion-Brush constructor method block but before the last two closing curly braces (that close the class block and the package block, respectively):

```
protected function onAddedToStage(e:Event):void{

}


protected function onFrame(e:Event):void {

}


protected function onRemovedFromStage(e:Event):
➥void {

}


public function getCanvas():Bitmap {

}
```

These four functions parallel the inventory items established for the MotionBrush class.

The onAddedToStage method starts your effect in motion once the symbol using the class is added to the Stage. If the symbol is added to the Stage by dragging it from the Library rather than instantiating it with ActionScript, the onAddedToStage will fire as soon as the frame with the symbol is played. Since an event listener calls your onAddedToStage method, it must accept a single parameter of type Event, which will be stored as a variable named e.

The onFrame method will be called regularly to reren-der your symbol. You'll use an ENTER_FRAME event to call the onFrame method on every frame, so onFrame must also accept a single parameter of type Event.

The onRemovedFromStage method will handle any cleanup necessary. This method will also be called from an event listener and therefore must accept a single parameter of type Event.

These first three methods utilize the protected access keyword because you'll want to permit any classes that extend MotionBrush to rewrite these methods to allow for new behaviors. None of these three methods return any values (hence the *void* keyword following each method). These methods are present to launch other actions into motion. The fourth method, however, is pres-ent precisely to return an object (the bitmap canvas).

Once executed, getCanvas will return the bitmap canvas that the MotionBrush has drawn on. This func-tionality allows even more visual effects to be created with the MotionBrush class (and subclasses), such as using the canvas as a mask for other artwork.

7. Make sure all the import statements are listed above the class declaration:

```
import flash.display.MovieClip;
import flash.display.Bitmap;
import flash.events.Event;
import com.anim.fx.SymbolCanvas;
```

You'll need to add com.anim.fx.SymbolCanvas by hand, but the code editor will likely have added the other import statements for you, since the classes have already been referenced in the code you've written.

8. Add the following property declarations above the constructor method (i.e., before the line that starts with public function MotionBrush):

```
protected var symbolCanvas:SymbolCanvas;
protected var hideSymbol:Boolean;
protected var clearCanvasOnUpdate:Boolean;
```

The first property, symbolCanvas, stores the reference for a class that will render the bitmap. You'll create that class in a moment. The next two properties, hideSymbol and clearCanvasOnUpdate, allow you to adjust how the symbolCanvas renders in future subclasses of Motion-Brush. Both properties will be simple toggle settings so they are typed to Boolean (*true* or *false*). All three properties are assigned as protected so they can be referenced and/or rewritten by future subclasses. The reason for this will become apparent when you write the first subclass for MotionBrush.

9. Add the following initialization method (after the constructor method) to be called when the class is constructed:

```
protected function init():void {
    hideSymbol = true;
    clearCanvasOnUpdate = false;
    initStageListeners();
}
```

The init method assigns true/false values to your Boolean properties. The first setting notifies the symbolCanvas that it won't need to display your original symbol, just the bitmap representation. The second setting notifies the symbolCanvas not to clear the canvas before rendering. This setting is central to achieving the write-on effect described at the beginning of this section. The init method also calls another method to initialize the listeners that will call the onAddedToStage and onRemovedFromStage methods. The initStageListeners method is primarily for organizational purposes. As a general rule, each method should perform one distinct task. Separating the listener initialization into a single method also makes the init method simpler to overwrite (and the code simpler to read).

Note that the init method is assigned protected access as well. Normally, an initialization method should be private, but in this case you want to allow for different assignments to the hideSymbol and clearCanvasOnUpdate properties in future subclasses, as

**TIP**

Having an initialization method instead of putting code into your constructor method is always good practice. An initialization method allows you to reset properties within your class without needing to generate a new instance of the class.

well as allow for the possibility of starting and stopping the bitmap rendering at points other than when the symbol is added to or removed from the Stage.

10. Add the `initStageListeners` method below the init block:

```
protected function initStageListeners():void {
    this.addEventListener(Event.ADDED_TO_STAGE,
➥onAddedToStage);
    this.addEventListener(Event.REMOVED_FROM_STAGE,
➥onRemovedFromStage);
}
```

Note that this method is also protected so that only a subclass can make changes.

11. After completing all the initialization code, you need to make sure that the constructor calls the init method. Add the highlighted code as shown:

```
public function MotionBrush() {
    init();
}
```

12. Flesh out the original four methods by adding the following highlighted code:

```
protected function onAddedToStage(e:Event):void{
    symbolCanvas = new SymbolCanvas(this,
➥hideSymbol, clearCanvasOnUpdate);
    this.addEventListener(Event.ENTER_FRAME,
➥onFrame);
    symbolCanvas.update();
}


protected function onFrame(e:Event):void {
    symbolCanvas.update();
}


protected function onRemovedFromStage(e:Event):
➥void {
    this.removeEventListener(Event.ENTER_FRAME,
➥onFrame);
    symbolCanvas.dispose();
```

```
        }

        public function getCanvas():Bitmap {
            return symbolCanvas.getBitmap();
        }
```

Most of the heavy lifting done in the preceding four methods is being passed along to the SymbolCanvas class. In the `onAddedToStage` method, you generate the SymbolCanvas instance using the *new* keyword and pass a reference to your symbol, and then the two properties that you assigned in the `init` method. You then add a listener for the ENTER_FRAME event and call the `update` method to immediately render the canvas.

The `onFrame` method calls the `update` method each time the ENTER_FRAME event fires. The frame rate of your document will determine how many times per second the ENTER_FRAME event is dispatched. The `onRemovedFromStage` and `getCanvas` methods also now contain the code to operate as previously described.

As a result of completing these methods, you now have an inventory for the first three methods to include in the SymbolCanvas class:

- ▶ `update`. To render the bitmap
- ▶ `dispose`. To get rid of the bitmap data that's being stored (and free up memory)
- ▶ `getBitmap`. To provide the bitmap canvas for outside use

The completed code for the MotionBrush class should read as follows:

```
package com.anim.fx {
    import flash.display.MovieClip;
    import flash.display.Bitmap;
    import flash.events.Event;
    import com.anim.fx.SymbolCanvas;

    public class MotionBrush extends MovieClip {
```

```
    protected var symbolCanvas:SymbolCanvas;
    protected var hideSymbol:Boolean;
    protected var clearCanvasOnUpdate:Boolean;

    public function MotionBrush() {
        init();
    }

    protected function init():void {
        hideSymbol = true;
        clearCanvasOnUpdate = false;
        initStageListeners();
    }

    protected function initStageListeners():void
{
        this.addEventListener(Event.ADDED_TO_
➥STAGE, onAddedToStage);
        this.addEventListener(Event.REMOVED_FROM_
➥STAGE,onRemovedFromStage);
    }

    protected function onAddedToStage(e:Event):
➥void{
        symbolCanvas = new SymbolCanvas(this,
➥hideSymbol, clearCanvasOnUpdate);
        this.addEventListener(Event.ENTER_FRAME,
➥onFrame);
        symbolCanvas.update();
    }

    protected function onFrame(e:Event):void {
        symbolCanvas.update();
    }

    protected function onRemovedFromStage
➥(e:Event):void {
        this.removeEventListener(
➥Event.ENTER_FRAME, onFrame);
        symbolCanvas.dispose();
    }
```

```
        public function getCanvas():Bitmap {
            return symbolCanvas.getBitmap();
        }



    }
}
```

Now you can update the Library item in your Flash document to use the MotionBrush class.

1. Return to your MotionBrushExample.fla document and open the symbol properties for the symbol you created in this section.

2. Open the Library item properties, select the Export for ActionScript check box, assign **com.anim.fx.MotionBrush** as the symbol's Class, and click OK.

3. Save your document.

Wait to test your movie, because you need to put the SymbolCanvas class into place first.

### The SymbolCanvas class

The SymbolCanvas class primarily utilizes the *private* access keyword rather than *protected*, since SymbolCanvas is less likely to be extended. Because other classes utilize SymbolCanvas via composition rather than subclassing, it will therefore be safer to add new methods to SymbolCanvas as you progress, as long as the old methods continue to function as expected. When you want to make a method or property available to another class, you will use the *public* keyword.

1. Create a new class named **SymbolCanvas**. Save the file as **SymbolCanvas.as** in the examples/com/anim/fx folder.

2. Update the first line in the script to reflect the proper package:

```
package com.anim.fx {
```

3. Let's first add the three methods that were established from writing the MotionBrush class. Add the following code just below the constructor block:

```
public function update():void{

}

public function dispose():void{

}

public function getBitmap():Bitmap {

}
```

4. Add the following properties above the constructor method:

```
private var offset:Point;
private var bmd:BitmapData;
private var bmp:Bitmap;
private var src:DisplayObject;
private var clearOnUpdate:Boolean;
private var hideOriginal:Boolean;
```

The first property, offset, will ensure that your effect always renders in the proper place on Stage (no matter how many symbols are nested above your symbol). The next two properties store the BitmapData and Bitmap objects that you'll use to render any and all effects. The last three properties store the information that you passed from the new SymbolCanvas instantiation in the MotionBrush class.

5. Update the constructor method to match the high-lighted code that follows:

```
public function SymbolCanvas(symbol:DisplayObject,
➥hideOriginalSymbol:Boolean=false,
➥clearCanvasOnUpdate:Boolean=true){
    initSymbolCanvas(symbol, hideOriginalSymbol,
➥clearCanvasOnUpdate);
}
```

This code informs the constructor function of how many and what types of arguments to accept. These parameters must match the arguments used in the MotionBrush class. The `symbol` parameter is typed to DisplayObject for forward compatibility. The DisplayObject class is a distant superclass of the MovieClip class. As a refresher, here is the inheritance chain for MovieClip: MovieClip > Sprite > DisplayObjectContainer > InteractiveObject > DisplayObject > EventDispatcher > Object.

Your MotionBrush class is of type `MotionBrush`, but it extends `MovieClip`, and by extension, all the classes listed in the inheritance chain. By typing the symbol parameter to `DisplayObject`, your SymbolCanvas class will also allow arguments for the symbol parameters that are Sprites, InteractiveObjects, and so on. This will be of use if you ever decide to pass the SymbolCanvas class a source object that's been instantiated using code rather than from the Library. As a general rule, typing a parameter to the lowest class in the chain makes your code more flexible for future features.

The line inside the constructor, the `initSymbolCanvas` method call, passes the arguments to an initialization function. You may have noticed that in addition to being strictly typed, the second two parameters defined for the SymbolCanvas constructor method also have values assigned. In addition to setting default values for these parameters, these assignments cause the `hideOriginalSymbol` and `clearCanvasOnUpdate` parameters to be optional. If these parameters are not passed when a new SymbolCanvas instance is created, the compiler will not generate an error and the parameters will be set to *false* and *true*, respectively, by default.

6. Let's append the following initialization method just below the constructor block:

```
private function initSymbolCanvas(symbol:
➥DisplayObject, hideOriginalSymbol:Boolean,
➥clearCanvasOnUpdate:Boolean):void{
    src = symbol;
```

```
    clearOnUpdate = clearCanvasOnUpdate;
    hideOriginal = hideOriginalSymbol;
    initBitmap();
    if(hideOriginal) src.visible = false;
}
```

Note that the parameters are exactly the same as those of the constructor. You'll then use the arguments from the three parameters to assign values to your `src`, `clearOnUpdate`, and `hideOriginal` properties. Your code will then call another initialization method to generate your bitmap. If it happens that `hideOriginal` resolves to a value of *true*, your code will render the source object invisible.

7. Now for some slightly more complex code (one reason you're encapsulating it in the SymbolCanvas class). Add the following method below the primary `initSymbolCanvas` method that you just added:

```
private function initBitmap():void {
    var targ:MovieClip = src.parent as MovieClip;
    bmd = new BitmapData(src.stage.stageWidth,
➥src.stage.stageHeight, true, 0xffffff);
    bmp = new Bitmap(bmd);
    bmp.cacheAsBitmap = true;
    offset = targ.globalToLocal(new Point(0, 0));
    bmp.x = offset.x;
    bmp.y = offset.y;
    targ.addChildAt(bmp, targ.getChildIndex(src));
}
```

Let's walk through the `initBitmap` method line by line. You first create a local variable named `targ` to store the parent of your source object. The `parent` is the object inside which your source object is nested (this will likely be the root of the Flash document). Your code then uses the *as* keyword to tell the compiler to type this existing object as a MovieClip. This is necessary to access methods within the MovieClip class without generating errors. At the moment, `targ` is a local variable, meaning it is assigned using the *var* keyword within the `initBitmap` method and will cease to exist once the

**Conditional Logic**

Conditional statements are used to determine if or when particular blocks of code should be executed.

The `if` statement is one of the most basic pieces of programming logic. The `if` statement only executes the code inside its code block if the conditions inside its parentheses are found to be true. No curly braces are necessary to enclose an `if` statement if the code block is only a single line (see the SymbolCanvas class for an example of a single-line `if` statement).

The counterpart to the `if` statement is the `else` statement. An `else` statement must immediately follow an `if` statement. The code contained in an `else` block will execute if the conditions for the `if` statement are found to be false. Similarly, there is also an `else-if` statement that you can use to test for additional conditions (see the BoundedMover class later in this chapter for an example of the `else-if` statement).

method has completed execution. Use local variables when possible to increase the speed at which your code executes.

Next, your code assigns the bmd property to a new BitmapData object. Every object onscreen has a reference to the Stage stored in the stage property. You then use that reference to set your new BitmapData object's width and height properties to match those of the Stage within the first two arguments passed to the BitmapData constructor. With the third argument, you're assigning the transparent property of the BitmapData to *true*, which is essential for your effect to render properly. With the last argument you set the fill color to a hex value representing white (since the BitmapData instances use transparency, you will not see the white).

In the next line, you then assign your bmp property to a new Bitmap object and pass your BitmapData object to the Bitmap object's constructor. The line following that turns on the cacheAsBitmap property for the Bitmap object. It may sound redundant to cache a bitmap as a bitmap, but it will be necessary if the bitmap canvas will be used for any advanced masking in the future.

The next three lines ensure that the bitmap starts at the top-left corner of the Stage, even if your source symbol's parent does not. A Point is a very basic object: just an x coordinate and a y coordinate. The new Point starts out with both x and y at 0 (the top-left corner of the Stage), and uses the globalToLocal method of the targ object to offset the coordinates based on the targ object's position on Stage. After the coordinate space of the Point object has been adjusted, the x and y values are assigned to the Bitmap object (**Figure 3.21**).

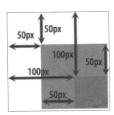

**Figure 3.21** The small purple square is nested inside the larger blue square's symbol. The local position of the purple square is x:50, y:50. The local position of the blue square is also x:50, y:50. The position of the purple square relative to the Stage is therefore x:100, y:100.

The last line within the `initBitmap` method adds your bitmap to the `targ` object's display list so that it will be visible onscreen. Your code uses the `addChildAt` method to ensure that bitmap is rendered just underneath your source symbol. By using the `getChildIndex` method to then assign your bitmap to the stacking position held by the source object, the source object is pushed up a level in the display list (right on top of the bitmap).

8. Let's fill in the `update`, `dispose`, and `getBitmap` methods with the following highlighted text:

```
public function update():void{
    if(clearOnUpdate) bmd.fillRect(bmd.rect, 0);
    var matrix:Matrix = src.transform.matrix;
    matrix.translate(-offset.x, -offset.y);
    bmd.draw(src, matrix, src.transform.
➥colorTransform, src.blendMode);
    bmp.bitmapData = bmd;
}


public function dispose():void{
    bmd.dispose();
    src.parent.removeChild(bmp);
    if(hideOriginal) src.visible = true;
}


public function getBitmap():Bitmap {
    return bmp;
}
```

The first line of the `update` method checks to see if `clearOnUpdate` is assigned a value of *true*, and if so, it clears the canvas using a simple fill. The second line stores the current matrix from the `src` object (which includes its position, scale, and rotation). The third line uses the `translate` method of the Matrix class, along with the `offset` point stored earlier, to determine where the `src` object should be rendered on the canvas (no matter how deep the source symbol is nested). Both the x and y coordinates have a minus sign (-) to compensate for the translation of the canvas in the initBitmap method. The fourth line renders an image of your source symbol onto the bitmap data using the transformation matrix that you translated, the color transform from the source symbol, and the blending mode from the source symbol, so it will appear as it does on Stage. The final line in the update method assigns the updated bitmap data to the bitmap object so it will render onscreen.

The dispose method is your housecleaning function. The first line removes the data stored within the BitmapData object (using the dispose method built into the BitmapData class) to free up memory. The second line removes the bitmap from the parent object's display list so it will no longer be rendered onscreen. The last line of the dispose method checks to see if the hideOriginal property was assigned a value of *true*, and if so, restores the visibility of the source object.

9. Confirm that the following import statements are all included at the top of your script. Add any that are missing:

```
import flash.display.DisplayObject;
import flash.display.MovieClip;
import flash.display.Bitmap;
import flash.display.BitmapData;
import flash.geom.Point;
import flash.geom.Matrix;
```

The SymbolCanvas class so far should read as follows:

```
package com.anim.fx {

    import flash.display.DisplayObject;
    import flash.display.MovieClip;
    import flash.display.Bitmap;
    import flash.display.BitmapData;
    import flash.geom.Point;
    import flash.geom.Matrix;

    class SymbolCanvas {
```

```
        private var offset:Point;
        private var bmd:BitmapData;
        private var bmp:Bitmap;
        private var src:DisplayObject;
        private var clearOnUpdate:Boolean;
        private var hideOriginal:Boolean;

        public function SymbolCanvas(symbol:
➥DisplayObject, hideOriginalSymbol:Boolean=false,
➥clearCanvasOnUpdate:Boolean=true){
            initSymbolCanvas(symbol,
➥hideOriginalSymbol, clearCanvasOnUpdate);
        }


        private function initSymbolCanvas(symbol:
➥DisplayObject, hideOriginalSymbol:Boolean,
➥clearCanvasOnUpdate:Boolean):void{
            src = symbol;
            clearOnUpdate = clearCanvasOnUpdate;
            hideOriginal = hideOriginalSymbol;
            initBitmap();
            if(hideOriginal) src.visible = false;
        }


        private function initBitmap():void {
            var targ:MovieClip = src.parent as
➥MovieClip;
            bmd = new BitmapData(src.stage.
➥stageWidth, src.stage.stageHeight, true, 0xffffff);
            bmp = new Bitmap(bmd);
            bmp.cacheAsBitmap = true;
            offset = targ.globalToLocal(new Point
➥(0, 0));
            bmp.x = offset.x;
            bmp.y = offset.y;
            targ.addChildAt(bmp, targ.getChildIndex
➥(src));
        }


        public function update():void{
            if(clearOnUpdate) bmd.fillRect
➥(bmd.rect, 0);
```

```
            var matrix:Matrix = src.transform.matrix;
            matrix.translate(-offset.x, -offset.y);
            bmd.draw(src, matrix, src.transform.
➥colorTransform, src.blendMode);
            bmp.bitmapData = bmd;
        }

        public function dispose():void{
            bmd.dispose();
            src.parent.removeChild(bmp);
            if(hideOriginal) src.visible = true;
        }

        public function getBitmap():Bitmap {
            return bmp;
        }
    }
}
```

The MotionBrush effect will also capture any animation inside your symbol.

You can now test the movie within your Flash document. Your symbol should now be drawing a path as it tweens (**Figure 3.22**).

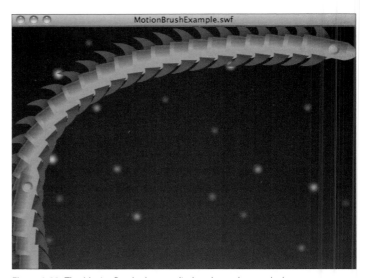

**Figure 3.22** The MotionBrush class applied to the rocket symbol.

To create a write-on effect, try drawing a shape or writing your name with the Pencil tool. You can select the path created with the Selection tool, cut it (Command+X/Ctrl+X), select your tweened symbol, and paste the path to the tween (Command+V/Ctrl+V). Test your movie again to see the effect (**Figure 3.23**).

**Figure 3.23** The MotionBrush class used as a write-on effect with a symbol containing a fire animation created using the Deco tool.

### The MotionTrail class

Now you'll generate the first variation on the MotionBrush theme. For starters, let's make the content painted onto the canvas fade as the source symbol moves farther away. This will render a trail, giving the impression that your brush symbol is moving a little too rapidly for the eyes. This effect is frequently used to create a trail for mouse cursors.

1. Save a new version of your MotionBrush document as **MotionTrailExample.fla**.

2. Create a new class called **MotionTrail**.

3. Save the class file as **MotionTrail.as** in the examples/com/anim/fx directory.

**TIP**

To explore the write-on effect further, check out the free Motion-Sketch extension (in the Extensions folder on the included CD or at http://ajarproductions.com/blog/2009/02/10/flash-extension-motionsketch/). MotionSketch can record your drawing in real time and translate it into a motion tween.

**CLOSE-UP**

#### Using a MotionBrush Object as a Mask

To use your symbol as a mask, you must first give instance names to your "brush" symbol instance and the symbol instance that you will be masking. Then you can use the following code (applied as a class or on a frame) (**Figure 3.24**):

```
import com.anim.fx.MotionBrush;
maskedInstance.cacheAsBitmap =
➥true;
maskedInstance.mask =
➥MotionBrush(brushInstance).
➥getCanvas();
```

**Figure 3.24** This animation creates the effect of wiping fog off a window using the MotionBrush applied as a mask.

4. Update the first line in the script to reflect the proper package:

```
package com.anim.fx {
```

5. You will be attaching MotionTrail to the Library symbol you created just as you did with the MotionBrush class. Update the class declaration so that your class extends MotionBrush:

```
public class MotionTrail extends MotionBrush {
```

6. The completed code for the MotionTrail class is considerably shorter than that of the MotionBrush class, because much of the behavior is inherited from the MotionBrush class. Complete the MotionTrail class by adding the highlighted code as follows:

```
package com.anim.fx {

    import flash.events.Event;
    import com.anim.fx.MotionBrush;

    public class MotionTrail extends MotionBrush {

        public var fadeAmount:Number = .5;

        public function MotionTrail() {
            init();
        }

        protected override function init():void {
            hideSymbol = false;
            clearCanvasOnUpdate = false;
            initStageListeners();
        }

        protected override function
    ➥onFrame(e:Event):void {
            symbolCanvas.fade(fadeAmount);
            super.onFrame(e);
        }

    }
}
```

Note that the `hideSymbol` and `clearCanvasOnUpdate` properties are assigned a value of *false*. Given that the MotionTrail will be manipulating the canvas, you'll keep the original symbol visible. Otherwise, the `init` function is identical to the `init` function in the Motion-Brush class. Also, note the use of the *override* keyword to rewrite the `init` function.

The `onFrame` method is also overwritten in the Motion-Trail subclass. The first line within the `onFrame` method calls a `fade` method on the SymbolCanvas instance that you will write in a moment. You'll pass the `fadeAmount` property value to the `fade` method. This will determine how much of the canvas's alpha value is faded on each new frame. Note that the `fadeAmount` property is public, meaning that this value can be assigned from any other part of your movie.

The second line in the `onFrame` method uses the *super* keyword to reference the `onFrame` method in the MotionBrush superclass and passes the event received by the overwriting `onFrame` method. In effect, you are augmenting the original `onFrame` method by adding a piece of functionality to the method and then running it as it normally would run inside of a MotionBrush instance.

**7.** Save your MotionTrail class and return to the SymbolCanvas class in the Code Editor. Add the following method toward the bottom of the SymbolCanvas class:

```
public function fade(alphaMult:Number=.5):void {
    if(clearOnUpdate) return;
    var cTransform:ColorTransform = new
➥ColorTransform();
    cTransform.alphaMultiplier = alphaMult;
    bmd.colorTransform(bmd.rect, cTransform);
}
```

This is the `fade` method that was referenced from the MotionTrail class. The `fade` method accepts one argument representing a value for how much transparency to apply on each frame. The closer the number is to 0, the more quickly the trail will fade out. The default value for this parameter is .5.

The first line inside the method checks to be sure that clearOnUpdate is not set to *true*; if it is, the code uses the *return* keyword to abort the function. Since clearOnUpdate will wipe the canvas clean each time the update method is executed, there would be no reason to adjust the transparency on a clean canvas, so there's no need to waste the processing power.

The second line within the fade method generates and stores a new ColorTransform object. In the third line, you apply the received argument to the alphaMultiplier property of the ColorTransform object. The last line then applies the ColorTransform to your BitmapData object, thus fading the entire image. The longer a particular representation of your symbol is onscreen, the more fades it will go through. Each fade will have an additive effect, rendering the older representations lighter than the new ones. The higher the alphaMultiplier property is set, the quicker the trail will fade.

8. Make sure that the following import statement has been added to the SymbolCanvas class:

   ```
   import flash.geom.ColorTransform;
   ```

9. Save your SymbolCanvas class and return to the MotionTrailExample.fla document.

10. Open the Symbol Properties for your symbol and update the Class field to read **com.anim.fx.MotionTrail**.

11. Test your movie (**Figure 3.25**).

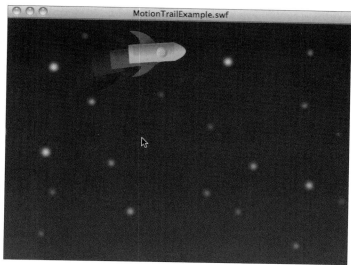

**Figure 3.25** The MotionTrail class applied to the rocket symbol.

Try adjusting the `fadeAmount` property in the Motion-Trail class and observe how the trail is altered (try values between 0 and 1). Note that the MotionTrail class is just as (if not more) complex an effect as the MotionBrush. But since the MotionBrush class was already written, it took significantly less effort to get the MotionTrail class off and running.

### The MotionBlurClip class

Now, rather than extending MotionTrail, you'll take the effect in a different direction by extending MotionBrush again. A motion blur effect will add a dose of realism to any animation. Motion blurring originates from motion pictures. The blur occurs when an object moves too fast for the camera to keep it in focus. This effect is a little more complex than MotionTrail, so it will require more new code, but several steps will look familiar at this point.

1.  Save a new version of your existing document as **MotionBlurExample.fla**.

2.  Create a new class called **MotionBlurClip**.

3.  Save the file as **MotionBlurClip.as** in the examples/ com/anim/fx directory.

4. Update the first line in the script to reflect the proper package:

```
package com.anim.fx {
```

5. Update the class declaration so that your class extends MotionBrush:

```
public class MotionBlurClip extends MotionBrush {
```

6. Add the following properties inside the package declaration (i.e., on a new line after public class MotionBlurClip extends MotionBrush { ):

```
protected var lastX:Number;
protected var lastY:Number;
protected var blurFilter:BlurFilter;
protected var blurIntensity:Number = 1;
```

These properties will store the information necessary to render the appropriate blur effect. The lastX and lastY properties will store the location of the symbol on the previous frame. Coupled with the blurIntensity properties, the lastX and lastY will be used to determine how much blur should be applied (because they reflect the current velocity of the symbol). The blurFilter property will store the actual BlurFilter object.

7. Add a new init method below the constructor method:

```
protected override function init():void {
    blurFilter = new BlurFilter(0, 0);
    lastX = this.x;
    lastY = this.y;
    hideSymbol = true;
    clearCanvasOnUpdate = true;
    initStageListeners();
}
```

The init method is similar to the previous init methods that you've written except that it also assigns values to the properties added to the MotionBlurClip class.

8. Make sure the constructor calls the init method by adding the following highlighted code:

```
public function MotionBlurClip() {
    init();
}
```

9. Add a new onFrame method (that will overwrite the onFrame method in the superclass):

```
protected override function onFrame(e:Event):void{
    var xdiff:Number = Math.abs(lastX - this.x) | 0;
    var ydiff:Number = Math.abs(lastY - this.y) | 0;
    lastX = this.x;
    lastY = this.y;
    setBlur(xdiff, ydiff);
    super.onFrame(e);
}
```

Similar to the onFrame method in the MotionTrail class, this onFrame method applies some code and then executes the onFrame method in the superclass (MotionBrush). The xdiff and ydiff variables store the difference between the previous location of the instance and the current location. Each line uses the absolute value method found in the Math class to ensure that the assigned values are positive. The bitwise OR operator (|) followed by the 0 ensures that if the preceding value is not a number, the xdiff and ydiff variables default to a value of 0. This is necessary for occasions when the lastX and lastY values have not been set (such as on the first frame).

10. Add the new setBlur method to implement the blur effect:

```
protected function setBlur(xAmount:Number,
➥yAmount:Number):void{
    blurFilter.blurX = xAmount * blurIntensity;
    blurFilter.blurY = yAmount * blurIntensity;
    symbolCanvas.filters = [blurFilter];
}
```

The setBlur method assigns the blurX and blurY values of the blurFilter using the position changes multiplied by the blurIntensity setting. The blurFilter is then passed to the symbolCanvas instance within an array.

This is set up to mimic the `filters` property used on display objects, which is always an array.

11. Ensure that the following import statements are included (you may have to add the line for MotionBrush):

```
import flash.filters.BlurFilter;
import flash.events.Event;
import com.anim.fx.MotionBrush;
```

The completed MotionBlurClip code should now read:

```
package   com.anim.fx {

    import flash.filters.BlurFilter;
    import flash.events.Event;
    import com.anim.fx.MotionBrush;

    public class MotionBlurClip extends
➥MotionBrush{

        protected var lastX:Number;
        protected var lastY:Number;
        protected var blurFilter:BlurFilter;
        protected var blurIntensity:Number = 1;

        public function MotionBlurClip() {
            init();
        }

        protected override function init():void {
            blurFilter = new BlurFilter(0, 0);
            lastX = this.x;
            lastY = this.y;
            hideSymbol = true;
            clearCanvasOnUpdate = true;
            initStageListeners();
        }

        protected override function
➥onFrame(e:Event):void{
            var xdiff:Number = Math.abs(lastX -
➥this.x) | 0;
```

```
                var ydiff:Number = Math.abs(lastY -
➥this.y) | 0;
                lastX = this.x;
                lastY = this.y;
                setBlur(xdiff, ydiff);
                super.onFrame(e);
            }


        protected function setBlur(xAmount:Number,
    ➥yAmount:Number):void{
                blurFilter.blurX = xAmount *
    ➥blurIntensity;
                blurFilter.blurY = yAmount *
    ➥blurIntensity;
                symbolCanvas.filters = [blurFilter];
            }


    }


}
```

12. Save your MotionBlurClip class and return to the Sym-
    bolCanvas class. Add the following methods below the
    getBitmap method in the SymbolCanvas class:

```
public function get filters():Array {
    return _filters;
}


public function set filters(filterArr:Array):void {
    _filters = filterArr;
    bmp.filters = _filters;
}
```

The preceding code uses two special types of methods
known as a *getter* and a *setter*. From the outside of the
class, these methods are applied as if they are a single
property. This allows you to keep your actual property
private, as well as allowing you to execute other code
after the value has been set. The get method is called
when no assignment operator (equal sign) is used;
thus, it returns the value as if it were a property. When

an assignment operator is used (e.g., symbolCanvas. filters = myFilterArray), the set method accepts the parameter to be set (which is whatever follows the assignment operator).

13. Add a private variable for the filters at the top of the SymbolCanvas code and below the package statement (after the existing properties):

```
private var _filters:Array;
```

14. Add this line inside the top of the initSymbolCanvas method to initialize the _filters property value:

```
_filters = new Array();
```

The (now totally) completed SymbolCanvas class should read:

```
package com.anim.fx {

        import flash.display.DisplayObject;
        import flash.display.MovieClip;
        import flash.display.Bitmap;
        import flash.display.BitmapData;
        import flash.geom.Point;
        import flash.geom.Matrix;
        import flash.geom.ColorTransform;
        import flash.filters.BitmapFilter;

        class SymbolCanvas {

            private var offset:Point;
            private var bmd:BitmapData;
            private var bmp:Bitmap;
            private var src:DisplayObject;
            private var clearOnUpdate:Boolean;
            private var hideOriginal:Boolean;
            private var _filters:Array;

            public function SymbolCanvas(symbol:
    ➥DisplayObject, hideOriginalSymbol:Boolean=false,
    ➥clearCanvasOnUpdate:Boolean=true){
```

**TIP**

It is common convention to use an underscore (_) at the beginning of a private property.

```
        initSymbolCanvas(symbol,
➥hideOriginalSymbol, clearCanvasOnUpdate);
        }


        private function initSymbolCanvas(symbol:
➥DisplayObject, hideOriginalSymbol:Boolean,
➥clearCanvasOnUpdate:Boolean):void{
            _filters = new Array();
            src = symbol;
            clearOnUpdate = clearCanvasOnUpdate;
            hideOriginal = hideOriginalSymbol;
            initBitmap();
            if(hideOriginal) src.visible = false;
        }


        private function initBitmap():void {
            var targ:MovieClip = src.parent as
➥MovieClip;
            bmd = new BitmapData(src.stage.
➥stageWidth, src.stage.stageHeight, true,
➥0xffffff);
            bmp = new Bitmap(bmd);
            bmp.cacheAsBitmap = true;
            offset = targ.globalToLocal(new
➥Point(0, 0));
            bmp.x = offset.x;
            bmp.y = offset.y;
            targ.addChildAt(bmp, targ.
➥getChildIndex(src));
        }


        public function update():void{
            if(clearOnUpdate) bmd.fillRect(bmd.
➥rect, 0);
            var matrix:Matrix = src.transform.
➥matrix;
            matrix.translate(-offset.x,
➥-offset.y);
            bmd.draw(src, matrix, src.transform.
➥colorTransform, src.blendMode);
            bmp.bitmapData = bmd;
        }
```

```
                    public function dispose():void{
                        bmd.dispose();
                        src.parent.removeChild(bmp);
                        if(hideOriginal) src.visible = true;
                    }


                    public function fade(alphaMult:Number=
➥.5):void {
                        if(clearOnUpdate) return;
                        var cTransform:ColorTransform =
➥new ColorTransform();
                        cTransform.alphaMultiplier =
➥alphaMult;
                        bmd.colorTransform(bmd.rect,
➥cTransform);
                    }

                    public function getBitmap():Bitmap {
                        return bmp;
                    }


                    public function get filters():Array {
                        return _filters;
                    }

                    public function set filters(filterArr:
➥Array):void {
                        _filters = filterArr;
                        bmp.filters = _filters;
                    }


            }
        }
```

15. Save your class and return to the MotionBlurExample.fla document.

16. Open the Symbol Properties for your symbol and update the Class field to read **com.anim.fx.MotionBlurClip**.

**17.** Test your MotionBlurExample movie and observe the new effect (**Figure 3.26**).

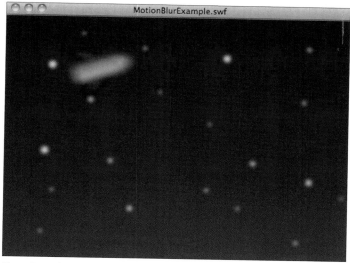

**Figure 3.26** The MotionBlurClip class applied to the rocket symbol.

### *The MotionBlurTrail class*

Now let's combine the MotionTrail effect with the motion blur. You'll start by extending the MotionBlurClip class and utilizing the code already written for the MotionTrail class.

**1.** Save a new version of your existing document as **MotionBlurTrailExample.fla**.

**2.** Create a new class called **MotionBlurTrail**.

**3.** Save the file as **MotionBlurTrail.as** in the examples/com/anim/fx directory.

**4.** Update the first line in the script to reflect the proper package:

```
package com.anim.fx {
```

**5.** Update the class declaration so that your class extends MotionBlurClip:

```
public class MotionBlurTrail extends
➥MotionBlurClip {
```

6. Update your class to match the following highlighted code to complete the MotionBlurTrail class:

```
package com.anim.fx {

    import flash.events.Event;
    import com.anim.fx.MotionBlurClip;

    public class MotionBlurTrail extends
➥MotionBlurClip {

        public var fadeAmount:Number = .5;

        public function MotionBlurTrail() {
            init();
        }

        protected override function init():void {
            super.init();
            hideSymbol = false;
            clearCanvasOnUpdate = false;
        }

        protected override function
➥onFrame(e:Event):void{
            symbolCanvas.fade(fadeAmount);
            super.onFrame(e);
        }

    }
}
```

The MotionBlurTrail class utilizes a fadeAmount property just like the MotionTrail class. The MotionBlurTrail init method starts by calling the init method in the superclass (MotionBlurClip) and then updates the hideSymbol property (to ensure the instance remains visible) and the clearCanvasOnUpdate property (to ensure the canvas is not cleared on each new frame). It is possible to set these properties after calling the superclass's init method because the SymbolCanvas is not instantiated until the onAddedToStage method is executed (after the init method is executed). The onFrame in this class then utilizes the same code found in the MotionTrail class.

7. Save your class and return to the MotionBlurTrailExample.fla document.

8. Open the Symbol Properties for your symbol and update the Class field to read **com.anim.fx.MotionBlurTrail**.

9. Test your movie to demo the new effect (**Figure 3.27**).

**Figure 3.27** The MotionBlurTrail class applied to the rocket symbol.

As you can see from the MotionBrush class and its subclasses, it's possible to construct fantastic visual effects with ActionScript classes. The more you can leverage object-oriented principles, the more effects you can create with progressively less new code.

The remaining examples in this chapter illustrate a different reusable behavior: character control.

## Class Examples: Character Control

As described at the beginning of the chapter, you'll start the character control classes by writing a simple Mover class. From the Mover class, you'll create subclasses to control different types of animated characters. These classes will allow for various types of user interaction.

For these classes, you'll need to add a new folder to your class package. Create a new folder called **character** inside the examples/com/anim/ directory.

### The Mover class

The Mover class will simply move an object based on keyboard input. It is recommended that you close any files that you have open from the previous examples before proceeding.

1. Create a new Flash ActionScript 3.0 document and save the file as **MoverExample.fla** in the examples folder.

2. Draw a circle on Stage using the Oval Primitive tool (found within the Shape tools on the Toolbar). Hold down the Shift key to constrain the proportions as you draw.

3. Select the circle and convert it to a MovieClip symbol (F8) named **character**. Make sure that the registration point (the dark square in the 9-square grid within the Convert to Symbol dialog box) is in the center before clicking OK.

4. Create a new ActionScript class named **Mover**.

5. Save the ActionScript file as **Mover.as** in the examples/com/anim/character folder.

6. Add the following highlighted code to have Mover subclass MovieClip:

```
public class Mover extends flash.display.MovieClip {
```

7. Update the package statement with the following highlighted code to match the saved location of the Mover.as file:

```
package com.anim.character {
```

8. Add the following variable declarations immediately following the class declaration (i.e., just before the `public function Mover` constructor line):

```
protected var vx:int;
protected var vy:int;
protected var normalSpeed:uint = 5;
protected var currentSpeed:uint = 0;
protected var currentScaleX:Number;
```

Let's review what you have so far. Steps 6 and 7 should be pretty familiar to you following the visual effects class examples. In step 8, you've set up several properties that will be accessed later in the code. All properties use the `protected` keyword to guarantee that their values can be altered by subclasses (and only by subclasses). The vx and vy variables will store the x (left and right) and y (up and down) velocities, respectively. Both variables are strictly typed to the *integer* data type (`int`). When strict typing a property, it is best to be as specific as possible. It's unlikely in the case of vx and vy that you'll need your object to move at less than 1 pixel per frame (that's quite slow), so integers will offer sufficient precision. The integer data type also allows negative values, which you'll need for your object to move up or left.

The next variable, `normalSpeed`, stores the default speed. This variable is typed to the *unsigned integer* data type (`uint`). Unsigned integer values do not include negative numbers, so this works great for speed, which will always be a positive number (since it's the absolute value of the velocity). You will use the speed, in combination with the direction, to determine the velocities.

**CLOSE-UP**

**The Flash Coordinate System**

The Flash coordinate system starts at the top-left corner of the Stage. Moving to the right increases the value of the x coordinate. Moving down increases the value of the y coordinate.

9. Add the following highlighted code to call the `init` method from the constructor:

```
public function Mover() {
    init();
}
```

10. Add the `init` method definition as follows below the constructor method:

```
protected function init():void {
    initSpeed();
    currentScaleX = this.scaleX;
```

```
        this.addEventListener(Event.ADDED_TO_STAGE,
➥onAddedToStage);
        this.addEventListener(Event.REMOVED_FROM_
➥STAGE, onRemovedFromStage);
}
```

Much of this init method will look familiar from the effects classes. So, let's just go through what's new. An initSpeed method is called. This is separated into its own method to make this aspect of the Mover class simpler to override. The next line initializes the currentScaleX value based on the current *x* scale of the symbol used. The currentScaleX property will be useful in subclasses when you want to alter the horizontal direction/orientation of the character. The two addEventListener method calls are identical to those in the classes you've already written in this chapter.

11. Add the following method after the init method to initialize the currentSpeed property:

```
protected function initSpeed():void {
    currentSpeed = normalSpeed;
}
```

12. Add the following code after the initSpeed method:

```
protected function onAddedToStage(e:Event):void {
    this.stage.addEventListener(KeyboardEvent.
➥KEY_DOWN, keyDown);
    this.stage.addEventListener(KeyboardEvent.
➥KEY_UP, keyUp);
    startMoving();
}

protected function onRemovedFromStage(e:Event):
➥void {
    this.stage.removeEventListener(KeyboardEvent.
➥KEY_DOWN, keyDown);
    this.stage.removeEventListener(KeyboardEvent.
➥KEY_UP, keyUp);
    stopMoving();
}
```

These methods have the same names as those used in the effects classes, but their content is different. The onAddedToStage method adds two event listeners to the symbol's stage property. These events fire when a key is pressed and when a key is released on the keyboard. The third line calls a (yet unwritten) method to start the Mover moving.

The onRemovedFromStage does the complete inverse of the onAddedToStage, removing the event listeners and calling a method to stop the Mover from moving.

13. Add the following three methods after the methods you've already written:

```
public function startMoving():void {
    this.addEventListener(Event.ENTER_FRAME,
➥updatePosition);
}

public function stopMoving():void {
    this.removeEventListener(Event.ENTER_FRAME,
➥updatePosition);
}

protected function updatePosition(e:Event):void {
    this.x += vx;
    this.y += vy;
}
```

The startMoving and stopMoving methods tend to the adding and removing of the ENTER_FRAME event. When the ENTER_FRAME event fires, it triggers the updatePosition method.

The updatePosition method adds the x and y velocities to the current x and y coordinates to move the symbol on each frame.

14. Then add the following code for the two methods that will handle the keyboard events:

```
protected function keyDown(e:KeyboardEvent):void {
    if (e.keyCode == Keyboard.LEFT) {
        vx = -currentSpeed;
```

```
        } else if (e.keyCode == Keyboard.RIGHT) {
            vx = currentSpeed;
        } else if (e.keyCode == Keyboard.UP) {
            vy = -currentSpeed;
        } else if (e.keyCode == Keyboard.DOWN) {
            vy = currentSpeed;
        }
    }


    protected function keyUp(e:KeyboardEvent):void {
        if (e.keyCode == Keyboard.LEFT || e.keyCode ==
    ➥Keyboard.RIGHT) {
            vx = 0;
        } else if (e.keyCode == Keyboard.DOWN ||
    ➥e.keyCode == Keyboard.UP) {
            vy = 0;
        }
    }
```

The keyDown and keyUp methods utilize conditional logic to respond differently based on which key was pressed. The keyCode property of the e parameter stores the key that was pressed when the keyboard event was fired. The keyCode value can then be compared against values stored in the Keyboard class. In this case, you're looking for the arrow keys: left, right, up, and down. This section of code utilizes else-if statements because the conditions are all mutually exclusive, since each event will reflect exactly one key press. The x or y velocity will then be set, depending on which key was pressed. The keyDown method uses the currentSpeed property as the basis for the velocities, and the keyUp method sets the values to 0.

15. Ensure that the following import statements are included just inside the package declaration:

```
import flash.display.MovieClip;
import flash.events.KeyboardEvent;
import flash.events.Event;
import flash.ui.Keyboard;
```

The completed Mover class should now read as follows:

```
package  com.anim.character {

    import flash.display.MovieClip;
    import flash.events.KeyboardEvent;
    import flash.events.Event;
    import flash.ui.Keyboard;

    public class Mover extends flash.display.
➥MovieClip {

        protected var vx:int;
        protected var vy:int;
        protected var normalSpeed:uint = 5;
        protected var currentSpeed:uint = 0;
        protected var currentScaleX:Number;

        public function Mover() {
            init();
        }

        protected function init():void {
            initSpeed();
            currentScaleX = this.scaleX;
            this.addEventListener(Event.ADDED_TO_
➥STAGE, onAddedToStage);
            this.addEventListener(Event.REMOVED_
➥FROM_STAGE, onRemovedFromStage);
            keyUp);
        }

        protected function initSpeed():void {
            currentSpeed = normalSpeed;
        }

        protected function onAddedToStage
➥(e:Event):void {
            this.stage.addEventListener
➥(KeyboardEvent.KEY_DOWN, keyDown);
            this.stage.addEventListener
➥(KeyboardEvent.KEY_UP, keyUp);
```

```
                                    startMoving();
                            }

                            protected function onRemovedFromStage
                    ➥(e:Event):void {
                            this.stage.removeEventListener(KeyboardEvent.
                    ➥KEY_DOWN, keyDown);
                            this.stage.removeEventListener(KeyboardEvent.
                    ➥KEY_UP, keyUp);
                                    stopMoving();
                            }

                            public function startMoving():void {
                                    this.addEventListener(Event.ENTER_
                    ➥FRAME, updatePosition);
                            }

                            public function stopMoving():void {
                                    this.removeEventListener(Event.ENTER_
                    ➥FRAME, updatePosition);
                            }

                            protected function updatePosition
                    ➥(e:Event):void {
                                    this.x += vx;
                                    this.y += vy;
                            }

                            protected function keyDown
                    ➥(e:KeyboardEvent):void {
                                    if (e.keyCode == Keyboard.LEFT) {
                                        vx = -currentSpeed;
                                    } else if (e.keyCode == Keyboard.
                    ➥RIGHT) {
                                        vx = currentSpeed;
                                    } else if (e.keyCode == Keyboard.UP) {
                                        vy = -currentSpeed;
                                    } else if (e.keyCode == Keyboard.DOWN) {
                                        vy = currentSpeed;
                                    }
                            }
```

```
        protected function keyUp(e:KeyboardEvent):
➥void {
            if (e.keyCode == Keyboard.LEFT ||
➥e.keyCode == Keyboard.RIGHT) {
                vx = 0;
            } else if (e.keyCode == Keyboard.DOWN
➥|| e.keyCode == Keyboard.UP) {
                vy = 0;
            }
        }


    }
}
```

**16.** Save your script, return to the MoverExample.fla document, and update the character symbol properties to use the **com.anim.character.Mover** class.

**17.** Save your document and test the movie (**Figure 3.28**).

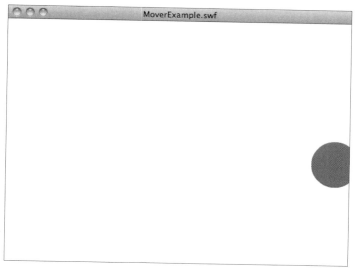

**Figure 3.28** The Mover class allows the arrow keys to move the character instance.

In the test window, press and hold the arrow keys to move the character around the Stage. Notice that you can navigate your character right off the edge of the screen. The

You could create a class with a different edge behavior, like one that will wrap your character to the opposite edge of the screen, or you could create a class with an edge behavior that can be altered on the fly.

first subclass to the Mover class will prevent your character from leaving the screen.

### The BoundedMover class

Depending on the type of experience you are designing, you'll need to decide what will happen when your character reaches the edge of the screen. For the examples in this chapter, you'll create a class that will prevent the Mover from leaving the screen.

1. Save a copy of your current document as **BoundedMoverExample.fla** in the examples folder.

2. Create a new class named **BoundedMover**.

3. Save the ActionScript file as **BoundedMover.as** in the examples/com/anim/character folder.

4. Add the following highlighted code to have BoundedMover subclass Mover:

```
public class BoundedMover extends Mover {
```

5. Update the package statement with the following highlighted code to match the saved location of the BoundedMover.as file:

```
package  com.anim.character {
```

6. Add the following variable declaration immediately following the class declaration:

```
protected var boundaries:Rectangle;
```

The boundaries property will store the rectangle that defines the edges of the area within which your character is allowed to travel.

7. Add the familiar onAddedToStage method below the constructor method:

```
override protected function onAddedToStage(
➥e:Event):void {
    var topCorner:Point = root.localToGlobal(new
➥Point(0,0));
    var w:Number;
    var h:Number;
```

```
    if(root.loaderInfo.loader == null){
        w = stage.stageWidth;
        h = stage.stageHeight;
    } else {
        w = root.loaderInfo.loader.parent.width;
        h = root.loaderInfo.loader.parent.height;
    }
    setBoundaries(new Rectangle(topCorner.x,
➡topCorner.y, w, h));
    super.onAddedToStage(e);
}
```

The onAddedToStage method is a little complicated, because you're writing it in a manner that will also work in your web portfolio (for Chapter 5) without needing any updates. So, your boundaries will be different if your SWF file is being loaded into another file (as it will in the web portfolio).

You first create a local variable, topCorner, to locate the top-left corner of the SWF that houses your BoundedMover instance. The *root* keyword will ensure that your topCorner point reflects the SWF containing the BoundedMover instance, not an outside movie that has loaded the SWF containing your BoundedMover (this will make more sense in Chapter 5). You then create two variables (w and h) to store the width and height of the container movie. To determine if your SWF has been loaded into another movie, you check the loader property of the loaderInfo object. If this property is *null* (not set), then your SWF has not been loaded into another movie, and you can use stage.stageWidth and stage.stageHeight for your default boundaries. If the loader property has been set, then the else block determines the w and h values based on the parent object of the loader.

The code then invokes a new method, setBoundaries, and passes a Rectangle object based on the corner point, width, and height determined above. Finally, the last line calls the onAddToStage of the superclass (Mover).

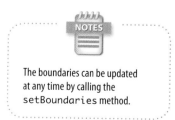

**NOTES**

The boundaries can be updated at any time by calling the setBoundaries method.

8. Add the following method after the method in the previous step.

```
override protected function updatePosition
➥(e:Event):void {
    checkEdges();
    super.updatePosition(e);
}
```

The new updatePosition method will check to see if your character is at or beyond the edges of the boundaries before calling the updatePosition from the superclass. You'll write the checkEdges method in a moment.

9. Add the setBoundaries method after the updatePosition method:

```
public function setBoundaries(rect:Rectangle):
➥void {
    boundaries = rect;
}
```

The setBoundaries method simply updates the boundaries property value. This value will be utilized in the checkEdges method that you are about to write.

10. Add the checkEdges method after the setBoundaries method:

```
protected function checkEdges():void {
    var characterEdges:Rectangle = this.
➥getBounds(this.stage);
    if(characterEdges.left <= boundaries.left &&
➥vx < 0) {
        vx = 0;
    } else if(characterEdges.right >= boundaries.
➥right && vx > 0) {
        vx = 0;
    }
    if(characterEdges.top <= boundaries.top &&
➥vy < 0) {
        vy = 0;
```

```
    } else if(characterEdges.bottom >= boundaries.
➥bottom && vy > 0){
        vy = 0;
    }
}
```

The first line inside the checkEdges method creates a new variable to store the rectangle containing the bounds around the character symbol. The conditional statements that follow check the left, right, top, and bottom edges, respectively.

Since your character can't be at the left edge and the right edge at the same time (as long as your Stage is wider than your character), it's best to use if-else blocks (rather than two if blocks). If the character is at or past the left edge, there's no reason to check the right edge. The same logic applies to the top and bottom. The code in the checkEdges method uses the *less than or equal to* (<=) and *greater than or equal to* (>=) operators to compare the edge of the character to the edge of the boundary rectangle.

In addition to checking the character's location, you should also confirm that the character is attempting to move beyond the boundary. If the character is headed away from the boundary, there's no reason to stop the character from moving. You can check the character's direction by determining if its x and y coordinates are positive or negative (if the velocity is 0, no action is needed).

If the *x* velocity is greater than 0, the character is moving to the right. If the *x* velocity is less than 0, the character is moving to the left. To check two conditions (the character's position relative to the boundary and the character's direction) in a single if statement, you need to use the conditional *and* operator (&&). To stop the character from moving, the relevant velocity is then set to 0.

NOTES

For simplicity, the checkEdges method in this chapter does not reset the character's position (just inside the boundary crossed) because it is not necessary for the examples shown. You may want to add this functionality to the class later, especially if you plan to call the setBounds method again (in case your character is then outside of the boundaries just set).

11. Ensure that the following import statements are included just inside the package declaration:

```
import com.anim.character.Mover;
import flash.events.Event;
import flash.geom.Rectangle;
import flash.geom.Point;
```

The completed BoundedMover class should read:

```
package com.anim.character {

    import com.anim.character.Mover;
    import flash.events.Event;
    import flash.geom.Rectangle;
    import flash.geom.Point;


    public class BoundedMover extends Mover {

        protected var boundaries:Rectangle;

        public function BoundedMover(){

        }

        override protected function
➥onAddedToStage(e:Event):void {
            var topCorner:Point = root.
➥localToGlobal(new Point(0,0));
            var w:Number;
            var h:Number;
            if(root.loaderInfo.loader == null){
                w = stage.stageWidth;
                h = stage.stageHeight;
            } else {
                w = root.loaderInfo.loader.parent.
➥width;
                h = root.loaderInfo.loader.parent.
➥height;
            }
            setBoundaries(new Rectangle(topCorner.x,
➥topCorner.y, w, h));
```

```
                super.onAddedToStage(e);
        }

        override protected function
➥updatePosition(e:Event):void {
                checkEdges();
                super.updatePosition(e);
        }

        public function setBoundaries
➥(rect:Rectangle):void {
                boundaries = rect;
        }

        protected function checkEdges():void {
                var characterEdges:Rectangle = this.
➥getBounds(this.stage);
                if(characterEdges.left <= boundaries.
➥left && vx < 0) {
                        vx = 0;
                } else if(characterEdges.right >=
➥boundaries.right && vx > 0) {
                        vx = 0;
                }
                if(characterEdges.top <=
➥boundaries.top && vy < 0) {
                        vy = 0;
                } else if(characterEdges.bottom >=
➥boundaries.bottom && vy > 0) {
                        vy = 0;
                }
        }

    }

}
```

**12.** Save your class, return to your BoundedMoverExample.fla
document, and update the character symbol properties to
have a Class value of **com.anim.character.BoundedMover**.

13. Save your document and test the movie. Move your character around and note that it will not leave the screen (**Figure 3.29**).

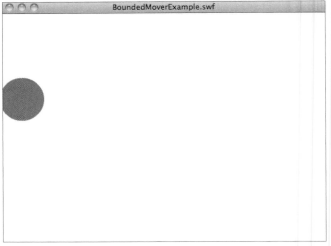

Figure 3.29 The BoundedMover class prevents the character from traveling beyond the edges of the Stage.

Now that you have a handle on controlling a character, let's start adding a bit more complexity to the character.

### Building the Wanderer symbol

In this section you'll build some character animation similar to that of an arcade classic. The Wanderer class will control a character that wanders around the screen (in search of food or possibly to evade tiny ghosts). You'll start by building a simple character with a hyperactive jaw.

1. Save a copy of your current (Mover.fla) document as **WandererExample.fla** in the examples folder.

2. Double-click on the character instance on the Stage to edit the symbol's Timeline.

3. Select the oval primitive shape that is already on Stage.

4. Set the Start angle and End angle settings in the Properties panel to **10** and **350**, respectively (**Figure 3.30**).

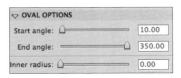

Figure 3.30 Setting the Start and End angle of the oval primitive shape will create the opening for the character's mouth.

Setting the Start and End angles will create a 20-degree opening for the character's mouth (**Figure 3.31**).

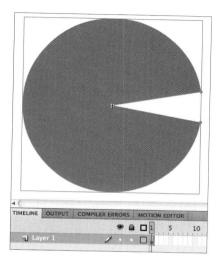

Figure 3.31 The oval primitive shape on frame 1 with a 20-degree opening.

5. Select frame 10 in the Timeline and add a new keyframe (F6).

6. Select the oval on frame 10.

7. Update the Start angle and End angle settings in the Properties panel to **40** and **320**, respectively. This will create a wider (80-degree) opening for when the character's mouth is completely open (**Figure 3.32**).

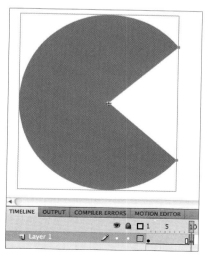

Figure 3.32 The oval primitive shape on frame 10 with an 80-degree opening.

8. Select frame 1 and create a Shape Tween (Insert > Shape Tween). If you scrub the Timeline at this point, you'll notice that the tween doesn't look like a mouth opening and closing (**Figure 3.33**).

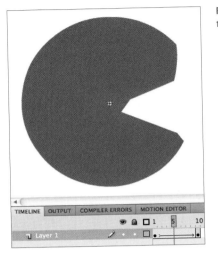

Figure 3.33 The shape tween needs a little work.

9. Select frame 1 again. Break the shape primitive into a raw vector shape (Command+B/Ctrl+B). This will allow you to add shape hints to help Flash interpolate the tweened frames.

10. Add three shape hints by choosing Modify > Shape > Add Shape Hint three times. The three hints will all have letters (a, b, and c) and will overlap when they are added.

**11.** Move the shape hints to the three points that compose the mouth. The points will be red for the moment (**Figure 3.34**).

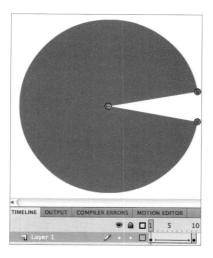

**Figure 3.34**  The shape hints in position on frame 1.

**12.** Select frame 10 on the Timeline and break that shape apart (Command+B/Ctrl+B).

**13.** Move the three shape hints to match the three points on frame 1. The points should turn green when they are in place (**Figure 3.35**).

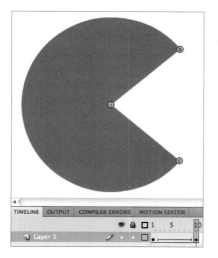

**Figure 3.35**  The shape hints in position on frame 10.

NOTES

When the shape hints on frame 10 are in place, the hints on frame 1 should turn yellow. You may have to move the first point away (release it) and move it back into position (on both frames 1 and 10) to have it turn yellow on frame 1 and green on frame 10.

**14.** Scrub the Timeline again. The mouth should now appear to open as you move from frame 1 to frame 10 (**Figure 3.36**).

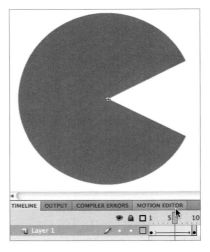

**Figure 3.36** The shape now tweens properly.

**15.** Ctrl-click/right-click on the first frame and choose Copy Frames.

**16.** Select frame 20, Ctrl-click/right-click and choose Paste Frames.

**17.** Ctrl-click/right-click on frame 10 and choose Create Shape Tween.

**18.** Add three new shape hints to frame 10 and move them to match the positions of the three shape hints already in place on frame 10 (**Figure 3.37**).

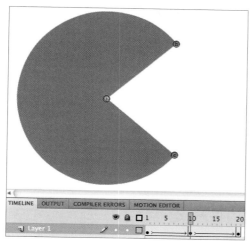

**Figure 3.37** The second set of shape hints added to frame 10.

**19.** Select frame 20 and move the three shape hints into position (**Figure 3.38**).

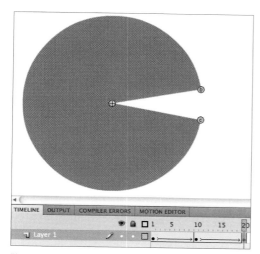

**Figure 3.38** The second set of shape hints in position on frame 20.

20. Scrub the Timeline.

You should now have a mouth that opens and closes. One last adjustment is needed: You'll want this mouth to loop (at the moment, frame 1 and frame 20 are identical and you only need one of them).

21. Select frame 19 and add a keyframe (F6). Note that two of the shape hints are now slightly out of place on frame 19.

22. Reposition the shape hints to match the points of the mouth (**Figure 3.39**).

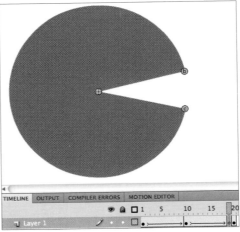

**Figure 3.39** The second set of shape hints repositioned on frame 19.

23. Ctrl-click/right-click on frame 20 and choose Remove Frames.

**24.** Add a new layer and create an eye for your character using the Oval tool. Make sure the eye doesn't overlap with the mouth on frame 10 (**Figure 3.40**).

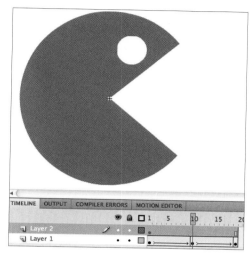

**Figure 3.40** The completed character with the eye in place.

**25.** Test your movie. You should now have a looping animation of your character.

### The Wanderer class

The Wanderer class will match the character's intention with the user's key presses. When the character changes directions, it will now orient toward that new direction. Additionally, the character's internal timeline will only animate when the character is in motion.

**1.** Create a new class named **Wanderer**.

**2.** Save the ActionScript file as **Wanderer.as** in the examples/com/anim/character folder.

**3.** Add the following highlighted code to have Wanderer subclass BoundedMover:

```
public class Wanderer extends BoundedMover {
```

4. Update the package statement with the following highlighted code to match the saved location of the Wanderer.as file:

```
package  com.anim.character {
```

5. Add the following updatePosition method below the constructor method to override the method (of the same name) in the superclass:

```
override protected function
➥updatePosition(e:Event):void {
    super.updatePosition(e);
    if(vx == 0 && vy == 0){
        this.stop();
    } else {
        this.play();
    }
}
```

The only update that this new method implements to the superclass's functionality is to either stop the animation on the symbol's Timeline if the object has no velocity (in any direction) or play the symbol's animation (mouth chomping in this example).

6. Add the following keyDown method below the updatePosition method:

```
override protected function
➥keyDown(e:KeyboardEvent):void {
    if (e.keyCode == Keyboard.LEFT) {
        vx = -currentSpeed;
        this.rotation = 0;
        this.scaleX = -currentScaleX;
    } else if (e.keyCode == Keyboard.RIGHT) {
        vx = currentSpeed;
        this.rotation = 0;
        this.scaleX = currentScaleX;
    } else if (e.keyCode == Keyboard.UP) {
        vy = -currentSpeed;
        this.rotation = -90;
        this.scaleX = currentScaleX;
    } else if (e.keyCode == Keyboard.DOWN) {
```

```
        vy = currentSpeed;
        this.rotation = 90;
        this.scaleX = currentScaleX;
    }
}
```

The logic in this method is exactly the same as the Mover class. The only updates are to assign values to the rotation and scaleX properties. These assignments are to orient the character to its direction. For example, since your character is facing right by default, you have to flip the character's horizontal scaling to have the character face to the left. To face the character up or down, you need to use rotation. Both scaleX and rotation are necessary, since only using rotation would cause the character to be upside down when traveling to the left (**Figure 3.41**).

**Figure 3.41** The character as shown if only **rotation** were used rather than setting the **scaleX** property.

**7.** Ensure that the following import statements are included just inside the package declaration:

```
import com.anim.character.BoundedMover;
import flash.events.KeyboardEvent;
import flash.ui.Keyboard;
import flash.events.Event;
```

The completed Wanderer class should read:

```
package   com.anim.character {

    import com.anim.character.BoundedMover;
    import flash.events.KeyboardEvent;
    import flash.ui.Keyboard;
    import flash.events.Event;

    public class Wanderer extends BoundedMover {

        public function Wanderer() {

        }

        override protected function
➥updatePosition(e:Event):void {
            super.updatePosition(e);
```

```
                if(vx == 0 && vy == 0){
                    this.stop();
                } else {
                    this.play();
                }
            }

            override protected function
    ➥keyDown(e:KeyboardEvent):void {
                if (e.keyCode == Keyboard.LEFT) {
                    vx = -currentSpeed;
                    this.rotation = 0;
                    this.scaleX = -currentScaleX;
                } else if (e.keyCode == Keyboard.
    ➥RIGHT) {
                    vx = currentSpeed;
                    this.rotation = 0;
                    this.scaleX = currentScaleX;
                } else if (e.keyCode == Keyboard.UP) {
                    vy = -currentSpeed;
                    this.rotation = -90;
                    this.scaleX = currentScaleX;
                } else if (e.keyCode == Keyboard.DOWN) {
                    vy = currentSpeed;
                    this.rotation = 90;
                    this.scaleX = currentScaleX;
                }
            }

        }
    }
```

8. Save your class, return to your WandererExample.fla document, and update the character symbol properties to have a Class value of **com.anim.character.Wanderer**.

9. Save your document and test the movie. Move your character around and note how the character changes direction when pressing a new arrow key and how the character stops animating when no keys are pressed (**Figure 3.42**).

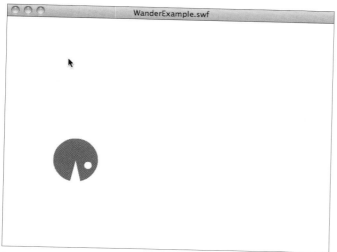

**Figure 3.42** The Wanderer in action, chomping away and facing in the intended direction.

Now you'll jump from the Wanderer to a much more advanced character. You can close any open Flash documents or scripts.

### The Runner class

Normally, you might want to develop an object that walks before it runs, but since you have your base classes built, you can always go back and add a Walker class. Like the Wanderer class, the Runner class will extend the Bounded-Mover class created earlier.

1. Create a new ActionScript 3.0 document and save it as **RunnerExample.fla** in the examples folder.

2. Open the walk cycle that you created in Chapter 2. Copy the symbol from the Library that contains your character and paste it into the RunnerExample document Library. Ctrl-click/right-click and ensure that the new symbol in your RunnerExample document is set to have a Type value of "Movie Clip" in the Symbol Properties.

3. Drag an instance of your character onto the Stage and position the instance near the bottom-left corner of the Stage (**Figure 3.43**).

**Figure 3.43** The symbol containing the walk cycle positioned near the bottom-left corner of the Stage.

4. Create a new ActionScript class named **Runner**.

5. Save the ActionScript file as **Runner.as** in the examples/com/anim/character folder.

6. Add the following highlighted code to make Runner a subclass of BoundedMover:

```
public class Runner extends BoundedMover {
```

7. Update the package statement with the following highlighted code to match the saved location of the Runner.as file:

```
package   com.anim.character {
```

8. Add the following properties just after the package declaration:

```
protected var runSpeedRatio:uint = 2;
protected var frameSkipRatio:uint = 2;
protected var shiftIsDown:Boolean = false;
```

The first property, runSpeedRatio, determines how fast the character moves compared to the character's normal walk speed. The second property, frameSkipRatio, determines how fast the character's walk cycle will animate. To simulate running, you will skip frames in the character's walk cycle. This will provide the illusion that the character's legs are moving faster. The last property, shiftIsDown, stores the status of the Shift key. If the Shift key is down (pressed), it causes your character to run rather than walk.

**9.** Add the updatePosition method just below the constructor method:

```
override protected function
➥updatePosition(e:Event):void {
    checkEdges();
    var velocity:int = vx;
    if(shiftIsDown) velocity *= runSpeedRatio;
    if(velocity == 0){
        this.stop();
    } else if (shiftIsDown){
        var newFrame:uint = this.currentFrame +
➥Math.round(runSpeedRatio/frameSkipRatio);
        var loopGap:int = newFrame - this.
➥totalFrames;
        if(loopGap > 0) {
            this.gotoAndPlay(loopGap);
        } else {
            this.gotoAndPlay(newFrame);
        }
    } else {
        this.play();
    }
    this.x += velocity;
}
```

This is the most complicated updatePosition method that you've written thus far, so let's go through each line. There's first a call to the checkEdges method to make sure the character is within the boundaries. Since you haven't overwritten the checkEdges method in this class, there's no need to use the *super* keyword.

NOTES

The checkEdges method is an inherited part of the Runner class, even though you haven't rewritten it.

Next, you create a local variable to store the *x* velocity. This variable can be manipulated without changing the value of the original vx property.

In the third line, if shiftIsDown is *true*, the velocity will be increased by the runSpeedRatio. So, if the user is pressing the Shift key, the character will run.

The next block, all the way down to before the last line (this.x += velocity;), is just a slightly more complex version of the if-else statement that appeared in the Wanderer class. In the if block, you're checking to see if the velocity is 0; if so, then you stop the walk-cycle animation. Now, examine the else block: Here you play the character's walk cycle (in the case that the velocity is not 0). Now look at the larger else-if block. This block runs only if the first if statement is *false* and if the shiftIsDown property is set to *true*. So, the conditionals in these blocks serve the following purposes: The if statement corresponds to when the character is not moving, the else-if for when the character is running, and the else for when the character is walking.

Let's look at the else-if block in detail. The first line defines a local variable named newFrame. The newFrame variable determines the next frame of the walk cycle that should be shown. Using the current property settings, runSpeedRatio divided by frameSkipRatio reduces to 2/2, or 1. You must round this number in case these values are changed later, because they could reduce to a number with a decimal and a frame must be a whole number. The 1 (from above) is then added to the current frame number (a property inherited from the MovieClip class).

The next variable, loopGap, stores the difference between the newFrame and the totalFrames available inside your walk cycle. This variable will be used to determine if you have gone beyond the last frame and must go back to the beginning of the cycle.

Lastly, inside the else-if block is a nested if-else statement. If the loopGap value is greater than 0, the newFrame value is beyond the total number of frames and you have to start playing your cycle from the beginning. Since the loopGap variable stores the number beyond the total number of frames, the loopGap becomes the starting frame. If you have not gone beyond the total number of frames, the else block will start playing at the newFrame value.

10. Add the keyboard listener methods below the updatePosition method:

```
override protected function
➥keyDown(e:KeyboardEvent):void {
    if (e.keyCode == Keyboard.SHIFT) {
        shiftIsDown = true;
    } else if (e.keyCode == Keyboard.LEFT) {
        vx = -currentSpeed;
        this.scaleX = -currentScaleX;
    } else if (e.keyCode == Keyboard.RIGHT) {
        vx = currentSpeed;
        this.scaleX = currentScaleX;
    }
}

override protected function
➥keyUp(e:KeyboardEvent):void {
    if (e.keyCode == Keyboard.LEFT || e.keyCode ==
➥Keyboard.RIGHT) {
        vx = 0;
    } else if (e.keyCode == Keyboard.SHIFT) {
        shiftIsDown = false;
    }
}
```

The UP and DOWN conditionals (used in the superclasses) have been removed, since your character is in profile and will only move left and right. Additionally, there's no need for the rotation used in the Wanderer class. Only the vx and the scaleX properties must be set. A condition has been added for SHIFT that simply toggles on (*true*) in the keyDown method and toggles off (*false*) in the KeyUp method for the shiftIsDown property.

**TIP**

You may want to extend the Runner class in the future and reinstate the UP and DOWN conditions to apply behaviors like jumping and crouching.

**11.** Ensure that the following import statements are included just inside the package declaration:

```
import com.anim.character.BoundedMover;
import flash.events.KeyboardEvent;
import flash.ui.Keyboard;
import flash.events.Event;
```

The completed Runner class should now read:

```
package com.anim.character {

    import com.anim.character.BoundedMover;
    import flash.events.KeyboardEvent;
    import flash.ui.Keyboard;
    import flash.events.Event;

    public class Runner extends BoundedMover{

        protected var runSpeedRatio:uint = 2;
        protected var frameSkipRatio:uint = 2;
        protected var shiftIsDown:Boolean = false;

        public function Runner() {

        }

        override protected function
➥updatePosition(e:Event):void {
            checkEdges();
            var velocity:int = vx;
            if(shiftIsDown) velocity *=
➥runSpeedRatio;
            if(velocity == 0){
                this.stop();
            } else if (shiftIsDown){
                var newFrame:uint = this.
➥currentFrame + Math.round(runSpeedRatio/
➥frameSkipRatio);
                var loopGap:int = newFrame -
➥this.totalFrames;
```

```
                    if(loopGap > 0) {
                        this.gotoAndPlay(loopGap);
                    } else {
                        this.gotoAndPlay(newFrame);
                    }
                } else {
                    this.play();
                }
                this.x += velocity;
            }


            override protected function
➥keyDown(e:KeyboardEvent):void {
                if (e.keyCode == Keyboard.SHIFT) {
                    shiftIsDown = true;
                } else if (e.keyCode == Keyboard.LEFT) {
                    vx = -currentSpeed;
                    this.scaleX = -currentScaleX;
                } else if (e.keyCode == Keyboard.
➥RIGHT) {
                    vx = currentSpeed;
                    this.scaleX = currentScaleX;
                }
            }


            override protected function
➥keyUp(e:KeyboardEvent):void {
                if (e.keyCode == Keyboard.LEFT ||
➥e.keyCode == Keyboard.RIGHT) {
                    vx = 0;
                } else if (e.keyCode == Keyboard.
➥SHIFT) {
                    shiftIsDown = false;
                }
            }

        }

}
```

12. Save your Runner class.

13. Return to the RunnerExample.fla document and open the symbol properties for your character. Select Export for ActionScript and input **com.anim.character.Runner** as the Class name.

14. Save your document and test the movie. Move your character around using the left and right arrow keys. Hold down the Shift key when you want your character to burn some rubber (**Figure 3.44**).

**TIP**

If you want to add functionality so your character can collect gold coins and run into enemies, do a web search for *as3 collision detection*.

Figure 3.44 The Runner class in action.

**CLOSE-UP**

**ActionScript Resources**

There are countless ActionScript resources on the web. Here are a few good sites to start with:

▶ http://flashthusiast.com (a blog managed by the Flash motion team)

▶ http://pixelfumes.blogspot.com (really cool effects classes)

▶ http://keyframer.com/forum (a community of animators)

▶ http://actionscript.org

▶ http://kirupa.com

▶ http://www.adobe.com/devnet/flash

▶ http://forums.adobe.com

▶ http://www.senocular.com

Now you have the tools to create some really amazing ActionScript animation on your own. Go forth and animate (with ActionScript if need be)!

## Using Classes from Other Sources

As you may already know, several animators and developers have provided their ActionScript 3.0 (AS3) classes for others to use. If you find that a certain task is beyond your current skill set, try a web search. There are tons of free classes on the web. The author will usually provide documentation on how to use the class. (You'll use a class from the web called TweenLite in Chapter 5.)

# 4

# Workflow Automation

**A**nimation is an intensely creative art. It requires an understanding not only of shape and color, but also of weight, movement, and timing. Animators often work in teams because creating the illusion of life on a two-dimensional screen is a laborious undertaking. Any minuscule loss of form, even for a fraction of a second, chips away at the illusion. To maintain this illusion for the audience, animators need to exercise a great deal of control over the medium. Every measure of control translates into a choice, which can quickly become overwhelming, especially when several steps are needed to enact each choice.

In this chapter, you'll learn how to make Flash do the heavy lifting for you by taking the complicated sets of choices and automating them into single steps. By simplifying the steps involved in creating your animation, you can focus on the choices that really matter—those involving shape, color, weight, movement, and timing.

The goals for this chapter include:

▶ Learn some Flash extensibility language basics

▶ Write scripts to automate common Flash animation tasks

▶ Integrate user interaction into the scripts

▶ Build a Flash panel from scratch

You'll also learn the basics of sharing what you've created in this chapter with others as well as where to look for additional resources. By the time you've finished this chapter you'll be an animator and an automator.

## Why Automate?

Suppose you're creating a three-minute animation in Flash that includes a character speaking onscreen for approximately half the duration of the piece. At 24 frames per second (fps), that's 2,160 potential mouth shapes needed to create the illusion of speech. Although altering every frame may not be necessary to create the illusion of speech, even the modification of every other frame would require 1,080 new mouth shapes.

Now suppose that for each of those 1,080 shapes you must do the following:

1. Scrub the Timeline over the current frame once or twice to hear the audio.

2. Select the symbol on Stage by clicking on it.

3. Highlight the first frame field in the Properties panel by clicking and dragging.

4. Remember the number of the frame inside the mouth symbol containing the mouth shape (which corresponds to the audio you heard on the frame).

5. Type the frame number into the keypad.

6. Press the Enter key.

7. Scrub the playhead to the next frame.

All told, this entire process translates to approximately one click, three to four click and drags, and two to three key presses on the keyboard. In addition, the mouse must be moved from the Timeline to the Stage to the Properties panel; all the while, your gaze needs to be darting back and forth between parts of the screen and the keyboard for each new mouth frame for 1,080 frames.

Clearly, the time spent on these actions adds up. If you assume that each frame requires at least 30 seconds to sync, you've just spent nine hours lip syncing (and you probably now have some repetitive strain injuries to boot). What if you could reduce the entire process to only four to five clicks—without dragging, keyboarding, and recalling frame numbers—and what if your mouse only needed to traverse an area of 200 by 350 pixels? This latter scenario might only require about ten seconds of your time per frame, which translates into only three hours of lip syncing! Now you've reduced your animating time by two-thirds with absolutely no loss of creative control. In fact, a greater proportion of your brain is likely to still be intact after only three hours of this process! Also, if you're getting paid a fixed amount of money for the project, you've just tripled your hourly income for that section of the job.

This more direct approach can be accomplished with a coding language called *JavaScript Flash* (JSFL). Actually, the rapid lip-syncing process just described can be achieved using a free extension called *FrameSync* that can be added to Flash (**Figure 4.1**). All the functionality in FrameSync was built with ActionScript and JSFL. The examples you'll work with throughout this chapter will be simpler than FrameSync in terms of coding, but like FrameSync, they'll be time-savers and are geared specifically toward animation tasks. As a general rule, anytime you find that you're doing the same thing more than two or three times in Flash, there's probably something JSFL can do to help you.

## What Is JSFL?

The term JSFL was introduced in Flash MX 2004. Normal user interactions that occur on the Stage, in the toolbar, on the Timeline, and elsewhere within Flash occur within the *authoring environment*. Specifically written to interact with the Flash Professional authoring environment, JSFL is a variant of JavaScript that functions much like a user, and as such, can do nearly everything that a user can do within Flash, such as create layers, create objects, select frames, manipulate Library items, open files, and save files. In addition, JSFL allows you to script a few tasks that users cannot normally perform (at least not easily or quickly). Anything made with JSFL can be referred to as an *extension*, because it extends the capabilities of Flash. You can effectively house extensions within the following regions of the authoring environment: in the Commands menu, in a SWF panel containing buttons and graphics, and as a tool in the toolbox. This chapter focuses primarily on commands.

**TIP**

See the section on lip syncing in Chapter 2 to learn more about FrameSync. You can download the extension from the Extensions folder on the CD included with this book or from http://ajarproductions. com/blog/flash-extensions.

**Figure 4.1** The FrameSync panel using JSFL to speed up the lip-syncing process.

**NOTES**

Extensions in other systems are sometimes referred to as plug-ins, macros, or add-ons. These terms all describe similar concepts that add functionality to an application.

Although this chapter is geared toward animators, JSFL is a scripting language. Don't worry if you don't understand every aspect of the language. Focus on completing the examples. It may take time for new concepts to sink in. The words *scripting, programming,* and *coding* will be used interchangeably to mean *writing code*. Refer to **Table 4.1** for any scripting terms that may be unfamiliar to you while reading the chapter.

TABLE **4.1**  Scripting terms used in this chapter

| TERM | DEFINITION |
| --- | --- |
| Variable | A named object with an associated value that can be changed |
| Function | A portion of code that performs a specific task |
| Method | A function associated with a particular object |
| Parameter | A piece of data that can be used within a function |
| Argument | A parameter that is sent to a function |
| Loop | A piece of code that is repeatedly executed |

You create a new JSFL script by choosing File > New and selecting Flash JavaScript File in the New Document dialog box. The file extension for a JSFL script is always *.jsfl*. It should be noted that JSFL is distinct from ActionScript. The latter is compiled into a SWF, and that SWF can play in the ubiquitous Flash Player. On the other hand, JSFL code is executed on the spot and is used to control the Flash Professional authoring environment. Both JSFL and ActionScript are based on a script standard known as *ECMAScript*. Whereas the "vocabulary" of JSFL is much smaller than that of ActionScript 3.0, much of the know-how gained in one language will be applicable in the other.

If you're familiar with other scripting languages, such as ExtendScript or AppleScript, you may be pleasantly surprised with how rapidly JSFL executes. The language is an integral part of the Flash application and is used by the Adobe Flash team to test features for quality assurance. The speed of execution makes JSFL excellent for batch processing and complex actions. In short, JSFL enables the animator to shed hundreds of redundant mouse clicks while saving heaps of time. To date, each Flash Professional update has included a few new commands for the JSFL Application Programming Interface (API), but most of the API has remained consistent since Flash MX 2004.

### Your Buddy, DOM

Everything that you can manipulate with code in JSFL is considered an *object*. The *Document Object Model* (DOM) is basically the hierarchy or structure (model) of objects within a particular document. If you've written JavaScript for a web browser, you're probably somewhat familiar with this idea. In the case of the browser, you're traversing the structure of an HTML document to gain access (and make changes) to tags and content.

The good news is that even though you may never have thought about it before, you're already familiar with the Flash DOM. There's an order to everything you do within a Flash document, and since you are reading this book, we can assume that you implicitly understand this order. Let's first consider some objects in Flash and how they relate to each other, starting with *frames* and *layers*. Which of the following options makes more immediate sense to you?

▶ A frame on a layer

▶ A layer on a frame

If the latter makes you scrunch up your nose and wonder how that might even be possible, you do possess an implicit awareness of the DOM. Without this organization of objects, it wouldn't be possible to make much sense of anything in Flash.

The most basic Stage object in Flash is called an *element*. All Stage objects—for example, bitmaps, groups, graphic symbols, and movieclip symbols—inherit the properties and methods of a basic element. Here's a representation of the hierarchy for an element that resides on the Flash Stage:

Flash > Document > Timeline > Layer > Frame > Element

In reverse order and translated into plain *Flenglish* (English for Flash users): An element is on a frame that is on a layer, and that layer is on a Timeline within a document that is open in Flash.

In JSFL, that same hierarchy is written as follows:

```
fl.documents[0].timelines[0].layers[0].frames[0].
➥elements[0]
```

Properties within objects, which can also be complex objects, are referenced using dot (.) syntax, just as they are in ActionScript. The object references in the code sample are actually arrays (collections of objects) containing several items. The square brackets are used to reference objects within an array. The zero, in array notation, denotes the first item in an array. So, in *Flenglish*, the preceding code references the first element, on the first frame, on the first layer, within the first Timeline (scene) of the first document that is open in Flash. Flash will not recognize any attempt to reference the first element on the first layer because a layer contains frames, not elements (not directly, at least). Each object in the DOM operates like a Russian doll that experiences a parent doll and a child doll (with the exception of the outermost and innermost objects). No object in the DOM has contact with what's inside its child object or outside of its parent object (**Figure 4.2**).

Figure 4.2 The Flash DOM hierarchy.

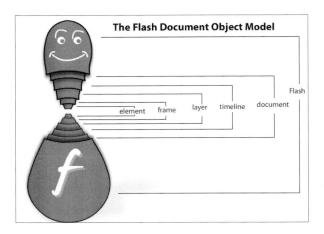

Consider this situation: Suppose an art director has a Flash file with an animated scene, and said art director wants you to hang a clock on the wall within that scene. You are told the layer on which to place the illustration, so that the clock doesn't end up obscuring the main character's face. However, nobody informed you that there's a transition at the beginning of the scene. Being a savvy animator, you scrub through the Timeline after inserting the clock to verify that everything looks OK, but you notice a problem. The clock is hanging in empty space on the first frame (**Figure 4.3**). As a fix, you move the starting keyframe for the clock to align it with the starting keyframes for the other layers with artwork (**Figure 4.4**). Everything looks good now, thanks to the fact that you were able to extend beyond the literal directions given to you.

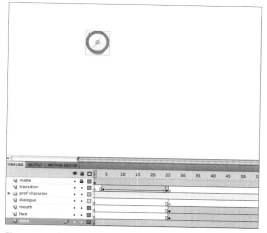

Figure 4.3 The clock hanging in empty space.

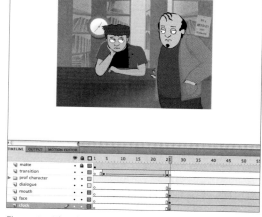

Figure 4.4 The clock hanging where it should be.

Keep in mind that the JSFL interpreter is not as smart as you are, so it will need you to spell out everything very clearly. If you instruct it to do something to an element on a layer, rather than to an element on a frame on a layer, it won't understand: Your script will stop executing and alert you with an error. The upside of JSFL's literal-mindedness is that it is quite reliable. Again, your skills on the Flash Stage already give you a leg up in understanding how to interact with the Flash DOM. You also have an eager friend who is ready to bridge the gap between the authoring environment and the scripting API: the History panel.

## Writing Scripts to Control Flash

The History panel is your conduit from animating on the Flash Stage to writing code in the Script Editor. The History panel stores all the actions you take within a Flash document: creating a new layer, editing a Library item, adding a new scene, drawing a shape, and so on. As such, the History panel is a great way to revert your document to an earlier state, but it's also a great way to peer inside Flash and see what steps can be automated.

### Getting Started with the History Panel

Let's take a look at the basic workings of the History panel and how you can use it to associate JSFL code with actions that are occurring on Stage.

1. Create a new Flash document by choosing File > New and then selecting ActionScript 3.0 in the New Document dialog box.

2. Open the History panel by choosing Window > Other Panels > History.

3. Select the Rectangle tool, make sure there is a fill color but no stroke color, and draw a rectangle on the Stage. Notice that this action is recorded in the History panel (**Figure 4.5**).

Figure 4.5 The new rectangle is recorded in the History panel.

4. Click the menu on the top right of the History panel to change the display format and tooltip display (**Figure 4.6**).

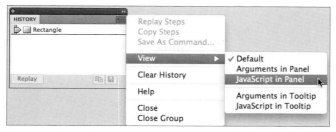

**Figure 4.6** Change the History panel display using the menu at the top right.

5. Change the display to show JavaScript in Panel if it's not selected already (**Figure 4.7**).

**Figure 4.7** JSFL code is displayed in the History panel.

NOTES

Not all actions in the History panel can be replicated with JSFL. If an action cannot be replicated with JSFL, it will appear with a red X in the History panel, and there will be a keyword or description in parentheses rather than a line of JavaScript.

6. Switch to the Selection tool. Select the rectangle on the Stage by clicking on it. Then delete the rectangle by pressing the Delete key on your keyboard.

7. On the left side of the History panel, drag the slider up so that it's parallel to the original rectangle command. Note that sliding the arrow undid the deletion of the rectangle. This slider acts as an undo and redo mechanism (**Figure 4.8**).

**Figure 4.8** Here the History slider is used as an undo.

**TIP**

You can select multiple steps in the History panel using the Command (Mac) or Ctrl (Windows) key. You can also select continuous steps by clicking on the first item, holding Shift, and then clicking on the last item.

8. Drag the slider down to the deleteSelection command (**Figure 4.9**). Select the original addNewRectangle command and click the Replay button. This will create a rectangle with the same dimensions as those of the original rectangle (**Figure 4.10**).

Figure 4.9 Here the slider is used as a redo (before clicking Replay).

Figure 4.10 After clicking the Replay button.

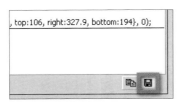

Figure 4.11 Save your script as a command from the History panel.

If this is as far down the rabbit hole as you'd like to venture, you can just save your script as a command. To save the command from the History panel, select the desired steps within the History panel and click the button showing the disk icon in the lower-right corner (**Figure 4.11**). As a result, you will be prompted to name your command, which will then be available via the Commands menu. Be sure to at least skim ahead in this chapter to the section on adding a keyboard shortcut to your command.

### Moving from the History Panel to a Script

The History panel is a great place to start automating, but it only allows you to repeat actions that you've already taken. Let's move the JSFL into the Script Editor so you can start generating new actions.

1. With only the addNewRectangle command still selected, click the Copy Steps button in the bottom right of the History panel (**Figure 4.12**).

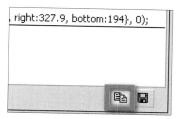

Figure 4.12 The Copy Steps button allows you to copy selected steps to your clipboard.

2. Drag the undo/redo slider to the very top of the History panel to revert the document to its opened state.

3. Choose File > New. When the New Document dialog box appears, select Flash JavaScript File and click OK.

4. Paste the stored command into the newly created script file by choosing Edit > Paste.

5. Click the Run Script button (**Figure 4.13**) at the top of the Script Editor and return to the Flash document.

Figure 4.13  The Run Script button inside the Flash Script Editor executes the current script.

Note that a rectangle has been drawn on the Stage in the same place and with the same dimensions as those of the initial rectangle drawn using the Rectangle tool (**Figure 4.14**).

Figure 4.14  The script successfully draws the rectangle.

**TIP**

To launch the help documents, choose Help > Flash Help. In the Adobe Community Help window, select Extending Flash Professional CS5. You'll see a list of contents on the left (mainly JSFL objects).

The help documents are a programmer's best friend. Get to know the Extending Flash help documents. It is highly recommended that you download a PDF to your local drive using the link provided on the help pages. The PDF is faster to navigate than any other format. There's no reason to memorize all the commands and properties within the JSFL API; just keep your PDF handy.

**TIP**

A new variable is created using the *var* keyword.

Now you're able to control the Flash Professional authoring environment, aka the Flash Integrated Development Environment (IDE), using a script, which is pretty cool in its own right. At this point, though, your rectangle has somewhat random and meaningless dimensions. In the next section, you'll leverage some information from the Flash DOM to make a rectangle using dimensions that will be more useful.

### Composing a Smarter Script

You'll now tweak the current script so that the new rectangle matches the current size of the Stage. Your rectangle will then be useful as a Stage background or a background for new symbols. By referring to the Extending Flash CS5 Professional help documents, you can see that a Flash document contains simple height and width properties, just like those of a Movieclip object in ActionScript. You'll utilize those properties when creating your rectangle.

1. Create a new variable to store the current document object by adding this code to the top of your script:

   ```
   var dom = fl.getDocumentDOM();
   ```

2. Replace `fl.getDocumentDOM()` in the original code with `dom`.

3. Set the top and left position for the rectangle to 0, and the right and bottom to `dom.width` and `dom.height`, respectively. The script should now read:

   ```
   var dom = fl.getDocumentDOM();
   dom.addNewRectangle({left:0, top:0,
   ➥right:dom.width, bottom:dom.height}, 0);
   ```

Now you have a rectangle you can use! Steps 1 and 2 just did a bit of housekeeping to organize your script and make it more readable, so it really only took you one step to make the History panel step more useful. By collecting data from the current document (like Stage height and width), you can make highly responsive scripts that will save you time. The next section shows you where to save your script so you can run it without opening the Script Editor.

**CLOSE-UP**

**Parameters in Square Brackets**

One way of getting the most out of the Flash help documents is knowing how to read the method usage descriptions. These descriptions will help you understand what arguments to send to each method:

▶ When a parameter is located within square brackets in a method definition of a help document page, it denotes that the parameter(s) is optional.

▶ In the following method usage description from the help documents, the parameter `boundingRectangle` is obligatory, but the parameter for suppressing the fill of the new rectangle as well as the parameter for suppressing the stroke are both optional:
`document.addNewRectangle(boundingRectangle, roundness [, bSuppressFill` ↩`[, bSuppressStroke]])`

▶ To suppress the stroke, an argument must initially be passed for the `bSuppressFill` parameter. Here's an example that suppresses the stroke, but not the fill:
`fl.getDocumentDOM().addNewRectangle({left:0,top:0,right:100,bottom:100},0, false,` ↩`true);`

## Saving a Script as a Command

To run your script conveniently from Flash, it helps to be able to access your script from within the Flash authoring environment. The simplest way to access a script inside of Flash is via the Commands menu. To add your script to the Commands menu, place the script file inside the Commands directory. The Commands directory is located within the Flash Configuration directory. The Extending Flash CS5 help document lists the following locations for the three common operating systems:

▶ **Windows Vista.** *boot drive*\Users\\*username*\Local Settings\Application Data\Adobe\Flash CS5\\*language*\Configuration\

▶ **Windows XP.** *boot drive*\Documents and Settings\\*username*\Local Settings\Application Data\Adobe\Flash CS5\\*language*\Configuration\

▶ **Mac OS X.** Macintosh HD/Users/*username*/Library/Application Support/Adobe/Flash CS5/*language*/Configuration/

If you still have trouble locating your Configuration directory, you can create and execute a simple new JSFL script with the following code:

```
fl.trace(fl.configDirectory);
```

This script displays the path to your Configuration directory in the Output panel. When you've found your configuration directory, save your existing script as **Create Stage Size Rectangle.jsfl** in the Configuration/Commands directory.

### Running a Saved Command

With your script saved as a command, you can now access the command!

1. Create a new Flash document by choosing File > New and selecting ActionScript 3.0.

2. Run the command by choosing Commands > Create Stage Size Rectangle (**Figure 4.15**).

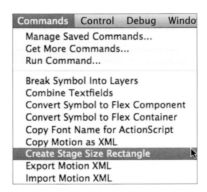

Figure 4.15 The command appears in the Commands menu.

*Voila!* You have a rectangle with dimensions that match the Stage. Once written, commands are quite easy to run. The power of a command as an automation tool lies in the fact that a command only has to be written once. The command can then be run instantly, whenever you need it.

### Creating a Matte

Animators and designers often find it necessary to use a matte or a mask to hide artwork at the edge of the Stage. A matte covers up areas that are not to be displayed. A mask operates by only showing content within the bounds

Copies of the finished scripts can be found in the Chapter 4 folder on the CD that accompanies this book.

Be careful when opening a JSFL script from your operating system's file browser. Rather than opening the script in Flash's Script Editor, Flash will actually execute the script. If you want to open the script for editing, choose File > Open inside Flash.

The rectangle was created using the currently selected fill and stroke colors from the toolbar. If you had object drawing mode selected when last using a drawing tool, your rectangle will be a shape object; otherwise, the rectangle will exist as raw vector data.

of the mask's shape. Both mattes and masks must sit on a layer above all others to function properly. Both devices are used to hide objects—typically those that are entering into or exiting from view—at the edge of the Stage. One reason to use a matte or a mask is to prevent these hidden objects from being seen when a SWF is scaled. The experience of seeing what is supposed to be hidden undermines the illusion that the artist is trying to create. This trespass across the imaginary wall separating an audience from the performance on a Stage is sometimes referred to as "breaking the fourth wall."

In Flash, it can be frustrating to work with masks because the mask and all the "masked" layers need to be locked for the mask to appear correctly on the Stage. A matte, on the other hand, appears on the Stage just as it will in the published SWF. So, a matte can also serve as Stage guidelines for the animator. For these reasons, some Flash users prefer to use mattes instead of masks.

Just as there are numerous approaches to accomplishing a task using the tools in the Flash authoring environment, there are a number of ways to accomplish the same end using JSFL. The approach to a problem in JSFL often parallels what a user would be doing onscreen in the authoring environment. So, let's consider this issue when creating a matte script.

Start by making a mental map of the steps that the script might follow. One way to create a matte involves drawing two rectangles and using the inside rectangle to cut a hole in the outer rectangle. You can refer to this strategy as the "two-rectangles" method. Once you have the two rectangles, you can approach the next step in two different ways. If the rectangles you drew are not shape objects and they have different color fills, simply deselecting the rectangles and deleting the inner rectangle will leave you with the matte appearance that you're seeking. Alternatively, you could draw two rectangles, make sure both rectangles are shape objects, and use `document.punch()` (Modify > Combine Objects > Punch) to generate your matte shape. You can verify that this works by replicating these steps on the Stage. If you copy the steps from the History panel, you'll be most of the way toward having a completed matte script.

### CLOSE-UP

### Identifying Raw Vector Data

Raw vector graphics are part of Flash's default Merge Drawing Model, which automatically merges shapes that overlap. A raw vector, when selected, appears as though it's covered with a dot pattern. In contrast, shape objects will appear with a "marquee" border when selected, just as a symbol or group would appear (**Figure 4.16**). Shape objects are part of the Object Drawing Model, which does merge shapes that overlap.

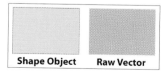

**Shape Object**    **Raw Vector**

Figure 4.16 Display differences with shape objects and raw vector data.

**TIP**

If you check the help page for `fl.objectDrawingMode`, which can toggle object drawing mode *on* or *off*, you'll notice that Flash 8 is listed under *Availability*. This means that the `fl.objectDrawingMode` property was not available in Flash MX 2004 (the version before Flash 8). Pay special attention to the availability of the properties and methods that you use if you intend to distribute your extension to others.

**TIP**

You can also work with the Create Stage Size Rectangle script and ActionScript to create an effect similar to your Stage matte script using masking. Do this by converting the rectangle into a movieclip symbol and using that symbol as an ActionScript mask for the Stage. Note that the masking set in ActionScript only shows when the file is compiled. The masking will not be apparent within the Flash authoring environment.

One problem with both of the two-rectangles approaches is that they require you to change the object drawing mode (and/or fill color) setting in the user interface. So you should first check to see whether object drawing mode is off or on (depending on the method), and then restore the setting when you're finished, so you don't interrupt your workflow (or the workflow of other users you might share the script with).

Let's go back to the proverbial drawing board and come up with a strategy that will create a matte without requiring you to fiddle with the user settings. This time let's consider something that would be difficult for a user to accomplish on Stage. Instead of worrying about object drawing mode, draw a rectangle, select it, and then break it apart into raw vector data (Modify > Break Apart). You could then draw a selection rectangle inside your rectangle on the Stage, and then delete that selection, leaving a hollow frame that surrounds the Stage area. A quick check in the documentation reveals that there is a `document.setSelectionRect()` method. Accomplishing this type of selection would be difficult (if not impossible) for a user, because the selection would start with a mouse click. As soon as the user clicks, the entire fill is selected. This is a case where JSFL can take an action that a user cannot. Let's now put this "single-rectangle" strategy to the test.

1. You'll build on the existing Create Stage Size Rectangle script (choose File > Open to open the script if you've closed it) to create your matte script. Choose File > Save As and save the script (also in the Commands directory) as **Create Stage Matte.jsfl**. This sequence will not overwrite your previous script as long as you choose **Save As**.

2. Copy the original `addNewRectangle` line and paste it below the first one:

```
dom.addNewRectangle({left:0, top:0,
➥right:dom.width, bottom:dom.height}, 0);
dom.addNewRectangle({left:0, top:0,
➥right:dom.width, bottom:dom.height}, 0);
```

3. Modify the second line so that it calls the `setSelection-Rect` instead. Change the second parameter to `true` to force the selection to replace any existing selections:

```
dom.addNewRectangle({left:0, top:0,
➥right:dom.width, bottom:dom.height}, 0);
dom.setSelectionRect({left:0, top:0,
➥right:dom.width, bottom:dom.height}, true);
```

4. Add a variable at the top of the script set to however many pixels you like to control matte thickness. Then update your original rectangle to account for the extra area created by the matte thickness, which will extend beyond the bounds of the Stage on all sides:

```
var matteThickness = 200;
dom.addNewRectangle({left:-matteThickness, top:
➥-matteThickness, right:dom.width+matteThickness,
➥bottom:dom.height+matteThickness}, 0);
```

5. Add a couple of optional arguments to keep the fill but suppress the stroke, since the stroke won't be needed for a matte:

```
dom.addNewRectangle({left:-matteThickness, top:
➥-matteThickness, right:dom.width+matteThickness,
➥bottom:dom.height+matteThickness}, 0, false,
➥true);
```

6. Check to see if object drawing mode is indeed turned on, and then break apart your rectangle before making a selection. To use the `breakApart()` command, you need to be certain that you've first made a selection. Add the following two lines of code between the `addNewRectangle` and `setSelectionRect` lines:

```
dom.selectAll();
if(fl.objectDrawingMode) dom.breakApart();
```

7. Using `selectAll` is imprecise because there might be something else on the layer you don't want to select, but you'll improve on that step in a moment. Delete your selection to form the cut-out part of the matte by adding this line to the end of the script:

```
dom.deleteSelection();
```

If you run the current script on a blank document, it works as intended. Unfortunately, if you run it in almost any other scenario, it will likely wreak havoc on your existing artwork. One thing you can do to improve your single-rectangle script is to situate the matte on its own named layer. Then you'll be sure to select the contents of that layer rather than selecting *all*. Ideally, this will prevent your selection rectangle (that you then delete) from also selecting artwork on other layers as well.

Jumping ahead a few steps, the astute reader may see a speed bump on the horizon. The selection rectangle selects content on all available layers, so when you delete your selection, you'll still be deleting content from other layers as well. You'll rectify that in the steps that follow.

### Improving the matte script

You can use several approaches to resolve the problem introduced by the selection rectangle:

▶ Loop through and remove items from the selection that are not contained on your new layer prior to deleting the selection.

▶ Use a mouse click to select only your rectangle (yes, JSFL can do that, too).

▶ Convert your rectangle into a shape object or a group, enter edit mode, and safely make your deletion there.

▶ Start over and try an entirely different approach.

Let's try the third option listed, the edit mode approach. Even if you make your object into a group, you still have to determine if your rectangle is a shape object once you're in edit mode. If you convert the rectangle into a shape object, you know you'll be dealing with a raw-vector rectangle inside edit mode. However, if your rectangle is a shape object from the beginning, the rectangle will be unaffected by being made into a shape object again, so you'll attempt to convert the rectangle to a shape object regardless. Test this out: Make an element into a drawing object by selecting the element on Stage and choosing Modify > Combine Object > Union. Then enter edit (in place) mode by double-clicking on the shape object. The shape within the shape object will be raw vector data regardless of whether the shape was a shape object to begin with.

1. Create a variable that will reference the current Timeline. Insert the following text just below the declaration of the dom variable near the top of the script:

```
var tl = dom.getTimeline();
```

2. Create a new layer below the `matteThickness` variable. The `addNewLayer` method will return the index of the new layer. The index refers to the position of the layer within its parent Timeline. You'll store the index so that you can use it later:

```
var newLayerNum = tl.addNewLayer("matte");
```

3. Make your selection more precise by assigning the elements contained on the first frame of your new layer (which will just be your rectangle) as the document's current selection. You're using the `elements` object because it's already in array format, and `dom.selection` only accepts an array. Replace the `selectAll` line with the following code:

```
dom.selection = tl.layers[newLayerNum].frames[0].
↪elements;
```

4. Remove the `breakApart` line entirely. You've rendered the break apart step obsolete.

5. Convert the selection into a shape object, and enter edit mode by adding these two lines right after the line in step 3:

```
dom.union();
dom.enterEditMode('inPlace');
```

6. To clean up, exit out of edit mode and lock your matte layer by adding these two lines to the end of the script:

```
dom.exitEditMode();
tl.setLayerProperty("locked", true);
```

If you want to make sure your matte layer is on top of the pile, you can add this line to the end of your script:

```
tl.reorderLayer(newLayerNum, 0);
```

7. Open a new ActionScript 3.0 document and run your script by choosing Commands > Create Stage Matte (**Figure 4.17**).

**Figure 4.17** The Stage matte in action after the Create Stage Matte command has been run.

The full script should now read as follows:

```
var dom = fl.getDocumentDOM();
var tl = dom.getTimeline();
var matteThickness = 200;
var newLayerNum = tl.addNewLayer("matte");
dom.addNewRectangle({left:-matteThickness,
➥top:-matteThickness, right:dom.width+matteThickness,
➥bottom:dom.height+matteThickness}, 0, false, true);
dom.selection = tl.layers[newLayerNum].frames[0].
➥elements;
dom.union();
dom.enterEditMode('inPlace');
dom.setSelectionRect({left:0, top:0, right:dom.width,
➥bottom:dom.height}, true, false);
dom.deleteSelection();
dom.exitEditMode();
```

```
tl.setLayerProperty("locked", true);
tl.reorderLayer(newLayerNum, 0);
```

If you were curious as to what your script would have looked like if you had initially followed the two-rectangles approach using object drawing mode, here it is with the drawing mode stored and then restored after all the other code has executed:

```
var dom = fl.getDocumentDOM();
var tl = dom.getTimeline();
var matteThickness = 200;
var storedODM = fl.objectDrawingMode;
var newLayerNum = tl.addNewLayer("matte");
fl.objectDrawingMode = true;
dom.addNewRectangle({left:-matteThickness,
➡top:-matteThickness, right:dom.width+matteThickness,
➡bottom:dom.height+matteThickness}, 0, false, true);
dom.addNewRectangle({left:0, top:0, right:dom.width,
➡bottom:dom.height}, 0, false, true);
dom.selection = tl.layers[newLayerNum].frames[0].
➡elements;
dom.punch();
tl.setLayerProperty("locked", true);
tl.reorderLayer(newLayerNum, 0);
fl.objectDrawingMode = storedODM;
```

The two-rectangles method has the same number of lines as the single-rectangle/edit-mode method. Both scripts are fairly robust (i.e., tough to "break" and will work in many scenarios). Both scripts require at least Flash 8, because they use aspects of the object drawing mode that were introduced with Flash 8.

There's at least one scenario in which the two-rectangles method could be a more robust script: Suppose you wanted to add a matte to a symbol's Timeline rather than to the main Timeline. If you're operating on a symbol's Timeline, then that places you in edit mode to start with, and exiting edit mode could potentially transport you to the main Timeline of the current scene instead of back to the symbol's Timeline (which you had been editing before you ran the script). The circumstances in which you might want to render a matte within a symbol may seem rare, but this type of scenario should be considered when developing scripts, especially when you plan to distribute your script to other users. Fortunately, if you test this scenario by running the current matte command while in symbol editing mode, the matte is drawn as expected (**Figure 4.18**).

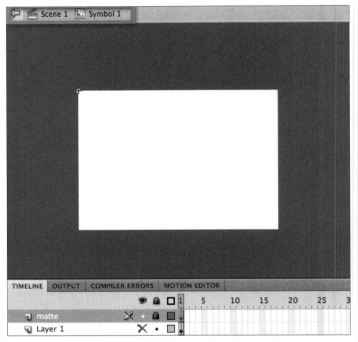

**Figure 4.18** Stage matte shown working properly within the edit mode of a symbol.

**Developing for Others**

As in all other development projects, it's good to think through how someone might cause your script to execute in a way that you did not intend. Try to "break" your script by testing it in as many different scenarios as you can imagine. Potential users who unintentionally run the script in a scenario that you had not imagined are likely to think of your script as breaking their workflow, not the other way around.

You will run into cases where a method functions differently in various scenarios or doesn't function exactly as anticipated in any scenario. In these cases, there are often still workarounds to accomplish your desired end. When seeking a new solution, it can be helpful to consider how you might accomplish the same task within the Flash interface. For instance, if `exitEditMode` did not produce the desired result, you could trigger a mouse double-click action on an empty part of the Stage to exit the current edit mode.

The process of creating a "smart" script is as much a process of creative thinking as anything else that can be done in Flash. As with any creative project, you may occasionally find that you need to scrap an idea entirely and start from scratch. With your matte script, a bit of persistence paid off and allowed you to move forward, but scenarios may arise during scripting in which there aren't ready alternatives. If you feel stuck, remember to comb the documentation further or post your questions on the help forums listed in the "More Resources" section at the end of this chapter.

**TIP**

If you're not worried about the backward compatibility of your script for any version prior to CS4, you can write a shorter version of the two-rectangles matte script using the *addNewPrimitiveRectangle* command. Rectangular Primitives will be shape objects by default.

### Adding a Keyboard Shortcut to a Command

The ability to add a shortcut to your commands allows for huge gains in workflow efficiency. Follow the steps here to add a new shortcut to one of the commands that you've written.

1. To open the Keyboard Shortcuts dialog box, choose Edit > Keyboard Shortcuts in Windows or Flash > Keyboard Shortcuts in Mac OS X (**Figure 4.19**).

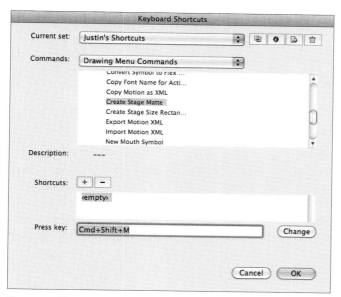

**Figure 4.19** The Keyboard Shortcuts dialog box allows you to add shortcuts to several items within the Flash authoring environment, including commands that you've written.

2. If you have not done so already, start by duplicating the default set of shortcuts and giving that set a unique name. The Duplicate button is the first on the left after the menu for the current set.

3. Choose Drawing Menu Commands from the Commands menu, and then twirl open the Commands item by clicking the adjacent arrow to reveal the list from your Commands menu.

4. Select the command to which you'd like to add a shortcut, and click the plus (+) button where it says Shortcuts. The word *<empty>* will appear in the "Press key" field and the Shortcut box.

5. Using the keyboard, perform the shortcut that you'd like to add. The shortcut keys will appear in the "Press key" field. If the shortcut is invalid or conflicts with another one of your shortcuts, a warning message will appear at the bottom of the dialog box.

6. When you are happy with a particular (valid) key combination, click the Change button to apply this shortcut to the <empty> item in the shortcut list. Note that you can click the plus (+) to add additional shortcuts to the same command.

7. Click the OK button to close the dialog box and save your settings when you've finished.

### Creating a Script with User Interaction

Three different types of basic user interactions are listed as global methods within the JSFL documentation: alert, confirm, and prompt. The alert method is the simplest. It accepts a single string parameter that is then displayed to the user (**Figure 4.20**). At this point, OK is the only user option, so alert is useful for cases in which you want to provide feedback such as error messages and script completion notifications to the user.

The confirm method adds a Cancel button to the alert. This is useful when you need the user to make a choice, such as whether or not to allow the script to continue to

Figure 4.20 The alert message box.

run, even though some precondition has not been met (**Figure 4.21**). The confirm method returns a value to notify you about which option the user selected.

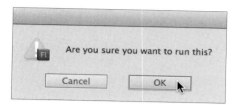

Figure 4.21
The confirmation message box.

The prompt method is the most sophisticated of the three. It allows the user to enter text and accepts two parameters when called (**Figure 4.22**). The first parameter is a prompt message. The second is optional and includes any text that you want to prepopulate into the user's text entry field. The prompt will then either return what was entered into the field or return a value of null if the user clicked Cancel. Although the prompt function has a number of applications, the most common is to allow the user to name something (e.g., a new symbol, a prefix for Library items, etc.).

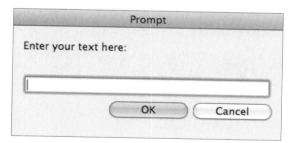

Figure 4.22  The Prompt message box.

## Bitmap Smoothing

Bitmaps can sometimes become pixelated, blurry, or otherwise "crunchy" when they are animated or scaled. Flash's default settings don't tend to display bitmaps well at any scale other than 100%. To fix this, you can open the bitmap Library item by Ctrl-clicking/right-clicking on the Library item and choosing Properties. In the Bitmap

CLOSE-UP

### Debugging Your Scripts

Debugging is the process of finding and reducing the number of bugs, or defects, in your script. You can use the following methods to generate feedback when parts of your script are not working:

▶ The alert method (described in this section) can be useful for providing you, the developer, with feedback when something is not working.

▶ The fl.trace method can also be used. It is similar to the trace method in ActionScript and prints the feedback into the Output panel instead of an alert message box. The fl.trace method will not clear the Output panel when you retest your script like the ActionScript trace method does when you retest a SWF. To clear the Output panel, use fl.outputPanel.clear() at the top of your script.

Properties dialog box, select the Allow Smoothing check box. If you're producing a project for broadcast or physical media (e.g., CD or USB drive) or if you are more concerned about quality than about file size, set the Compression to Lossless (PNG/GIF) instead of Photo (JPEG) (**Figure 4.23**). Setting these properties on every bitmap can be a headache if you have a lot of bitmaps in your Library, so let's script it!

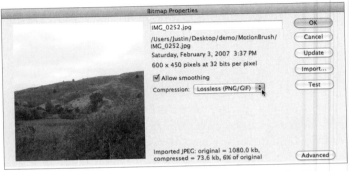

**Figure 4.23** The Bitmap Properties dialog box allows you to control settings on individual bitmaps within the Library.

1. Create a new JSFL file (File > New > Flash JavaScript File) and save it in the Commands directory as **Smooth and Lossless Bitmaps.jsfl**.

2. Define variables for the Library and the items currently selected in the Library:

```
var lib = fl.getDocumentDOM().library;
var items = lib.getSelectedItems();
```

3. Loop through the contents of your items variable using a for in loop and store the current Library item as you go:

```
for(var i in items) {
    var it = items[i];
}
```

4. You need to set the allowSmoothing and compressionType properties of each variable. Before doing so, check to make sure the current item is a bitmap, since only

a bitmap will possess these properties (attempting to apply these properties to any other types of Library items will generate an error). Add the following lines after the declaration line for the `it` variable inside the for in loop:

```
if(it.itemType == "bitmap") {
    it.allowSmoothing = true;
    it.compressionType = 'lossless';
}
```

The script will run fine at this point, but the user remains uninformed about what's going on behind the curtain. Even when you're scripting just for you, it's nice to have confirmation that the script ran as intended. While you're at it, check to see if any Library items are selected in the first place. If there are no items selected, give the user the option to apply this command to all the bitmaps in the Library.

5. To see if the user wants to apply the command to all Library items, use a `confirm` box if no Library items are selected. If the user clicks OK, you'll reassign your `items` variable to the entire list of Library items. Add the following lines just after the line containing the declaration of the `items` variable:

```
if(items.length < 1) {
    var confirmed = confirm("No items are
➥selected. Do you want to run this on all library
➥items?");
    if(confirmed) items = lib.items;
}
```

6. Add a variable at the top of your script that will keep track of the number of bitmap items you've altered:

```
var runCounter = 0;
```

7. You'll now increment this variable by 1 for each time a bitmap is encountered in your list of items. When your loop is complete, you'll display the resulting number to the user in the form of an `alert` message. Add the highlighted code as shown:

```
for(var i in items) {
    var it = items[i];
    if(it.itemType == "bitmap") {
        it.allowSmoothing = true;
        it.compressionType = 'lossless';
        runCounter++;
    }
}
alert(runCounter + " items affected.");
```

If nothing is selected in the Library, the user will see the message that you added in step 5 (**Figure 4.24**). Now the user has more control and receives some feedback from your script (**Figure 4.25**).

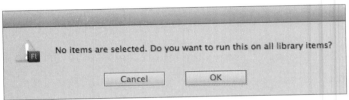

**Figure 4.24** The confirmation message appears and informs the user that no Library items are selected.

**Figure 4.25** The alert message tells the user how many bitmaps were affected by the script.

### Generating a Ready-made Mouth Symbol

For setting up and organizing files, JSFL is a great tool. Perhaps you have a common set of layers or Library folders that you always use for your files. Any repeated activities used to set up a file or assets within a file will lend themselves well to scripting. Standards make files simpler to work with. Aside from the organization benefits, standards take away the burden of memorization. For instance, if you have a standard set of mouth shapes for your character, you won't have to memorize a new set when working with each new character. In this example, you'll set up a mouth symbol with ready-made frame labels for lip syncing an animated character (**Figure 4.26**).

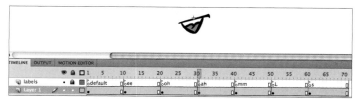

Figure 4.26 Frame labels as they will appear when the script is complete.

1. Create a new JSFL file and save it in the Commands directory as **New Mouth Symbol.jsfl**.

2. Define variables for the current document's DOM and Library:

```
var dom = fl.getDocumentDOM();
var lib = dom.library;
```

3. You'll define two settings for your script. The first variable will store all your standard mouth shapes (which tend to represent phonemes, basic units of sound) as a string with the values separated by commas. You can add to or subtract from this list to fit your needs. The second variable will tell the script how many frames you want between each label, which will enable you to easily read each label. Add the following two variable declarations to your script:

```
var labelString = "default,ee,oh,ah,mm,L,s";
var framesPerLabel = 10;
```

4. Prompt the user to name the new symbol and to store that name by adding this code immediately after the code in the previous step:

```
var namePath = prompt("Symbol name: " );
```

5. You'll add a graphic symbol to the Library using the name given by the user. The new Library item will automatically be selected. You'll edit the symbol from there. Add these two lines after the code in the previous step:

```
lib.addNewItem('graphic', namePath);
lib.editItem(namePath);
```

6. Since you've called `editItem()`, you're now inside the symbol, and by requesting the current Timeline, you'll receive the symbol's Timeline. Add the following line after the lines in the previous step:

```
var tl = dom.getTimeline();
```

7. You'll create a new variable and convert your `labelString` into an array so that you can loop through each label. Then you'll use the length of that array and the `framesPerLabel` variable to determine the number of frames that the symbol should have on its Timeline. Add the following lines to your script:

```
var labels = labelString.split(',');
tl.insertFrames(labels.length * framesPerLabel);
```

8. Add the following lines to create a new layer to store your labels, as well as create a variable to store your new layer for easy referencing:

```
var newLayerNum = tl.addNewLayer("labels");
var newLayerObj = tl.layers[newLayerNum];
```

9. Loop through all your labels and assign a frame number to each label based on your `framesPerLabel` setting and the number of times that your loop has run by adding this block of code:

```
for (var i=0; i < labels.length; i++){
    var frameNum = i * framesPerLabel;
}
```

10. For each iteration of the loop, you also want to add a keyframe (except on the first frame, because there's already a keyframe there by default). You also want to set the name of the current frame in your loop to the current label in the loop. Setting the name of the frame is equivalent to assigning the label name via the Properties panel. Add these next two lines within the `for` loop after the first line, but before the closing curly brace:

```
if(frameNum != 0) tl.insertKeyframe(frameNum);
newLayerObj.frames[frameNum].name = labels[i];
```

*Improving the mouth symbol script*

Your script will work just fine as it is right now, but you should probably do a little housekeeping:

1.  Lock the new layer to make sure no content is accidentally placed on the "labels" layer by adding the following line to the end of the script:

    ```
    newLayerObj.locked = true;
    ```

2.  You'll use the next bit of code to move the playhead back to the first frame and target "Layer 1" so the user can immediately begin adding artwork after running the script. This can be accomplished in a single step by setting the selected frame.

    There are two different ways to pass a selection to the `setSelectedFrames()` method. Method A accepts arguments for a `startFrameIndex`, an `endFrameIndex`, and a toggle about whether to replace the current selection (the toggle is optional and `true` by default). Method B accepts a selection array as its first argument and the same toggle from method A as the second argument. Because you want to specify the layer that you're selecting, you'll use method B with a three-item array that includes the layer that you want to select, the first frame, and the last frame. Layer index numbering starts with zero at the top of the stack. To access the layer below your "labels" layer, you need to add 1 to the layer index that you stored. Add this next line to the bottom of the script:

    ```
    tl.setSelectedFrames([newLayerNum + 1, 0, 1]);
    ```

3.  If the user clicks Cancel when asked for the symbol name, you need to be sure to abort the rest of the script. You'll do this by wrapping most of your code in a function. You can then exit that function at any point in time. Add the following function definition before the declaration of the `namePath` variable:

    ```
    function createNewSymbol(){
    ```

4.  You still need to make sure that you close your function and that the script actually calls the function that you

255

just defined. Do so by adding the following to the end of the script:

```
}
createNewSymbol();
```

5. You're now able to exit the function if and when the user clicks Cancel. Clicking Cancel causes the prompt() to return a value of null. To exit the function if the user cancels, add the following line immediately after the namePath prompt:

```
if(namePath == null) return;
```

6. Save your script (Command+S/Ctrl+S) and test it by opening a new document and choosing Commands > New Mouth Symbol.

Rather than wrapping your code in a function (as you just did), you could have wrapped your code in an if statement block, which would have checked to see if namePath was *not* set to null. The advantage of wrapping everything in a function is that it's easy to then exit the function for any number of reasons. For example, you could add another prompt before the symbol name to determine if the user wants to add (or remove) any labels to your set. This is an easy feature to add because you originally defined your label set as a string, not an array. The prompt will also return a string. You thus have the option to abort the script if the user clicks Cancel within the Prompt box. If you had used a second if statement instead of a function, you'd in turn have to wrap everything in another set of brackets, rendering everything more difficult to read.

7. Return to your script. By adding the following snippet inside the beginning of the createNewSymbol function block, the command will present the user with your set of labels and allow the user to add or remove labels:

```
var returnedLabels = prompt("Labels: ",
➥labelString);
labelString = returnedLabels;
if(labelString == null) return;
```

8. Save your script, return to the open document, and run the command again. Your script will now include a prompt that allows the user to add or remove frame labels (**Figure 4.27**).

Your completed New Mouth Symbol script should look like this:

```
var dom = fl.getDocumentDOM();
var lib = dom.library;
var labelString = "default,ee,oh,ah,mm,L,s";
var framesPerLabel = 10;

function createNewSymbol(){
var returnedLabels = prompt("Labels: ", labelString);
labelString = returnedLabels;
if(labelString == null) return;
var namePath = prompt("Symbol name: " );
if(namePath == null) return;
lib.addNewItem('graphic', namePath);
lib.editItem(namePath);
var tl = dom.getTimeline();
var labels = labelString.split(',');
tl.insertFrames(labels.length * framesPerLabel);
var newLayerNum = tl.addNewLayer("labels");
var newLayerObj = tl.layers[newLayerNum];
for (var i=0; i < labels.length; i++){
    var frameNum = i * framesPerLabel;
    if(frameNum != 0) tl.insertKeyframe(frameNum);
    newLayerObj.frames[frameNum].name = labels[i];
}
newLayerObj.locked = true;
tl.setSelectedFrames([newLayerNum + 1, 0, 1]);
}

createNewSymbol();
```

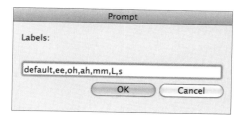

**Figure 4.27** The prepopulated prompt that allows users to add or remove labels.

## Extending Flash Even Further

Several topics capable of improving your workflow have been covered to this point, but there are even more powerful techniques yet to be discovered. This section gives you a taste of additional techniques that you can use to extend Flash beyond the topics covered thus far in this chapter.

### Advanced Dialog Boxes

So far, we've touched upon some very simple user interactions, but you can create more complex interactions using the XMLUI object (**Figure 4.28**). The XMLUI object allows you to create complex dialog boxes using a simple XML configuration file. An XML file is a simple text file that uses tags to describe data. Similar to HTML, XML tags begin with a less than sign (<) and end with a greater than sign (>), and a slash (/) is used to close a tag. Here's the XML that describes the structure of a dialog box for a command that combines textfields in Flash:

Figure 4.28 The dialog box produced by an XMLUI file that appears for the Combine TextFields command.

```xml
<?xml version="1.0" encoding="UTF-8"?>
<dialog id="combineTF" title="Combine TextFields"
➥buttons="accept,cancel">
        <vbox>
                <label value="Sort from:" />
                <radiogroup id="sortby" tabindex="5">
                    <radio label="top" accesskey="t"
➥selected="true"/>
                        <radio label="left" accesskey="l" />
                        <radio label="bottom" accesskey="b" />
                        <radio label="right" accesskey="r" />
                </radiogroup>
        </vbox>
        <spacer />
        <hbox>
                <label value="Separator:" />
                <textbox id="separator" maxlength="20"
➥multiline="false" value="" tabindex="1" size="12"
➥literal="false" />
        </hbox>

</dialog>
```

Once the XML file is saved, the file location can be passed as an argument using the document.xmlPanel() method, which launches the dialog box. You can access the user selections made within the dialog box after the dialog box has been closed just as you can with the `confirm` and `prompt` methods.

Adobe has almost no official documentation of how these XML files work. The only complete documentation can be found in *Extending Macromedia Flash MX 2004: Complete Guide and Reference to JavaScript Flash* by Todd Yard and Keith Peters (friends of ED, 2004). You can also find a great article by Guy Watson at www.devx.com/webdev/Article/20825.

### Panels

The JSFL knowledge covered in this chapter carries over to Flash panels as well. A Flash panel is simply a published SWF that can be loaded into the Flash Professional interface and accessed by choosing Window > Other Panels. You can design custom panels to look like the panels that come installed with Flash, or you can make them entirely unique. To have your SWF show up as a panel, you'll need to place it in the Configuration/WindowSWF folder. If you have Flash open when you paste (or save) the SWF into the folder for the first time, you must restart Flash to make the panel available.

From a SWF, there is one primary way for ActionScript to talk with JSFL, which is to use the `MMExecute()` function. This function passes a string to be interpreted as JSFL. When you pass this code as a string, you'll have to be careful to escape any characters such as quotation marks (using a backslash, e.g., `/"`) that will disrupt the string in ActionScript. If you use double-quotes for JSFL, you can use single quotes to wrap your string, and vice versa:

```
MMExecute("alert('hello');");
```

When you publish your SWF by choosing Control > Test Movie, you won't see any indication that the JSFL code has executed. If you place the SWF inside the WindowSWF folder, restart Flash, and locate the panel by choosing Window > Other Panels (the panel name will be the filename minus the .swf extension), you will then see an alert box that displays "hello" (**Figure 4.29**).

Figure 4.29  An alert box generated by a SWF panel using MMExecute.

**Complex ActionScript-to-JSFL Interactions**

For more complex interactions, it is recommended that you place all your JSFL functions in a script file and call individual functions within the script using the `fl.runscript()` method (from MMExecute) rather than including all your JSFL inside your ActionScript and sending large strings with MMExecute.

▶ The method usage for `fl.runscript()` is documented as follows:
   `fl.runScript(fileURI [, funcName [, arg1, arg2, ...]])`

▶ To execute an entire script, pass the file location of the script as the only argument.

▶ To call a function within a script, also pass the name of the function as the second argument.

▶ All arguments after the second one are for arguments that you are passing to the function that you are calling.

▶ By keeping your JSFL in a separate script, you avoid the need to republish your SWF (and copy it to the WindowSWF folder) with every update.

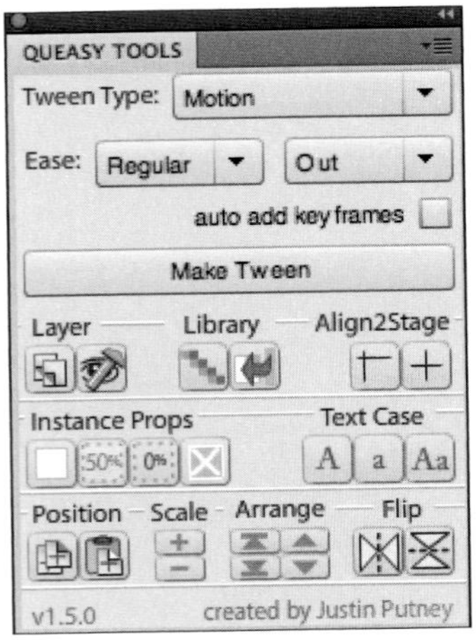

*Building the Animation Tasks panel*

There are several reasons to design a SWF panel. Action-Script has several capabilities to analyze and display content that JSFL does not. Sometimes, however, house-cleaning for your Commands menu is reason enough. As more commands are collected, the Commands menu list can be so extensive that it becomes difficult to locate the desired command. Since the name of the game is efficiency, there's good reason to keep the Commands list manageable (**Figure 4.30**). Let's take some of the commands that you developed in this chapter and design a simple SWF panel.

**Figure 4.30** The Queasy Tools panel started out as a way to clean up the Commands menu and has evolved into a powerful SWF panel.

1. Create a new JSFL script and save it as **Animation Tasks.jsfl** in a folder of your choosing.

2. Copy the content from Create Stage Size Rectangle.jsfl, Create Stage Matte.jsfl, Smooth and Lossless Bitmaps.jsfl, and New Mouth Symbol.jsfl scripts that you saved previously, and paste each into the Animation Tasks script.

3. Wrap each block of code from the scripts you copied within the following function names respectively: `stageRectangle`, `stageMatte`, `smoothBMPs`, and `newMouthSymbol`.

4. Consolidate any variable declarations for the document, Library, and Timeline (except the one in the middle of the `newMouthSymbol` function) at the top of the script.

Your Animation Tasks script should now read as follows:

```
var dom = fl.getDocumentDOM();
var tl = dom.getTimeline();
var lib = dom.library;


function stageRectangle(){
    dom.addNewRectangle({left:0, top:0,
➥right:dom.width, bottom:dom.height}, 0);
}


function stageMatte(){
    var matteThickness = 200;
    var newLayerNum = tl.addNewLayer("matte");
    dom.addNewRectangle({left:-matteThickness,
➥top:-matteThickness,
➥right:dom.width+matteThickness,
➥bottom:dom.height+matteThickness},
➥0, false, true);
    dom.selection = tl.layers[newLayerNum].
➥frames[0].elements;
    dom.union();
    dom.enterEditMode('inPlace');
    dom.setSelectionRect({left:0, top:0,
➥right:dom.width, bottom:dom.height}, true,
➥false);
    dom.deleteSelection();
    dom.mouseDblClk({x:10, y:10}, false, false,
➥false);
    tl.setLayerProperty("locked", true);
    tl.reorderLayer(newLayerNum, 0);
}
```

```
function smoothBMPs(){
    var items = lib. getSelectedItems();
    if(items.length < 1) {
        var confirmed = confirm("No items are
➥selected. Do you want to run this on all library
➥items?");
        if(confirmed) items = lib.items;
    }
    var runCounter = 0;
    for(var i in items) {
        var it = items[i];
        if(it.itemType == "bitmap") {
            it.allowSmoothing = true;
            it.compressionType = 'lossless';
            runCounter++;
        }
    }
    alert(runCounter + " items affected.");
}

function newMouthSymbol(){
    var labelString = "default,ee,oh,ah,mm,L,s";
    var framesPerLabel = 10;
    var returnedLabels = prompt("Labels: ",
➥labelString);
    labelString = returnedLabels;
    if(labelString == null) return;
    var namePath = prompt("Symbol name: " );
    if(namePath == null) return;
    lib.addNewItem('graphic', namePath);
    lib.editItem(namePath);
    var tl = dom.getTimeline();
    var labels = labelString.split(',');
    tl.insertFrames(labels.length *
➥framesPerLabel);
    var newLayerNum = tl.addNewLayer("labels");
    var newLayerObj = tl.layers[newLayerNum];
    for (var i=0; i < labels.length; i++){
        var frameNum = i * framesPerLabel;
        if(frameNum != 0) tl.insertKeyframe
➥(frameNum);
```

```
        newLayerObj.frames[frameNum].name =
➥labels[i];
    }
    newLayerObj.locked = true;
    tl.setSelectedFrames([newLayerNum + 1, 0, 1]);
}
```

5. Create a new ActionScript 3.0 document and save it as **Animation Tasks.fla** (in the same folder with the corresponding JSFL script).

6. In the Properties panel under the Properties heading, click the Edit button next to Size, change the size of the document to **200 x 150**, and click OK.

7. Use the color selector within the Properties panel to change the background color of the Stage to a light gray color, like #CCCCCC.

8. Open the Components panel (Window > Components), twirl open the User Interface folder, and drag four instances of the Button component onto the Stage.

9. Select all four buttons (Command+A/Ctrl+A), set their width properties to **200** in the Properties panel, and arrange the buttons evenly on the Stage (**Figure 4.31**).

**Figure 4.31** Button instances evenly spaced on the Stage.

10. Give the buttons the following instance names using the Properties panel (from top to bottom): **rect_btn**, **matte_btn**, **bmp_btn**, and **mouth_btn**.

11. Give the buttons the following labels using the Component Parameters area of the Properties panel: **Create Stage Rectangle**, **Create Stage Matte**, **Smooth Bitmaps**, and **New Mouth Symbol** (**Figure 4.32**).

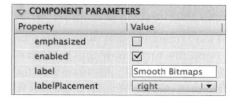

**Figure 4.32** Setting the button label in the Properties panel.

**12.** Create a new layer and name it **actions**. Lock the layer and select the first frame.

**13.** Open the Actions panel (Window > Actions) and type the following ActionScript into the Actions panel:

```
rect_btn.addEventListener(MouseEvent.CLICK,
➥rect_click);
matte_btn.addEventListener(MouseEvent.CLICK,
➥matte_click);
bmp_btn.addEventListener(MouseEvent.CLICK,
➥bmp_click);
mouth_btn.addEventListener(MouseEvent.CLICK,
➥mouth_click);

function rect_click(event:MouseEvent):void {

}

function matte_click(event:MouseEvent):void {

}

function bmp_click(event:MouseEvent):void {

}

function mouth_click(event:MouseEvent):void {

}
```

This code uses the instance names you added to the buttons to create mouse click listeners. When the SWF is rendered and a user clicks one of the four buttons, your panel will summon the corresponding function. Each one of these functions will trigger a function inside of your Animation Tasks JSFL script.

**14.** To save some typing, funnel all the JSFL communication through a single ActionScript function. Add the following highlighted code to the click functions:

```
function rect_click(event:MouseEvent):void {
    jsFunct("stageRectangle");
}

function matte_click(event:MouseEvent):void {
    jsFunct("stageMatte");
}

function bmp_click(event:MouseEvent):void {
    jsFunct("smoothBMPs");
}

function mouth_click(event:MouseEvent):void {
    jsFunct("newMouthSymbol");
}
```

Now you'll write the function that will communicate with your JSFL script. This function will accept a JSFL function name from your script as an argument, and then your ActionScript function will call the function within the JSFL script.

**15.** Add the following code at the end of the ActionScript within the Actions panel:

```
function jsFunct(fname:String):void{
    var jsfl:String = "fl.runScript('" +
➥scriptPath + "','" + fname + "');";
    trace(jsfl);
}
```

Notice how complex the jsfl string is with all the single and double quotations. You need JSFL to recognize parts of your message as a string, hence the use of the single quotes within the double quotes that define your string. You'll be sending a message for JSFL to run a function from within a script.

**16.** Add this line of ActionScript to the top of your code to define the location of the JSFL script:

```
var scriptPath:String = this.loaderInfo.url.
➥replace(".swf",".jsfl");
```

This line retrieves the name of your SWF and replaces the .swf extension with a .jsfl extension to locate the path for your JSFL script (which is in the same folder).

For the moment, you're using the `trace` method instead of `MMExecute`, so that you can preview your JSFL strings in the Output panel.

**17.** Ensure that Control > Test Movie > in Flash Professional is selected and press Command+Return/ Ctrl+Enter to test the movie.

**18.** Click all four buttons. Your Output window should trace text resembling the following:

```
fl.runScript('file:////Volumes/Macintosh%20HD/
➥Users/YourName/Desktop/AnimatingWithFlash/
➥jsfl%5Fscripts/Animation%20Tasks.jsfl',
➥'stageRectangle');
fl.runScript('file:////Volumes/Macintosh%20HD/
➥Users/YourName/Desktop/AnimatingWithFlash/
➥jsfl%5Fscripts/Animation%20Tasks.jsfl',
➥'stageMatte');
fl.runScript('file:////Volumes/Macintosh%20HD/
➥Users/YourName/Desktop/AnimatingWithFlash/
➥jsfl%5Fscripts/Animation%20Tasks.jsfl',
➥'smoothBMPs');
fl.runScript('file:////Volumes/Macintosh%20HD/
➥Users/YourName/Desktop/AnimatingWithFlash/
➥jsfl%5Fscripts/Animation%20Tasks.jsfl',
➥'newMouthSymbol');
```

Verify that the two arguments being sent to `fl.runScript` are in single quotes and that there are no other quotation marks.

**19.** Close the test window and update your code to replace the `trace` method with `MMExecute`:

```
MMExecute(jsfl);
```

**20.** Test your movie again, click each button, and ensure that there are no errors in the Compiler Error or Output panels.

**21.** Locate the folder containing Animation Tasks.fla. There will be a corresponding Animation Tasks.swf file that was generated as a result of testing your movie in Flash. Copy the Animation Tasks.swf and Animation Tasks.jsfl files into your Configuration/WindowSWF directory. Restart Flash.

**22.** Open a new ActionScript 3.0 document. You can now open your SWF panel by choosing Window > Other Panels > Animation Tasks (**Figure 4.33**). Verify that each button completes its task (**Figure 4.34**).

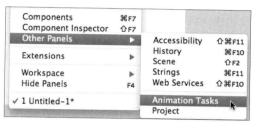

**Figure 4.33**  Locating the newly created Flash panel by choosing Window > Other Panels.

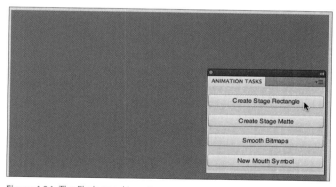

**Figure 4.34**  The Flash panel in action.

Because you've successfully grouped these four commands in a panel, you can now delete the original commands from your Configuration/Commands directory to free some space in the Commands menu.

**TIP**

You can also delete (or rename) commands by choosing Commands > Manage Saved Commands.

### Tools

You can also create custom tools for the Flash toolbar using JSFL. Tool files reside in the Configuration/Tools directory. Tool files have special functions not generally used in other JSFL scripts, like mouse event handlers and Properties panel settings. The PolyStar tool that comes with Flash (found with the shape tools in the toolbar) is actually an example of an extensible tool. You won't be developing any tools in this book, but you can view the code that powers the PolyStar tool by opening Configuration/Tools/PolyStar.jsfl.

## Packaging Extensions for Distribution

The first step toward making your extension available (and easily installable) to others is creating an MXI descriptor file. An MXI file is a special XML file that contains information about the extension (title, author, version, copyright, license agreement, which files it includes, where to install the files, etc.). Here's sample text from an MXI file:

> **NOTES**
>
> The file extension for an MXI file is .mxi.

```
<?xml version="1.0" encoding="UTF-8"?>
<macromedia-extension
    name="Sample Extension"
    version="1.0.0"
    type="command">
    <author name="Your Name Here" />
    <products>
        <product name="Flash" version="7" primary=
➥"true" />
    </products>
    <description>
    <![CDATA[
    This extension does A and B.
    ]]>
    </description>
    <ui-access>
    <![CDATA[
    The command can be found in 'Commands > Sample
➥Extension'
    ]]>
```

```
    </ui-access>
    <license-agreement>
    <![CDATA[
    ]]>
    </license-agreement>
    <files>
        <file source="Sample Extension.jsfl"
➥destination="$flash/Commands" />
    </files>
</macromedia-extension>
```

The highlighted text needs to be customized for each extension using a text editor like TextEdit in Mac OS X or Notepad in Microsoft Windows.

After you've edited your MXI file in a text editor, open it in the Adobe Extension Manager (**Figure 4.35**). The Extension Manager comes free with any of the Adobe Creative Suite applications. The Extension Manager will ask where you want to save your packaged file. Once you've given your file a name and location, the Extension Manager will package all the files referenced in the `<files>` tag of the MXI file and include them in a single MXP (or ZXP for CS5-specific extensions) file. That new file can then be distributed to other users and installed using the Extension Manager.

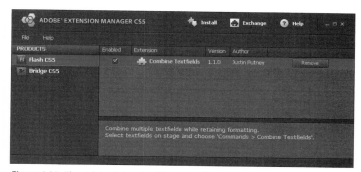

**Figure 4.35** The Adobe Extension Manager allows you to package extensions for others as well as save and manage extensions on your own system.

## More Resources

This chapter covered the basics of writing commands and creating a handy SWF panel for accelerating your Flash animation workflow, but we've still only scratched the surface of Flash extensibility. This last section provides you with additional resources to continue extending your Flash animation workflow.

### Other People's Extensions

There's a wealth of cool stuff that's already available and free to use. If you're on a tight deadline and you don't have time to write your own script, don't be shy about checking to see if anyone has gotten there before you. Conversely, if you just want to write the script as a challenge or to make something work *exactly* the way you want, then go for it. You can always learn from comparing your solution to others on the web.

### Books

There's only one book to-date that is completely dedicated to JSFL. It hasn't been updated since the release of JSFL in 2004. Luckily, very little of the language has changed since 2004. Coupled with the (up-to-date) help documentation, *Extending Macromedia Flash MX 2004: Complete Guide and Reference to JavaScript Flash* by Todd Yard & Keith Peters (friends of ED, 2004) is an invaluable reference.

### Forums

Forums are a great way to start a conversation. Sometimes a web search is all that is needed to find a solution, but other times you really need a back-and-forth interaction with someone who understands your problem. Many of the Flash forums are packed with knowledgeable people willing to give free advice. If you're looking for existing extensions or help with JSFL, here are a few good sites to start with:

▶ http://forums.adobe.com/

▶ http://www.keyframer.com/forum/

- http://bbs.coldhardflash.com/
- http://www.actionscript.org/forums/

### Sites with Flash Extensions

Looking for sites with Flash extensions? Check out these sites:

- http://www.adobe.com/exchange/
- http://ajarproductions.com/blog/
- http://theflashblog.com/
- http://www.animonger.com/flashtools.html
- http://www.dave-logan.com/extensions
- http://www.toonmonkey.com/extensions.html
- http://www.5etdemi.com/blog/archives/2005/01/toolsextensions-for-flash-mx-2004/

### Sites with JSFL Help

Here are a few other sites to visit for JSFL techniques:

- http://summitprojectsflashblog.wordpress.com/
- http://www.bit-101.com/blog/
- http://www.adobe.com/devnet/flash/articles/invisible_button.html
- http://www.adobe.com/go/em_file_format (MXI documentation in PDF format)

# 5

# Sharing Your Animation

If you're creating animated movies or games in Flash, chances are you'd like someone to see what you've produced. Whether your goal is to tell a story, express yourself creatively, or sell a product, you'll need a way to share your handiwork with an audience. Fortunately, sharing is a fundamental part of the Flash platform.

This chapter gives you the industrial-strength tools necessary to share your Flash creations with the world. You'll construct a Flash portfolio to display the character animation and visual effects you created in the preceding chapters of this book. To craft your portfolio, you'll utilize ActionScript techniques from Chapter 3 and even use a bit of JavaScript Flash (JSFL) to render some of your artwork.

The goals for this chapter include:

▶ Create a website to showcase your animated projects

▶ Learn how to load content into your Flash movie dynamically using XML

▶ Learn how to dynamically style text using CSS

▶ Add animation to your site using ActionScript

▶ Learn about other ways to share your animation (broadcast, mobile, and desktop)

## Showcasing Your Animation on the Web

If you're looking for a job or hoping someone will notice your work, there are few tools as effective as an online portfolio. It's a simple, inexpensive way to show potential clients or employers what you can offer. For a few dollars a month, you can have your own website with a unique URL to host your content. An online portfolio has become an expected part of any digital artist's professional presentation. This section shows you how to build an easy-to-update portfolio to serve as a platform for your work on the web.

### Planning Your Portfolio

A digital portfolio can be laborious and time-consuming to build and maintain (especially when you're busy with client work and/or a full-time job). Proper planning can make the difference between a portfolio that requires a complete rebuild in six months and a portfolio that will be viable for years (with minor updates).

While planning your portfolio, it's important to first determine which parts of your site will change frequently and which parts will remain fairly constant. For instance, you will probably want to update your work samples often, but your name will likely remain unchanged. To facilitate easy upkeep, you'll want to separate frequently updated portions of your site from portions that will not change (at least in terms of how the file and the ActionScript are set up). This type of modularity (having independent parts) also has additional benefits. Site visitors will benefit from only needing to load those pieces of your site that they actually see.

As you begin to plan your site, consider the following questions about potential visitors to your portfolio:

▶ Who is your intended audience? Art directors? Business people?

▶ Is your audience technically savvy?

▶ What do you want your visitors to take away from your site?

The answers to these questions will inform the require-ments for your site. Once you've addressed the preceding questions, you'll want to generate a list of the attributes required for your portfolio.

Here are the site requirements for the portfolio you will build in this chapter:

▶ Easy to edit and update (keeps work recent)

▶ Concise (limited window of time to catch the viewer's eye)

▶ Reasonably low-bandwidth (load indication for large content)

▶ A space reserved for text (to describe the work and your role in the project, as well as credit for anyone else involved)

▶ Must show some design and animation skills but not draw attention away from the work itself

▶ A reasonably large area for displaying work samples

▶ Readable text

After you've listed the site requirements, make a list of methods for meeting those requirements.

Solutions (site specifications) include:

▶ Arranging buttons vertically to accommodate varying numbers of work samples

▶ Using a two-color design, which is less likely to clash with the colors in the work samples

▶ Using vector artwork for the site, which is low band-width, but including a preloader for work samples that may be larger

▶ Adding an area for descriptive text with the capability of including links

▶ Loading content from an XML file that can be edited without opening Flash

▶ Using a sans-serif typeface (Myriad Pro) that is easy to read onscreen

▶ Controlling the site animation with ActionScript, which is also easy to update

**Flash Player Version**

Deciding which Flash Player version to publish to is usually a decision between the latest/greatest features and maximum compatibility. As a general rule, you'll want to publish to the lowest version that includes all the features (and ActionScript methods) used in your project. If your intended audience is a Flash-based design or animation studio, backward compatibility will be less of a concern.

For statistics on the acceptance of a specific Player version, see the following site: www.adobe.com/products/player_census/flashplayer/version_penetration.html.

Additionally, you want to consider the monitor size and the likely Flash Player version that your visitors will have installed.

After you've established some of your technical specifications, you can start thinking about how your site will look. As you start to envision your site, you'll want to consider the organization of the visual elements onscreen. Which areas will deserve more attention than others? Certain areas of the screen will command more of the viewer's attention. You'll want to make these areas correspond with the content that you most want the viewer to see.

It's easy enough to write an explicit list of items that you want the viewer to see: clear title, easy to locate links/options, prominently displayed work samples, and so on. Then sketch the elements of your site (on paper or onscreen) and see if you can make the elements work together as a cohesive whole (**Figure 5.1**). It may take a couple of attempts to render a visually pleasing layout that meets the site requirements that you've listed (**Figure 5.2**).

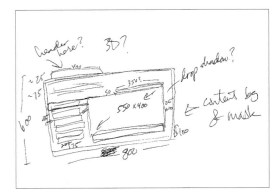

**Figure 5.1** A rough pencil mockup and notes for the portfolio site.

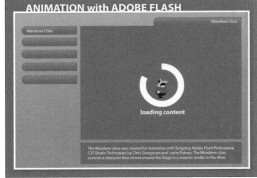

**Figure 5.2** A more polished digital mockup created in Flash.

## Setting Up the Flash Document and Creating Artwork

You'll begin by creating those aspects of your site that will remain more or less unchanged. In general, even these elements will be organized in a manner that will allow for reasonably easy updates.

Start by setting up your site directory and Flash file.

1. Create a new folder named **website** to house all the files you create in this section.

2. Create a new ActionScript 3 document and save it as **site.fla** in your website folder.

3. In the Properties panel under the Properties heading, click the Edit button next to Size, change the size of the document to **800 x 600** pixels, and click OK.

   Dimensions of 800 x 600 pixels will allow for plenty of space for your work samples, buttons, and text description while still fitting on nearly every (nonmobile) screen quite nicely.

Now that your document has been established, you can start creating artwork within the document.

1. Rename Layer 1 to **background**.

2. Select the Rectangle Primitive tool. In the Properties panel, set the fill color to **#6699FF** and the stroke to white (**#FFFFFF**), set the Stroke value to **6**, set the Cap to Square, and set Join to Miter (**Figure 5.3**).

3. Draw a rectangle on Stage and use the Properties panel to adjust the rectangle to have a position of X: **0**, Y: **50** and have a size of W: **800**, H: **550** (**Figure 5.4**).

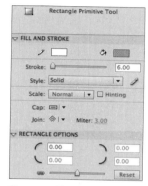

Figure 5.3 The Rectangle Primitive settings for the background shape.

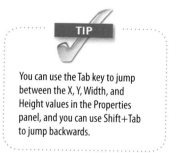

**TIP**

You can use the Tab key to jump between the X, Y, Width, and Height values in the Properties panel, and you can use Shift+Tab to jump backwards.

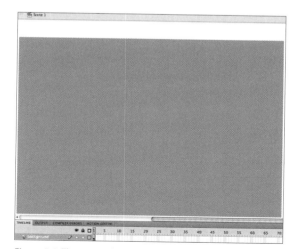

Figure 5.4 The rectangle will serve as the background for the portfolio artwork.

4. Convert your rectangle into a Movie Clip symbol (F8). Name the symbol **background** and make sure the Registration is set to the top left (**Figure 5.5**).

Figure 5.5 The Convert to Symbol dialog box settings for the background symbol.

5. Expand the Filters group in the Properties panel (if necessary) and add a new Drop Shadow filter (**Figure 5.6**) to the background instance. Update the following properties on the Drop Shadow: Blur X: **10**, Blur Y: **10**, Strength: **30%**, Quality: Medium.

Figure 5.6 Use the New Filter button to add a Drop Shadow filter to the background instance.

Now you'll create the shape that will house the externally loaded work samples. Later, using ActionScript, you'll make your dynamically loaded content visible by nesting it inside the symbol instance you are about to create.

1. Lock the background layer. Create a new layer named **content**.

2. Use the Rectangle Primitive tool to draw another rectangle.

3. In the Properties panel, update the new rectangle so it has no stroke and a fill color of **#3366FF**, X: **225**, Y: **100**, W: **550**, and H: **400**.

4. Convert the current rectangle to a Movie Clip symbol (F8) named **content** with a top-left Registration.

5. Ctrl-click (right-click) on the first frame in the content layer and choose Copy Frames.

6. Create a new layer named **content_mask**.

7. Ctrl-click (right-click) on the first frame in the content_mask layer and choose Paste Frames.

8. Ctrl-click (right-click) on the content_mask layer and choose Mask.

   This mask ensures that any offstage artwork from the dynamically loaded content is hidden (**Figure 5.7**).

**NOTES**

Observe that the content rectangle matches the default size of a Flash document (and the size of the documents you created in previous chapters). This allows you to load that content without needing to scale it.

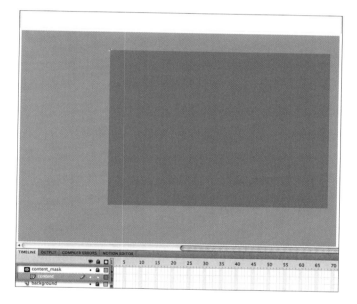

**Figure 5.7** The content layer is indented under the content_mask layer to indicate that it is masked by the content_mask layer.

9. Unlock the content layer and use the Selection tool to select the symbol instance. In the Properties panel, give the rectangle an instance name of **content_mc**.

10. Re-lock the content layer.

**TIP**

One convention to distinguish instance names from symbol names is to add a suffix (e.g., "_mc" for Movie Clips).

Recall that you'll need an area to display a text description for each work sample. You'll now create the artwork that will display the description just below the content region.

1. Create a new layer named **description** and move it above the content_mask layer.

2. Use the Rectangle Primitive tool and the Properties panel to add a rectangle at X: **225**, Y: **510** with the dimensions W: **550** and H: **75**.

3. Convert the new rectangle to a Movie Clip symbol named **description**.

4. Add an instance name of **description_mc** using the Properties panel, and lock the description layer (**Figure 5.8**).

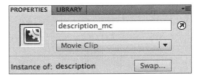

**Figure 5.8** The instance name of description_mc has been added using the Properties panel.

In addition to the description area, you'll create a symbol that will house the title of the work sample that is currently being displayed.

1. Create a new layer named **title**.

2. Use the Rectangle Primitive tool and the Properties panel to add a rectangle at X: **475**, Y: **70** with dimensions of W: **300** and H: **30**.

3. In the Rectangle option of the Properties panel, click the chain icon to allow each corner radius to be set to a different value. Then set the upper-left corner to a value of **20**.

4. Convert the new rectangle to a Movie Clip symbol named **title**.

5. Name the instance **title_mc** and lock the title layer.

**6.** Drag the title layer below the content layer and toward the left so it is not masked by the content_mask layer (**Figure 5.9**).

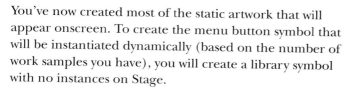

**Figure 5.9** Flash indicates where the layer will land so you can avoid accidentally masking the layer.

You've now created most of the static artwork that will appear onscreen. To create the menu button symbol that will be instantiated dynamically (based on the number of work samples you have), you will create a library symbol with no instances on Stage.

**1.** In the Library panel, Ctrl-click (right-click) on the title symbol and choose Duplicate. In the Duplicate Symbol dialog box, name the new symbol **menuItem** and select the Export for ActionScript check box (**Figure 5.10**).

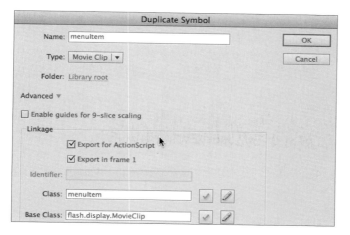

**Figure 5.10** The Export for Action-Script check box automatically populates the Class field with the symbol name.

When you click OK in the Duplicate Symbol dialog box, you will be prompted with a message telling you that the menuItem class was not found and that Flash will automatically create one for you (**Figure 5.11** on the next page). Click OK to allow Flash to generate a class automatically.

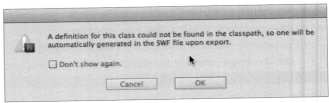

**Figure 5.11** Flash will prompt you if the name in the Class field does not correspond with an existing file that it can locate.

**Figure 5.12** The curved edge rendered using the Rectangle options.

2. Double-click the menuItem icon in the Library to edit the symbol.

3. Select the rectangle primitive and update the bottom-left corner in the Rectangle options within the Properties panel to a value of **20**. The rectangle should now be completely curved on the left side (**Figure 5.12**).

4. Update W to a value of **180** and lock Layer 1.

5. Ctrl-click (right-click) on the first frame inside the menuItem symbol and choose Copy Frames.

6. Create a new layer named **shine**.

7. Ctrl-click (right-click) on the first frame of the shine layer and choose Paste Frames.

8. Select the shape on the shine layer and open the Color panel (Window > Color).

9. Change the color type to Linear Gradient. By default, this will create a black-to-white gradient with a black color pointer at the left (at the bottom of the Color panel) and a white pointer at the right. The selected color pointer will have a black tip (**Figure 5.13**).

**Figure 5.13** The settings in the Color panel correspond to the selected pointer with the black tip.

**10.** Update the pointer on the left to be white with an alpha value of **0%** and move the pointer about 1/5th of the way to the right. Update the pointer on the right to white with an alpha (the A under RGB) of **25%** (**Figure 5.14**).

**11.** Use the Gradient Transform tool (by default it's grouped with the Free Transform tool) to rotate the gradient counterclockwise 90 degrees (by dragging the circular handle), and collapse the gradient height (by dragging the square handle with the arrow) to match the height of the artwork (**Figure 5.15**).

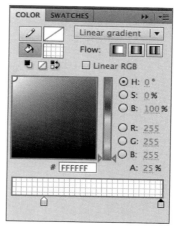

Figure 5.14 The updated gradient settings for the shine shape.

Figure 5.15 The collapsed gradient now covers the shine shape exactly.

**12.** Adjust the position of the shine shape to X:**2** and Y:**2** with dimensions of W:**176** and H:**26** to indent the shine within the shape (**Figure 5.16**).

Figure 5.16 The indent completes the shine effect and gives the button some depth.

Now that you have the artwork laid down for the menu-Item symbol, you'll add a dynamic textfield. A dynamic textfield, unlike a static textfield, can be edited at runtime using ActionScript. Employing a dynamic textfield allows you to populate your movie with content that will be added to an external file later in the chapter. Given that the contents of your dynamic textfield are uncertain (and unfixed) when your movie is published, Flash won't know which characters to include in your file; thus, you'll need to embed font characters so that your text can be properly displayed.

**Font Embedding**

When your published movie plays on a user's computer, there is no guarantee that the fonts you applied will be available on another user's machine. To ensure that your text maintains the appearance that you intended (regardless of the machine on which your movie is viewed), you can embed entire fonts or specific subsets of characters from a font. Once a font is embedded, you can use that font anywhere in your published movie.

Flash CS5 has a spiffy new Font Embedding dialog box. Also, beginning with Flash CS5, Flash automatically embeds all characters used by any text objects that contain text.

1. Choose Text > Font Embedding, type **siteFont** into the Name field, and type **Myriad Pro** into the Family field. Then select the check boxes for Uppercase, Lowercase, Numerals, and Punctuation, and click the plus sign (+) to add the font. Click OK to save (**Figure 5.17**).

You'll now be able to access siteFont* (the asterisk indicates an embedded font) from the Font Family menu.

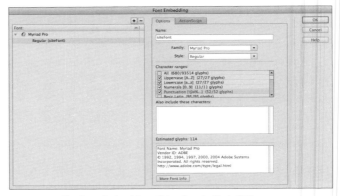

**Figure 5.17** The Font Embedding dialog box in Flash CS5.

**Figure 5.18** The Properties panel settings for the textfield instance inside the title symbol.

2. Create a new layer named **text** inside the menuItem symbol.

3. Draw a new textfield using the Text tool. In the Properties panel, set the Text engine to Classic Text, the Text type to Dynamic Text, and type in **txt** as the Instance Name.

4. Update the respective position and size of the textfield to X:**15**, Y:**5** and W: **160**, H: **20**. In the Character section of the Properties panel, set the Family to **siteFont*** (the font you created), the Size to **14**, and the Color to white. Make sure the anti-aliasing is set to "Anti-alias for readability," and toggle the Selectable button off (**Figure 5.18**).

**Classic Text vs. TLF Text**

Flash CS5 now has native support for the Text Layout Framework (TLF) that was introduced with Flash CS4. A TLF textfield can support several new formatting features, including ligatures, multicolumn layout, linked textfields, and more.

Classic text refers to the text engine that has been available in all of the previous versions of Flash.

When you publish a movie that contains a TLF textfield, an SWZ file is added to the directory with your SWF file. The SWZ file contains code necessary for the TLF textfield to function, and it weighs in at about 160 KB. Because you won't be using any of the TLF features in your portfolio, you'll stick with classic text for this project. But keep TLF in mind for future projects that require large amounts of text (or special formatting).

You're now finished editing the menuItem. Because the menuItem will be instantiated using ActionScript, no instances need to be added to the Stage.

You'll also use the shine and the textfield that you just created (slightly adjusted) in your title and background symbols.

1.  Select the frames on the text and shine layers, Ctrl-click (right-click), and choose Copy Frames.

2.  In the Library, double-click the icon next to the title item to edit the symbol.

3.  Lock Layer 1 and create a new layer. Ctrl-click (right-click) on the first frame in the new layer and choose Paste Frames. You should now have a shine layer and a text layer.

4.  Update the textfield properties to have a width of **275** and a Paragraph format of Align Right.

5.  Update the shine shape to have a width of **296** and set the bottom-left corner radius back to **0** to match the shape in Layer 1.

6. In the Library, double-click the icon next to the description item to edit the description symbol.

7. Lock Layer 1 in the description symbol's Timeline and create a new layer. Ctrl-click (right-click) on the first frame in the new layer and choose Paste Frames. You should now have a shine layer and a text layer. Delete the shine layer.

8. Update the textfield with the following values in the Properties panel: Y: **15**, W: **520**, and H: **50**. In the Paragraph section, update the Line Spacing to **1** pt, and choose Multiline for the Behavior.

9. Return to the main Timeline by clicking Scene 1 at the top of your Stage. Deselect all (Command+A/Ctrl+A) and use the Stage color selector within the Properties panel to change the background color of the Stage to the following hex value: **#3366FF**. Your Stage should now be blue.

10. In the Library, double-click the icon next to the background item to edit the symbol.

11. Again, lock Layer 1 and paste the stored frames into a new layer.

12. Use the Text tool to type **ANIMATION with ADOBE FLASH** into the textfield on the text layer (or use your own name if you'd like).

13. Convert the Text type to Static Text. Change the Family to Myriad Pro, the Style to Bold, and the Size to **40**.

14. Adjust the X to **37** and the Y to **−34** so the text sits on and blends into the white border of the background symbol. Adjust the width of the textfield as well so that the text sits on one line (**Figure 5.19**).

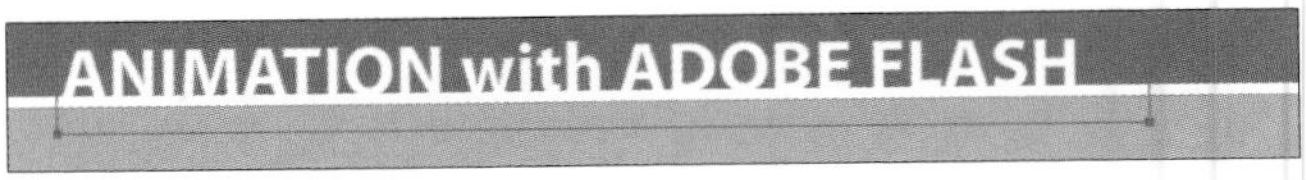

ANIMATION with ADOBE FLASH

Figure 5.19 The textfield sits on a single line along the white border.

15. Select the shine shape and use the Properties panel to adjust the respective Position and Size values to the

following: X: **4**, Y: **4** and W: **792**, H: **540**. Also, click the Reset button in the Rectangle options to restore pointed corners to the rectangle shape.

**16.** Resize the shine gradient using the Gradient Transform tool so the gradient spans the entire shine shape. You may need to move the center point of the gradient down to do so (**Figure 5.20**).

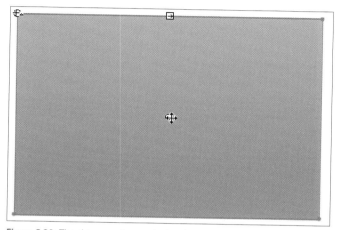

**Figure 5.20** The shine gradient scaled and positioned within the background symbol.

**17.** Save your document.

Congratulations! You've completed all the necessary artwork for the web portfolio. Let's just add one piece of flair.

### Building an animated preloader

A preloader is a way to provide visitors with feedback by letting them know that the content they requested is loading. This will be one place in this particular portfolio where you'll show off some Timeline animation.

**1.** Create a new layer above all the existing layers and name it **preloader**.

**2.** Select the Oval Primitive tool and draw a circle on Stage (hold down the Shift key to constrain the proportions).

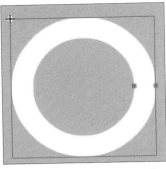

**Figure 5.21** The circle primitive with a hollow center was created by adjusting the Inner Radius in the Properties panel.

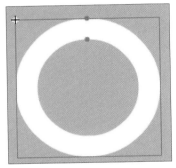

**Figure 5.22** The rotated oval primitive.

3. Your oval should have a white fill with no stroke. In the Properties panel, update the following values: X: **425**, Y: **200**, W: **150**, and H: **150**. In the Oval options, assign a value of **70** to the Inner Radius. Your circle should now have a hollow center like that of a ring (**Figure 5.21**).

4. Convert the oval to a new Movie Clip symbol named **preloader**. Name the symbol instance **preloader_mc**.

5. Switch to the Selection tool and double-click on the preloader instance on the Stage to edit it in place.

6. Use the Transform panel (Window > Transform) to rotate the oval shape **–90** degrees. This will place the two dots that appear in the oval selection at the top of the oval (**Figure 5.22**). This rotation will cause your animation to begin at the top of the circle.

There are several ways to animate this ring so it appears to be actively drawn in a circle. Tweening is generally a good way to save time (recall the mouth within the Wanderer example in Chapter 3). Unfortunately, in this case, tweening this effect would take at least four new keyframes, several shape hints, and a mask (because the resulting tween would remain slightly deformed). Alternatively, adjusting the End angle of the shape would create the desired effect and would produce a clean animation; however, you would need an inordinate number of keyframes. In this case, 100 keyframes would be required. Each keyframe would correspond to 1 percent of loaded content. This process would also be a bit tedious, so let's script it with JSFL.

7. Create a new Flash JavaScript file and save it as **AnimateOvalPrimitive.jsfl**.

8. Input the following code:

```
var dom = fl.getDocumentDOM();
var tl = dom.getTimeline();
var sel = dom.selection[0];
var targEndAngle = 360;
var frameDuration = 100;

if(sel.isOvalObject){
```

```
    var startFrame = tl.currentFrame;
    var endFrame = startFrame + frameDuration - 1;
    var startEndAngle = sel.endAngle;
    var angleChange = targEndAngle -
➥startEndAngle;
    var frameChange = endFrame - startFrame;
    var anglePerFrame = angleChange/frameChange;
    for(var i=0; i < frameDuration; i++){
        tl.insertKeyframe();
        tl.setSelectedFrames(tl.currentFrame,
➥tl.currentFrame + 1);
        var newAngle = Math.min((i+1) *
➥anglePerFrame, 360);
        dom.setOvalObjectProperty("endAngle",
➥newAngle);
    }
}
```

Let's briefly consider what you accomplish with the code you've entered. You first create variables to store the current document and current Timeline. Then you create a variable, sel, to store the first item in the selection array. The next variable, targEndAngle, specifies the End angle that your oval will reach at the end of the frame sequence. Finally, frameDuration determines how many frames to create for the sequence.

To be on the safe side, the rest of the code has been wrapped in an if block that will only execute if the (first) selected object is an oval primitive. Inside the if block, several additional variables are created. Most of these variables are included so that this script is easy to reuse (and repurpose) in the future. For example, you will be starting on frame 1, but your script won't assume that you're starting on frame 1, and instead will check for the current frame. Then the script will determine the endFrame based on the current frame and the frameDuration assigned above. You must subtract one frame from this total to include the current frame in the total duration (i.e., for a frame duration of 100, starting on frame 1: 1 + 100 = 101; therefore, subtract 1). The startEndAngle for the animation is then determined

NOTES

The Math.min method is used to ensure that the newAngle value does not exceed 360 degrees. The Math.min method accepts as many arguments as you care to feed it (separated by commas) and returns the lowest value. Additionally, 1 is added to i because the loop starts at 0 and the frame sequence starts at 1.

using the `endAngle` property on the oval primitive that is selected on Stage. The total `angleChange` and `frameChange` values are then determined and are used to calculate the angle change per frame.

The `for` loop then iterates a certain number of times based on the `frameDuration`. For each iteration, a keyframe is added (which contains the content from the previous frame), the new frame is selected, the angle for that frame is determined by multiplying the `anglePerFrame` value with the iteration value (i.e., the number of times the loop has run), and finally the `endAngle` property is assigned on the oval within the current frame.

9. Save your script and return to your site document. Select the oval and enter a value of **0.50** for the End angle. This will serve as the starting frame for the animation.

10. Now return to the JSFL script you just wrote and click the Run Script button.

11. When your script is finished executing, return to your document. You should now have a 100-frame animation (**Figure 5.23**). Press Return/Enter to see a preview of the animation.

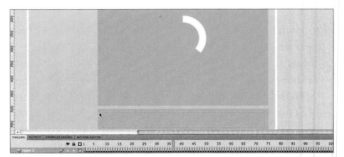

**Figure 5.23** The 100-frame loader ring animation generated by the JSFL script.

12. Lock the current layer and create a new layer named **character**.

**13.** Open the document containing the run cycle that you created in Chapter 2 (the driver from Sausage Kong) or open the run_cycle.fla in the Chapter 5/assets folder on the accompanying CD.

**14.** Copy an instance of the character and paste it into the character layer in the site.fla document. Move the playhead to frame 100. Position and scale the character so he fits inside the ring (**Figure 5.24**).

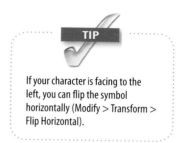

**Figure 5.24** The character positioned inside the loader ring.

**15.** Ensure that the Instance behavior in the Properties panel is set to Movie Clip (so that the run-cycle animation loops independently of the ring animation).

**16.** Add a new layer named **text** and use the Text tool to add a static textframe that reads **loading content**.

**17.** Adjust the size (**20** pt) and position (X: **4**, Y: **164**) of the textfield so it sits below the ring and lines up close to the edges (**Figure 5.25**).

**Figure 5.25** The preloader content with the textfield in position.

**18.** Save your document.

Congratulations, you've completed the artwork for a sophisticated preloader! Now it's time to set up the content that will be loaded into your site.

### Preparing the Site Content

It's time to start collecting the artwork (and animation) that you'll display in your portfolio. You'll start by collecting files from previous chapters, but you'll soon see how easy it is to update the portfolio to highlight whatever pieces you'd like.

1. Create a folder inside the website directory named **content**. The content folder will hold all the examples that will be loaded into the portfolio.

You only need to copy the output files into the content directory (i.e., SWFs not FLAs).

2. Copy any examples that you'd like to include in the portfolio. You can use the examples you created from previous chapters or use the following files from the Chapter 5/assets folder on the CD: MotionBlurExample.swf, MotionBlurTrailExample.swf, MotionBrushExample.swf, MotionTrailExample. swf, RunnerExample.swf, and WandererExample.swf (**Figure 5.26**).

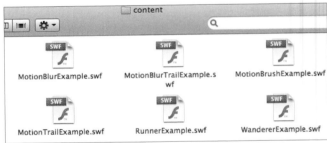

**Figure 5.26** The content directory will contain all the work samples for the portfolio.

3. Create a **config** folder in your website directory. The config directory will hold the configuration files for the portfolio.

Now that you have your work samples collected in a single directory, you can write the XML text that will reference these files.

Note: You'll be employing SWFs in this chapter, but your portfolio will also be able to load JPEGs, GIFs, and PNGs with no alterations to the code.

When you add new content, you will place the files in the content directory.

## Dynamic Content Using XML

As you may recall from the previous chapter, *XML* is short for Extensible Markup Language. An XML file is a simple text file that uses tags to describe data. Similar to HTML, XML tags begin with a *less than* sign (<) and end with a *greater than* sign (>), and a slash (/) is used to close a tag. Collectively, an opening tag, the corresponding closing tag, and everything in between is referred to as a *node* when the XML content is converted into an ActionScript object. An XML object must possess a root node (a node that encompasses all the data) to be properly read into ActionScript.

1. Create a new text file using a simple text editor (like TextEdit on Mac, or Notepad on Windows, or you can use Dreamweaver to create a new XML file). Save the file as **config.xml** in your website/config directory.

2. Enter the following text into the config.xml file:

```xml
<?xml version="1.0" encoding="UTF-8"?>
<site>
    <item name="" url="" ></item>
    <item name="" url="" ></item>
    <item name="" url="" ></item>
    <item name="" url="" ></item>
    <item name="" url="" ></item>
    <item name="" url="" ></item>
</site>
```

**NOTES**

If you use TextEdit on the Mac, you need to choose Format > Make Plain Text before saving your file. When you save your file, deselect Hide Extension and manually type in the *.xml* extension. After you click Save, TextEdit will ask you to confirm that you want to use the *.xml* extension; click "Use .xml" to save the file. You will need to follow these same steps to properly save your *.css* file later in the chapter as well.

The preceding code defines the structure for your XML document. The XML document will determine what is shown in your portfolio.

The first line of the XML file is called the *XML declaration*. The declaration indicates to any system that tries to use the file that what follows is XML content. The next line contains the opening <site> tag. Note that there is a corresponding closing tag that contains a forward slash (</site>) at the end of the file. The <site> tag will serve as the root node.

There are six opening and closing <item> tags. Inside the opening tags are two *attributes*. Attributes provide additional information about a tag element. The *name* attribute will be displayed on a menu item button and on the content title within the Flash movie. The *url* attribute will tell the Flash file where to look for content that will be loaded when the corresponding menu item button is clicked. The address that you add to the url attribute will be relative to the location of the Flash document.

Since each item node refers to a menu item, adding or removing work samples to your portfolio will be as simple as adding or removing an item node in this file. This approach allows you to make updates without requiring you to update and republish your Flash movie.

**NOTES**

Adjust the *name* and *url* attributes to customize whatever content you want to use in your portfolio.

3. Update your attributes on each item tag to match the files in the content directory by adding the following highlighted text:

```
<item name="MotionBrush" url="content/
➥MotionBrushExample.swf" ></item>
<item name="MotionTrail" url="content/
➥MotionTrailExample.swf" ></item>
<item name="MotionBlur" url="content/
➥MotionBlurExample.swf" ></item>
<item name="MotionBlurTrail" url="content/
➥MotionBlurTrailExample.swf" ></item>
<item name="Wanderer" url="content/
➥WandererExample.swf" ></item>
<item name="Runner" url="content/
➥RunnerExample.swf" ></item>
```

**TIP**

You can add attributes containing other information that you'd like to keep track of, such as *date_added*, *project_type*, and so on. These additional attributes can then be displayed by updating your Flash file (and code), or they can remain unseen and yet retained for your personal reference.

Next, you'll add a description that will appear in the box below the content in your portfolio. To accomplish this, you will add your text between each opening and closing item tag. Your text will potentially contain characters reserved by XML (e.g., < and &); this will especially be the case when you include HTML text. Thus, you will wrap your text in a *CDATA* tag to prevent it from being *parsed* (i.e., interpreted) as XML. A CDATA section starts with `<![CDATA[` and ends with `]]>`.

4. Add the following highlighted descriptions to each item:

```
<item name="MotionBrush" url="content/
➥MotionBrushExample.swf" ><![CDATA[The MotionBrush
➥class allows you to draw on screen using a
➥symbol.]]></item>
<item name="MotionTrail" url="content/
➥MotionTrailExample.swf" ><![CDATA[The MotionTrail
➥class creates a trail that follows an animated
➥symbol.]]></item>
<item name="MotionBlur" url="content/
➥MotionBlurExample.swf" ><![CDATA[The MotionBlur
➥class blurs a symbol based on its velocity.]]>
➥</item>
<item name="MotionBlurTrail" url="content/
➥MotionBlurTrailExample.swf" ><![CDATA[The
➥MotionBlurTrail combines the functionality of the
➥MotionTrail and MotionBlur classes.]]></item>
<item name="Wanderer" url="content/
➥WandererExample.swf" ><![CDATA[The Wanderer class
➥allows you to control an animated character.]]>
➥</item>
<item name="Runner" url="content/RunnerExample.
➥swf" ><![CDATA[The Runner class allows you
➥to control an animated character at varying
➥speeds.]]></item>
```

You may want to add links or formatting to your description text. Links are useful if you want to credit another artist for some portion of the work shown or if you want to link to a live website that contains your work.

5. Add the following highlighted HTML link to the first item description:

```
<item name="MotionBrush" url="content/
➥MotionBrushExample.swf" ><![CDATA[The MotionBrush
➥class allows you to draw on screen using a
➥symbol. MotionBrush can be used in combination
➥with the <a href="http://ajarproductions.com/
➥blog/2009/02/10/flash-extension-motionsketch/"
➥target="_blank">MotionSketch extension</a>.]]>
➥</item>
```

If you want to add bold or italic formatting to content that will appear in a textfield with an embedded font, you will also need to embed the bold and italic variations of the font family in the Font Embedding dialog box. Alternatively, embedding will not be necessary if your textfield uses Device Fonts with a common web font (e.g., Arial or Verdana).

The anchor (<a…>) tag in the preceding text will create a link in the description field. The *target* attribute (set to _blank) will force the link to open in a new window.

6. Save your XML file.

Now that your content and configuration files are ready, you can write the document class that will drive the entire site.

## The Site Document Class

There are a number of ways to approach the coding of your site. If you feel that you could potentially reuse many of the behaviors on the site or that you might be developing similar sites in the future, you may want to structure your project to be heavily object-driven (broken into smaller, more reusable classes). Given that the interactions in this project are pretty simple and will all take place well within reach of the site document, this chapter will approach the coding of this site using a document class. This is a somewhat subjective decision that will be largely affected by your needs as a Flash artist.

1. Return to your site.fla document in Flash. Deselect all (Command+Shift+A/Ctrl+Shift+A).

2. In the Properties panel, type in **Site** as the document class and click the Edit class definition button (the pencil icon) (**Figure 5.27**). The first time you click this button, Flash warns you that the class doesn't exist and that it will create one automatically; click OK.

3. Click the Edit class definition button a second time. Flash shows you the document class that it generated. Save this class as **Site.as** in your website folder.

4. Add the following property declarations just inside the class block:

```
private var menuItemStart:Point = new Point(25,
➥100);
private var menuItemSpacing:uint = 10;
private var configFile:String = "config/
➥config.xml";
```

**Figure 5.27** The Edit class definition button in the Properties panel.

```
private var styleFile:String  = "config/site.css";
private var dataLoader:URLLoader  = new
➥URLLoader();
private var styleLoader:URLLoader = new
➥URLLoader();
private var xml:XML;
private var stylesheet:StyleSheet = new
➥StyleSheet();
private var contentLoader:Loader;
private var currentMenuItem:MovieClip;
```

These properties will be used later in the Site class.
Defining these properties at the top makes the file
easy to update, and it renders the properties available
to all the methods you're going to write. Since this is
a document class, all the methods and properties will
be *private*, because no other class will need (or have
reason) to access them.

The `menuItemStart` property will store the position of
the first menu button, and that position will determine
the position of all the subsequent buttons. It is more
efficient to store this position as a Point object rather
than having separate properties for x and y values. The
`menuItemSpacing` property will determine how much
vertical space (in pixels) is added between each button.
The `configFile` and `styleFile` properties will store the
relative locations of the XML file you just created and
a CSS file that you will create later on. The `dataLoader`
and `styleLoader` objects will take the file locations and
load them into the Flash file. The `xml` object will store
the data from the loaded XML file, and the `stylesheet`
object will store the data from the loaded CSS file.
The `contentLoader` will be responsible for loading and
storing the content that will be loaded based on the
`url` attributes in the XML. Finally, `currentMenuItem` will
store the active menu item once it's been clicked.

5. Define the `init` method and call it from the constructor, as shown in the following highlighted code:

```
public function Site(){
    init();
}
```

```
private function init():void {
    preloader_mc.visible = false;
    dataLoader.addEventListener(Event.COMPLETE,
➥onDataLoaded);
    styleLoader.addEventListener(Event.COMPLETE,
➥onStylesLoaded);
    styleLoader.load(new URLRequest(styleFile));
    dataLoader.load(new URLRequest(configFile));
}
```

The init method starts by hiding the preloader_mc instance (since you only want it to appear when content is loading). The init method then adds two event listeners to handle the loaded XML file and CSS style sheet. Finally, the load method of each loader is called, and the links are sent as URLRequest objects.

6. Add the methods (after the init method) that will be called as a result of the init method:

```
private function onDataLoaded(e:Event):void {
    xml = new XML(e.target.data);
    trace(xml.toXMLString());
}
```

```
private function onStylesLoaded(e:Event):void {
    stylesheet.parseCSS(e.target.data);
    description_mc.txt.styleSheet = stylesheet;
}
```

The onDataLoaded method uses the event data that has been passed to the method to populate the xml object. The trace method will provide confirmation that your XML data has been loaded successfully (this method will be removed in a moment). The onStylesLoaded method parses the data provided into the stylesheet object and then applies the parsed CSS to the stylesheet property of the description textfield.

7. Ensure that the following classes are imported at the top of your class package:

```
import flash.display.MovieClip;
import flash.geom.Point;
import flash.net.URLLoader;
```

```
import flash.display.Loader;
import flash.text.StyleSheet;
import flash.net.URLRequest;
import flash.events.Event;
```

8. Save your script and test your movie
   (Command+Return/Ctrl+Enter).

   When you test your movie, you'll see a significant
   amount of text in the Output panel. You'll see an
   Unhandled ioError pointing to your nonexistent CSS file
   (you may have to scroll up in the Output panel). That
   will be resolved later, after you've created the CSS file.
   Don't worry about this error message for now. If Flash
   is able to parse your XML, you'll also see the text from
   your XML file in the Output panel. If Flash cannot
   parse your XML, you'll receive an XML parser failure
   message in the Output panel, and you'll need to check
   your XML file for typos.

9. Once you have your XML loading successfully, you can
   replace the trace method call:

```
private function onDataLoaded(e:Event):void {
    xml = new XML(e.target.data);
    generateMenu();
}
```

10. Now define the generateMenu method below the
    onStylesLoaded method:

```
private function generateMenu():void {
    var items:XMLList = xml.item;
    var itemY:Number = menuItemStart.y;
    for(var i:uint=0; i < items.length(); i++) {
        var mi:menuItem = new menuItem();
        mi.x = menuItemStart.x;
        mi.y = itemY;
        mi.txt.text = items[i].@name;
        mi.index = i;
        mi.addEventListener(MouseEvent.CLICK,
➥onMenuItemClick);
        addChild(mi);
        itemY += mi.height + menuItemSpacing;
    }
}
```

The generateMenu method creates a local variable, items, to store the item nodes in the XML object. Note the simplicity and power of the dot syntax used to reference this list of nodes (xml.item). The items variable is typed to XMLList because it has no root node (it's just a list of the item nodes inside the XML object). Next, a local variable is used to store the y position for the item. This position will change for each menu item.

A for loop is utilized to traverse the items list. Note the parentheses on length(). These are necessary to retrieve the length of the items list because length is a method in the XMLList (and XML) class, whereas it is a property in the Array class. Within the loop, a new menuItem instance is created from the menuItem symbol in the Library. This instance is given a position based on the stored x value and the current itemY value. The text property is then assigned on the textfield within the menu item. The name attribute of the current item in the loop is then referenced using the @ operator. Then a new property is created dynamically on the menu item to store the current index in the loop. This index allows you to reference the correct item node in the XML when the button is pressed. A click listener is added to detect when the button has been clicked. The button is then added to the display list using the addChild method. Finally, the itemY value is increased, both to account for the height of the button that was just added and to add space for a new button that is still to be added.

You'll now begin writing the code that will load in your external content.

1. Within your Site.as ActionScript file, add the onMenuItemClick method below the generateMenu method:

```
private function onMenuItemClick(e:MouseEvent):
➥void {
    currentMenuItem = e.currentTarget as
➥MovieClip;
}
```

**NOTES**

Using the index number on each menu button to trigger new content is a smart means of achieving forward compatibility. If you decide you want *back* and *next* buttons or a different navigation system entirely, you'll still be able to easily load content from places other than the menu item button.

**CLOSE-UP**

**Accessing XML Attributes**

There are two ways to access attribute content on an XML node:

▶ node.@attributeName

▶ node.attribute("attributeName");

The first method is shorthand and is generally very readable. The second method is longer but slightly more tolerant if your attribute happens to be missing. Whichever method you use is project-specific and the choice is largely based on personal preference.

The clicked button is obtained by accessing the `currentTarget` property of the MouseEvent. The `currentMenuItem` will be stored as a Movie Clip so that you can use methods and properties of the MovieClip class without offending the compiler.

**2.** Ensure that `flash.events.MouseEvent` has been added to your `import` statements at the top.

**3.** Save your script and test your movie. You should now see six buttons with text corresponding to the item names in your XML file (**Figure 5.28**).

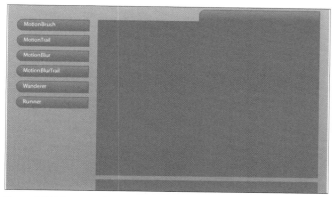

**Figure 5.28** The menu buttons are now loaded in and arranged dynamically with ActionScript.

**4.** Add the following highlighted code to your `onMenuItemClick` method:

```
private function onMenuItemClick(e:MouseEvent):
➥void {
    currentMenuItem = e.currentTarget as
➥MovieClip;
    loadItem(currentMenuItem.index);
}
```

The `index` property that you stored in the `generateMenu` method will now be used to load the item content, title, and description into the corresponding symbols within your Flash document.

5. Add the `loadItem` method below the `onMenuItemClick` method:

```
private function loadItem(n:uint):void {
    var xmlItem:XML = xml.item[n];
    loadContent(xmlItem.@url);
    loadDescription(xmlItem.toString());
    loadTitle(xmlItem.@name);
}
```

The first line on the `loadItem` method uses Array access notation to locate the desired item node within the stored XML object. The node is then accessed to populate the arguments for the method calls that follow. The description content is obtained by using the `toString` method on the item node.

6. Add the following method definitions below the `loadItem` method:

```
private function loadDescription(
➥captionStr:String):void {
    description_mc.txt.htmlText = captionStr;
}

private function loadTitle(titleStr:String):void {
    title_mc.txt.text = titleStr;
}

private function loadContent(link:String):void {
    trace("link: " + link);
}
```

The `htmlText` property is used for the description (rather than the `text` property) to ensure that the content will be displayed as HTML rather than as plain text.

7. Save your script and test your movie. Click each menu button. You should see the title and description appear in their proper places as you click each menu item, and the link to the content should appear in the Output panel (**Figure 5.29**).

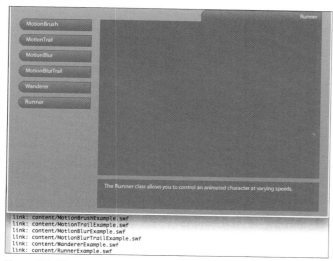

**Figure 5.29**  The Output panel displays the links from the menu button clicks.

8.  Now replace the `trace` call in the `loadContent` method with the following highlighted code:

```
private function loadContent(link:String):void {
    unloadContent(contentLoader);
    contentLoader = new Loader();
    contentLoader.load(new URLRequest(link));
    content_mc.addChild(contentLoader);
    contentLoader.contentLoaderInfo.
➥addEventListener(Event.OPEN, onContentLoadStarted);
    contentLoader.contentLoaderInfo.
➥addEventListener(Event.COMPLETE, onContentLoaded);
    contentLoader.contentLoaderInfo.
➥addEventListener(ProgressEvent.PROGRESS,
➥onContentLoadProgress);
    contentLoader.contentLoaderInfo.
➥addEventListener(IOErrorEvent.IO_ERROR,
➥onContentLoaded);
}
```

The `loadContent` method looks complex, but what it's doing is actually pretty simple. An `unloadContent` method clears out any content that has been loaded previously. Next, a fresh Loader object is assigned to the `contentLoader` property, and the link is loaded as a `URLRequest`. The `contentLoader` is then added to the display list within the `content_mc` instance on Stage. The next four lines use the `contentLoaderInfo` property of the loader to add event listeners for the following scenarios: when the content starts loading, finishes loading, progresses in loading, and fails to load.

9. Add the following two methods after the `loadContent` method:

```
private function onContentLoadStarted(e:Event):
➥void {
    preloader_mc.visible = true;
    preloader_mc.gotoAndStop(1);
}

private function onContentLoadProgress(
➥e:ProgressEvent):void {
    var percent:uint =
➥Math.ceil((e.bytesLoaded/e.bytesTotal) * 100);
    preloader_mc.gotoAndStop(percent);
}
```

When the load is started, the `onContentLoadStarted` method will make the preloader visible and move the preloader to the first frame. As the load progresses, the `onContentLoadProgress` method will calculate the percentage loaded and will move the preloader to the corresponding frame. Moving the preloader's frame will animate the ring you created while the content loads. The code utilizes the `bytesLoaded` and `bytesTotal` properties of the ProgressEvent to calculate the percentage, which is then translated to a frame number by multiplying the decimal by 100 and rounding that value up to a whole number using the `Math.ceil` method (i.e., "ceiling"; because there is no frame 0, that value should always be rounded up to the nearest integer).

10. Add the `unloadContent` method below the previous two methods:

```
private function unloadContent(loader:Loader):void{
    try { loader.close(); } catch (e:*) {}
```

```
        try { loader.unload(); } catch (e:*) {}
        try { removeChild(loader);  } catch (e:*) {}
        try { loader = null;  } catch (e:*) {}
    }
```

The unloadContent method utilizes try and catch
statements. Try-catch statements are similar to if-else
statements except that each try statement *must* have a
corresponding catch statement. If the code inside the
try block fails, the catch block will be executed. In the
preceding code, each try-catch block has been con-
densed to a single line. The catch statement requires
a single parameter, which has been typed here with
an asterisk (*). The asterisk denotes that the argument passed can be of any type. In these try-catch
statements, the catch block is empty. In this case, the
purpose of using try-catch is simply to avoid generating
errors. The try-catch statements are a quick solution for unloading content, because you won't know
exactly what state the contentLoader is in when the
unloadContent method is called. The contentLoader
could be loading content, done loading, or undefined.
This unloadContent method is a nice one-size-fits-all
solution.

**11.** Finally, add the onContentLoaded method below the
previous method:

```
private function onContentLoaded(e:*):void {
    preloader_mc.visible = false;
    if(e.type == IOErrorEvent.IO_ERROR){
        trace(e.text);
    }else {

    }
}
```

The incoming parameter is typed using an asterisk,
because it could be an error event or a complete event.
The preloader is hidden in any case. If the incoming event is an error, the message will be sent to the
Output panel.

Thus far, your Site class should read as follows (be sure to add any missing `import` statements):

```
package  {

    import flash.display.MovieClip;
    import flash.geom.Point;
    import flash.net.URLLoader;
    import flash.text.StyleSheet;
    import flash.net.URLRequest;
    import flash.events.Event;
    import flash.display.Loader;
    import flash.events.MouseEvent;
    import flash.events.ProgressEvent;
    import flash.events.IOErrorEvent;

    public class Site extends MovieClip {

        private var menuItemStart:Point = new
    ➥Point(25, 100);

        private var menuItemSpacing:uint = 10;
        private var configFile:String = "config/
    ➥config.xml";
        private var styleFile:String  = "config/
    ➥site.css";
        private var dataLoader:URLLoader  = new
    ➥URLLoader
        private var styleLoader:URLLoader = new
    ➥URLLoader();
        private var xml:XML;
        private var stylesheet:StyleSheet = new
    ➥StyleSheet();
        private var contentLoader:Loader;
        private var currentMenuItem:MovieClip;

        public function Site(){
            init();
        }
```

```
        private function init():void {
            preloader_mc.visible = false;
            dataLoader.addEventListener(Event.
➥COMPLETE, onDataLoaded);
            styleLoader.addEventListener(Event.
➥COMPLETE, onStylesLoaded);
            styleLoader.load(new URLRequest(
➥styleFile));
            dataLoader.load(new URLRequest(
➥configFile));
        }

        private function onDataLoaded(e:Event):
➥void {
            xml = new XML(e.target.data);
            generateMenu();
        }

        private function onStylesLoaded(e:Event):
➥void {
            stylesheet.parseCSS(e.target.data);
            description_mc.txt.styleSheet =
➥stylesheet;
        }

        private function generateMenu():void {
        var items:XMLList = xml.item;
        var itemY:Number = menuItemStart.y;
        for(var i:uint=0; i < items.length(); i++)
{
            var mi:menuItem = new menuItem();
            mi.x = menuItemStart.x;
            mi.y = itemY;
            mi.txt.text = items[i].@name;
            mi.index = i;
            mi.addEventListener(MouseEvent.CLICK,
➥onMenuItemClick);
            addChild(mi);
            itemY += mi.height + menuItemSpacing;

        }
    }
```

```
            private function onMenuItemClick(e:MouseEvent):
➥void {
        currentMenuItem = e.currentTarget as
➥MovieClip;
        loadItem(currentMenuItem.index);
    }

    private function loadItem(n:uint):void {
        var xmlItem:XML = xml.item[n];
        loadContent(xmlItem.@url);
        loadDescription(xmlItem.toString());
        loadTitle(xmlItem.@name);
    }

    private function loadDescription(captionStr:
➥String):void {
        description_mc.txt.htmlText = captionStr;
    }

    private function loadTitle(titleStr:String):
➥void {
        title_mc.txt.text = titleStr;
    }

    private function loadContent(link:String):void
    {
        unloadContent(contentLoader);
        contentLoader = new Loader();
        contentLoader.load(new URLRequest(link));
        content_mc.addChild(contentLoader);
        contentLoader.contentLoaderInfo.
➥addEventListener(Event.OPEN, onContentLoadStarted);
        contentLoader.contentLoaderInfo.
➥addEventListener(Event.COMPLETE, onContentLoaded);
        contentLoader.contentLoaderInfo.
➥addEventListener(ProgressEvent.PROGRESS,
➥onContentLoadProgress);
        contentLoader.contentLoaderInfo.
➥addEventListener(IOErrorEvent.IO_ERROR,
➥onContentLoaded);
    }
```

```
        private function onContentLoadStarted(e:Event):
    ➥void {
            preloader_mc.visible = true;
            preloader_mc.gotoAndStop(1);
        }


        private function onContentLoadProgress(
    ➥e:ProgressEvent):void {
            var percent:uint = Math.ceil(
    ➥(e.bytesLoaded/e.bytesTotal) * 100);
            preloader_mc.gotoAndStop(percent);
        }


        private function unloadContent(loader:Loader):
    ➥void{
            try { loader.close(); } catch (e:*) {}
            try { loader.unload(); } catch (e:*) {}
            try { removeChild(loader);  } catch (e:*) {}
            try { loader = null;   } catch (e:*) {}
        }


        private function onContentLoaded(e:*):void {
            preloader_mc.visible = false;
            if(e.type == IOErrorEvent.IO_ERROR){
                trace(e.text);
            }else {

            }
        }

    }

}
```

12. Save your script and test your movie. Click on each
    menu item. You should now see your content files
    loaded into your portfolio (**Figure 5.30** on the
    next page).

**Figure 5.30** The content is now successfully being loaded into the portfolio.

At this point, your content should be loading just fine, but since you're loading files directly from your local machine, you may not have any indication that the preloader is working.

### Testing Using Bandwidth Profiler and Simulate Download

The Bandwidth Profiler and Simulate Download features allow you to test different download speeds for your Flash movie. This is the best way to test the bandwidth of your content and how it will load at various speeds.

1. Test your movie.

2. With the test window still open, open the Bandwidth Profiler by choosing View > Bandwidth Profiler (**Figure 5.31**).

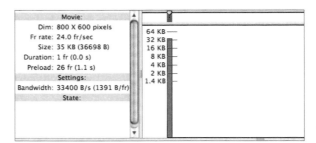

**Figure 5.31** The Bandwidth Profiler appears at the top of your test movie window and provides information about the movie and how many kilobytes are on each frame.

3. Adjust the download speed to test for a DSL connection rate by choosing View > Download Settings > DSL (32.6 KB/s) (**Figure 5.32**).

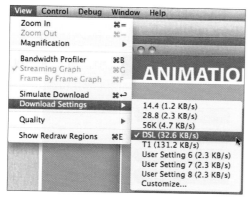

**Figure 5.32** The Download Settings can be adjusted to simulate different Internet connection speeds.

4. Choose View > Simulate Download. Your test window will go white for a moment while the site.swf file loads.

5. Click on the menu items to see your preloader in action (**Figure 5.33**).

**Figure 5.33** The preloader is visible while simulating a DSL connection speed, and beneath the Streams heading, the Bandwidth Profiler displays information about the content that is being loaded.

6. When you're done testing, hide the Bandwidth Profiler (View > Bandwidth Profiler) and close the test window. You won't need the Bandwidth Profiler for the remaining steps in this chapter.

Now that you know your preloader is running smoothly, you can write the CSS file that will style your description text.

### Dynamic Styling Using CSS

**NOTES**

Flash utilizes only a subset of CSS. To see all the CSS properties available to Flash, visit http://help.adobe.com/en_US/FlashPlatform/reference/actionscript/3/flash/text/StyleSheet.html.

There are a number of ways to style a textfield in Flash. But there are two main advantages to loading an external CSS file. First, just like your XML file, a CSS file is just a simple text file, which makes it very easy to edit and requires no republishing of your Flash file. Second, you can also use the same CSS file for the HTML document that contains your Flash movie, which facilitates easy coordination of your text styling and colors (between HTML and Flash).

The reason for using CSS in this project is rather simple: to highlight any links in the description text. At the moment, the hand cursor appears when hovering over the link that you've added, but the user has no other visual indication that there is a link in the textfield (**Figure 5.34**).

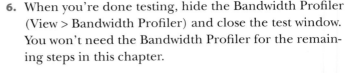

**Figure 5.34** The hand cursor is the only indication that there is a link in the textfield.

To better accentuate any links in your description text, you'll create a CSS file and add styling for the anchor tag.

1. Create a new text file and save it to the website/config folder as **site.css**.

2. Add the following text to the site.css file:

**NOTES**

The hover state in CSS is akin to a rollover state in Flash.

```
a {
    color:#FFFF33;
}

a:hover {
    text-decoration:underline;
}
```

3. Save the file and return to your site.fla document.

4. Test your movie. Click the MotionBrush menu item. Note that the link from your XML file is now yellow and shows an underline when you roll over it (**Figure 5.35**).

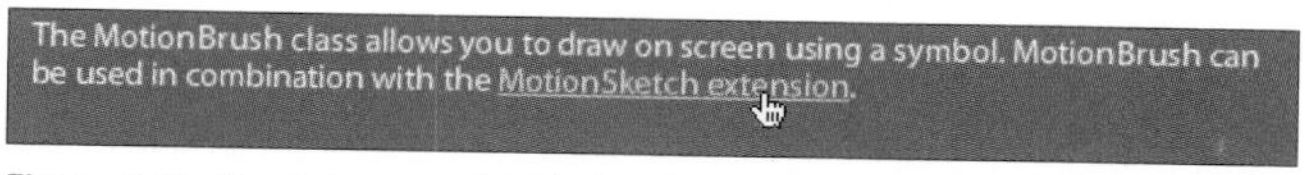

**Figure 5.35** The link is now highlighted in yellow, and an underline appears when you roll over the link.

Your Output panel should now be empty (no error regarding the missing CSS file).

Admittedly, this approach to styling an anchor tag within this single textfield may be overkill. This method of loading an external CSS file is included partially as a proof of concept, in case you would like to use it in future projects (or expand it as your portfolio grows).

Now that everything you've built so far is in working order, it's time to start adding animation to your ActionScript.

## Adding Animation with ActionScript

Animating with ActionScript has two distinct advantages over Timeline animation. First, ActionScript animation can easily be altered. Timeline animation offers a great amount of precision, but that precision often comes at the cost of flexibility. Second, ActionScript animation can easily be written to be dynamic (i.e., the animation can change based on circumstance). Timeline animation works well when everything is fixed, but what happens when user interaction or dynamic content from XML is introduced? For these reasons, you'll be employing ActionScript animation in your portfolio.

Animation classes are also known as *tween* classes. Flash comes with its own Tween class (in the `fl.transitions` package). The built-in Tween class can be useful when you don't want to keep track of extra ActionScript files, but it has a number of limitations. Fortunately, there are several tween libraries (all written by different developers) that

**NOTES**

For more documentation on TweenLite, visit http://greensock.com/tweenlite.

you can choose from. Some of the freely available libraries are Tweener, gTween, TweenLite, and Twease. Each library was designed for a slightly different purpose, and thus, each library has slightly different advantages.

**CLOSE-UP**

### Easing

Each tween library can take advantage of a concept known as *easing*. Easing alters the rate at which your animation occurs. Almost nothing in nature goes from a stop to full speed for a set amount of time, and then immediately returns to a stop. Easing simulates more realistic movements by varying an object's speed based on its distance (or time) from its final destination. An *ease-in* starts slowly before reaching its target speed. An *ease-out* drops an object from its max speed and slows it to a stop as the object approaches its destination. An *ease-in-out* starts slowly before reaching its max speed and then slows to a stop.

There are several different types of eases; a few common eases include Quadratic, Cubic, Back, and Elastic. Each one of these types includes ease-in, ease-out, and ease-in-out variations. For realistic animation, you'll want to choose the easing that best fits the type of movement you're trying to simulate. This sometimes requires you to treat inanimate objects like living things and imagine how they *might* move. A little ease goes a long way in adding personality to any animation.

**TIP**

Jack has several free ActionScript classes available, as well as several other cool classes that are available as part of a subscription on his site at http://greensock.com.

For this project, you'll be using TweenLite, which was written by Jack Doyle. TweenLite has a small footprint and a simple syntax (with a nice built-in ease), and it allows for sequencing and delays (which you'll use in your portfolio).

The basic syntax of TweenLite is as follows:

```
TweenLite.to(instance_mc, timeInSeconds,
➥{propertyValuesToTween});
```

Let's jump right in!

### Using TweenLite

You'll add the TweenLite classes to your project folder, just as you did with the classes that you developed in Chapter 3, but you will be accessing TweenLite through ActionScript alone.

1. Download the latest ActionScript 3.0 (AS3) version of TweenLite from www.greensock.com/tweenlite/ or copy it from the Chapter 5/assets folder on the CD included with this book.

2. Unzip the greensock-as3.zip file and copy the *com* folder into your website directory. This will make the TweenLite classes available to your Site class.

3. Open your Site.as file in Flash. Add the following `import` statements after the existing `import` statements:

```
import com.greensock.*;
import com.greensock.easing.*;
```

The asterisks (*) instruct the compiler to include any classes within the preceding package that are referenced in the ensuing code. This method of importing classes is slightly imprecise but is very handy when you need to reference several classes from a single package.

4. Start by adding a simple fade-in for your content. Add the following highlighted code to the `onContentLoaded` method:

```
private function onContentLoaded(e:*):void {
    preloader_mc.visible = false;
    if(e.type == IOErrorEvent.IO_ERROR){
        trace(e.text);
    }else {
        contentLoader.alpha = 0;
        TweenLite.to(contentLoader, .75, {alpha:1});
    }
}
```

The highlighted code is added to the `else` statement to ensure that the code only executes when there is no load error. The first line sets the alpha of the `contentLoader` to 0, rendering the content entirely transparent. The next line animates the `contentLoader` over a period of .75 seconds, tweening the `alpha` property to 1 (100% opaque).

5. Save your script and test your movie. Click on the menu items. Note the subtle fade-in that occurs on the loaded content when you click each item.

**NOTES**

The asterisk only instructs the compiler to import classes within a package. Classes within subpackages will not be imported (e.g., `import com.yoursite.utils.*` will not import `com.yoursite.utils.text.TextUtils`).

Now let's utilize the TweenLite class further and create a sequenced animation.

1. Update the `loadTitle` method with the following highlighted code:

```
private function loadTitle(titleStr:String):void {
    var startY:Number = title_mc.y;
    TweenLite.to(title_mc, .25, {y:startY+
➥title_mc.height, ease:Quad.easeIn,
➥onComplete:function(){title_mc.txt.text =
➥titleStr;}});
    TweenLite.to(title_mc, .75, {y:startY,
➥delay:.25, overwrite:false});
}
```

The first line stores the y position of the `title_mc` instance so that the position can be returned to at the end of the animation. The second line tweens `title_mc` over a duration of .25 seconds, moving the title down to a position equal to its current position plus its height. An ease-in is applied rather than the default ease-out. An `onComplete` method is assigned to the content that previously populated the `loadTitle` method. The net result is that the `title_mc` object slides behind the content rectangle and then updates the title's content (in private, so to speak). Finally, `title_mc` is tweened again, this time over a period of .75 seconds. The y position is returned to its original value. A delay is added to match the first tween of `title_mc`, and `overwrite` is given a value of `false`. Setting `overwrite` to false prevents the second tween from overwriting (and destroying) the first tween.

2. Save your script and test your movie. When you click on a menu item, the old title should now slide down behind the content rectangle and slide back into position with the new title (**Figure 5.36**).

Figure 5.36 The title sliding down below the content area.

3. Now create a similar effect on the description, this time using 3D rotation. Update the `loadDescription` method with the following highlighted code:

```
private function loadDescription(
➥captionStr:String):void {
    TweenLite.to(description_mc, .25,
➥{rotationX:90, onComplete:function(){
➥description_mc.txt.htmlText = captionStr;}});
    TweenLite.to(description_mc, .75,
➥{rotationX:360, delay:.25, overwrite:false});
}
```

This code is similar to the code used to animate the title except it utilizes the `rotationX` property rather than the `y` property. This subtle difference results in a very different animation (**Figure 5.37**).

Figure 5.37 The description rotating in 3D space.

4. Save your script and test your movie. Your description should now flip around in 3D space and update the description text in the process. You may notice that your description text remains blurry after completing its animation. This blurriness is partially due to the fact that Flash converts the content into a bitmap in order to render 3D effects (**Figure 5.38**).

> The MotionBrush class allows you to draw on screen using a symbol. MotionBrush can be used in combination with the MotionSketch extension.

Figure 5.38 The 3D rotation causes the text to remain blurred.

5. Update the `loadDescription` method with the following highlighted code:

```
private function loadDescription(
➥captionStr:String):void {
    TweenLite.to(description_mc, .25,
➥{rotationX:90, onComplete:function(){
➥description_mc.txt.htmlText = captionStr;}});
```

```
    TweenLite.to(description_mc, .75,
➡{rotationX:360, delay:.25, overwrite:false,
➡onComplete:function(){
        var position:Point = new
➡Point(description_mc.x, description_mc.y);
        description_mc.transform.matrix3D =
➡null;
        description_mc.x = position.x;
        description_mc.y = position.y;
    }});
}
```

This new code runs when the tween has completed. It stores the current position, removes any 3D properties applied to the object, and then restores the object's position. As a result of the removal of the 3D properties, the text is now clear when the animation completes (**Figure 5.39**).

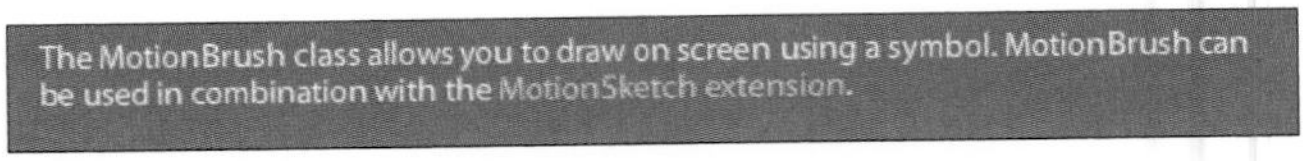

The MotionBrush class allows you to draw on screen using a symbol. MotionBrush can be used in combination with the MotionSketch extension.

Figure 5.39 The text no longer has a blur after being rotated.

Now that the basic animation is in place, there are just a few more items to wrap up.

### Adding the Finishing Touches

You'll now add a little bit of button behavior to your menu items and give them a nice animation as they appear onscreen.

1. In your document class, update the generateMenu method to include the following highlighted code:

```
private function generateMenu():void {
    var items:XMLList = xml.item;
    var itemY:Number = menuItemStart.y;
    for(var i:uint=0; i < items.length(); i++) {
        var mi:menuItem = new menuItem();
        mi.x = -mi.width;
        mi.y = itemY;
        mi.txt.text = items[i].@name;
```

```
        mi.index = i;
        mi.buttonMode = true;
        mi.useHandCursor = true;
        mi.mouseChildren = false;
        mi.addEventListener(MouseEvent.ROLL_OVER,
➥onMenuItemRollOver);
        mi.addEventListener(MouseEvent.ROLL_OUT,
➥onMenuItemRollOut);
        mi.addEventListener(MouseEvent.CLICK,
➥onMenuItemClick);
        addChild(mi);
        itemY += mi.height + menuItemSpacing;
        TweenLite.to(mi, 1, {x:menuItemStart.x,
➥delay: i*.1, ease:Back.easeOut});
    }
}
```

The preceding highlighted code starts by setting the x position of each menu item so that each item sits off the left edge of the Stage. To show the hand cursor when hovering over each button, the buttonMode and useHandCursor properties are both toggled to true. The mouseChildren property is toggled to false so that the textfield nested in each menu item does not affect the cursor. Event listeners are added for rolling over and rolling off each menu item. Finally, each item is tweened over a 1-second duration to its proper x position. A delay is added based on the item's location in the loop. Items later in the loop will have a longer delay. A *back* ease is added to cause each item to overshoot its position before snapping back (hence the name) to its final location. Postpone testing your movie for a moment, because you still need to define the methods called by the event listeners.

2. Add the following two methods before the onMenuItemClick method:

```
private function onMenuItemRollOver(e:MouseEvent):
➥void {
    var btn:MovieClip = e.currentTarget as
➥MovieClip;
```

```
        var btnGlow:GlowFilter = new GlowFilter(
➥0x6699ff, .75, 8, 8, 2, 3, true);
    if(btn.enabled) btn.filters = [btnGlow];
}


private function onMenuItemRollOut(e:MouseEvent):
➥void {
        var btn:MovieClip = e.currentTarget as
➥MovieClip;
    btn.filters = null;
}
```

Each method retrieves the menu item from the incoming event and types it to a MovieClip so that the filters property can be accessed. The rollover method creates a light blue inner glow and assigns the filter to the active menu item, but only in the case that the menu item's enabled property resolves to true. The rollout method then resets the item's filters when the item is no longer active.

3. Now update the onMenuItemClick method with the following highlighted code:

```
private function onMenuItemClick(e:MouseEvent):
➥void {
    if(currentMenuItem) {
        currentMenuItem.enabled=true;
        TweenLite.to(currentMenuItem, .25,
➥{x:menuItemStart.x, ease:Quad.easeIn});
    }
    currentMenuItem = e.currentTarget as MovieClip;
    currentMenuItem.enabled = false;
    currentMenuItem.filters = null;
    TweenLite.to(currentMenuItem, .5,
➥{x:menuItemStart.x+20});
    loadItem(currentMenuItem.index);
}
```

The if block at the top executes if currentMenuItem has been assigned a value. If so, the currentMenuItem is reenabled and tweened back to its original location. Then, per the original code, the currentMenuItem property is updated to the item that was just clicked. That item is then disabled (so that the filter is not shown when the current item is rolled over) and its filters (that were assigned within the rollover method) are cleared. The menu item is then tweened so that it sits against the content.

A completed version of the Site.as file can be found on the CD in the Chapter 5/finished/website/folder.

4. Save your document class and test your movie. You should now see the buttons slide in (**Figure 5.40**), glow when rolled over (**Figure 5.41**), and slide against the content region when clicked (**Figure 5.42**).

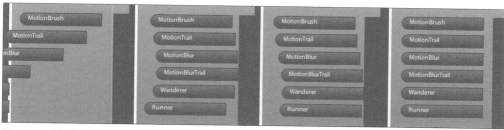

**Figure 5.40**  The buttons form a rubbery wave as they animate onto the Stage.

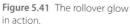

**Figure 5.41**  The rollover glow in action.

**Figure 5.42**  The clicked menu button slides against the content region.

Congratulations! You've completed the portfolio. You can now customize it and make it your own. Play around with your files and see what you can come up with. Here are some suggestions to get you started:

▶ Try updating the code to scale artwork that is larger or smaller than the 550 x 400 content area, and see if you can load artwork of different sizes and shapes (hint: think about constraining proportions).

▶ Try different types of easing on your tweens, like Elastic.easeOut on the tween within your generateMenu method.

▶ Try creating different types of transitions, such as blurring and unblurring the description rather than rotating it.

▶ Give the content_mask an instance name and animate the mask rather than the content.

Have fun and alter the portfolio until it provides a good representation of you and your work. Because your site is so flexible, you can try all kinds of variations. When you have the portfolio just the way you want it, you're ready to upload it for the world to see.

## Uploading Your Site to the Web

When your files are ready to share, you can use an application (like Transmit, FileZilla, or Dreamweaver) with File Transfer Protocol (FTP) capabilities to transfer your files to your web server. You'll only need to transfer the output files (e.g., SWF, HTML, XML, CSS, JS) in order for your site to function. Your source files (e.g., FLA, AS, PSD) do not need to (and in most cases should not) be uploaded.

Before uploading your files, you want to make sure that you've published your HTML document. Testing your movie in the authoring environment only generates a SWF file.

1. Choose File > Publish Settings and click on the HTML heading at the top.

2. Set the Dimensions menu to Pixels and update the Width and Height to **830** and **630** pixels, respectively. The increased dimensions will make room for a stroke and drop shadow around the background symbol.

3. Set the HTML alignment to Top, set Scale to No scale, and set both the Horizontal and Vertical Flash alignment settings to Center (**Figure 5.43**).

4. Click the Publish button to publish both the SWF and the HTML file, and then click OK to save your Publish settings.

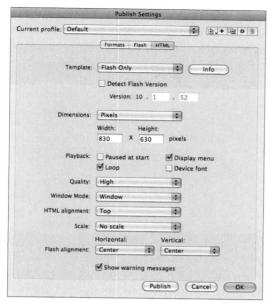

**Figure 5.43** The updated HTML Publish Settings.

5. Navigate to your website directory on your hard drive. You should see a site.html file. Open the site.html file in your web browser by double-clicking on the file. Note that there is plenty of room for the stroke and drop shadow (**Figure 5.44**).

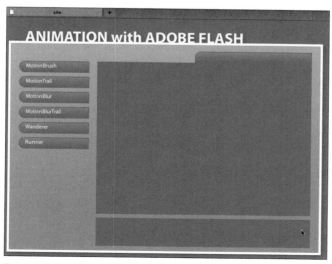

**Figure 5.44** The site.html file viewed in a web browser.

6. Open the site.html file again, this time in a plain text editor (like TextWrangler on a Mac, Notepad in Windows, or Dreamweaver code view). You should now see the raw HTML text (**Figure 5.45**).

```
<!DOCTYPE html PUBLIC "-//W3C//DTD XHTML 1.0 Strict//EN"
"http://www.w3.org/TR/xhtml1/DTD/xhtml1-strict.dtd">
<html xmlns="http://www.w3.org/1999/xhtml" lang="en" xml:lang="en">
    <head>
        <title>site</title>
        <meta http-equiv="Content-Type" content="text/html; charset=utf-8" />
        <style type="text/css" media="screen">
        html, body { height:100%; background-color: #3366ff;}
        body { margin:0; padding:0; overflow:hidden; }
        #flashContent { width:100%; height:100%; }
        </style>
    </head>
    <body>
        <div id="flashContent">
            <object classid="clsid:d27cdb6e-ae6d-11cf-96b8-444553540000" width="830" height="630"
            id="site" align="top">
                <param name="movie" value="site.swf" />
                <param name="quality" value="high" />
                <param name="bgcolor" value="#3366ff" />
                <param name="play" value="true" />
                <param name="loop" value="true" />
```

**Figure 5.45** The raw HTML text in TextWrangler (with customized color coding).

7. Edit line 9 in the site.html file to match the following highlighted code:

`#flashContent { margin-left:-415px; padding-left:`
`➥50%; width:100%; height:100%;}`

Flash wraps your movie in a `<div>` tag with an `id` attribute set to `flashContent` by default when you publish your HTML file. The text that you just added to the HTML is actually CSS embedded in the HTML page. By giving the `flashContent` element a negative left margin that is half the width of your embedded Flash movie, and padding the left side of the element by 50%, you have effectively centered your movie horizontally (even when the user changes the scale of the browser window).

8. Save the HTML file.

9. Refresh the site.html page in your web browser (or reopen it if you closed it). The style update in the previous step will have centered your Flash content horizontally, blending the Flash more seamlessly into the matching HTML background (**Figure 5.46**).

**TIP**

While you're editing the HTML code, also consider updating the text within the `<title>` tag. This text will appear at the top of your browser tab or window when the page is loaded.

You can find TextWrangler (a free code editor for the Mac OS) at www.barebones.com/products/textwrangler.

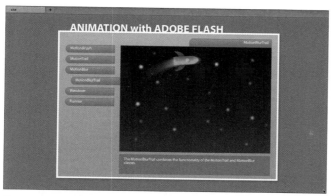

**Figure 5.46** The site.html page centered horizontally in the web browser.

10. Use an FTP application of your choice and upload the following files and folders: site.swf, site.html, the content folder (and the files contained within), and the config folder (and its files).

When your files have been uploaded, you can send the link to your desired clients/employers, friends, and family, and show them the great work you've done.

Now that you have a solid web portfolio up and running, it's time to look at a few other ways to get others to notice your work.

NOTES

Before uploading your files, be sure to test them on as many operating systems and browsers as you have available to make sure everything is working properly.

## Publishing for Broadcast

Your intended output format will help dictate how you set up your Flash document and in some cases how you will create your animation. There are countless animation studios using Flash for the development of CD and broadcast television. The early years of using Flash were focused solely on Timeline animation and exporting to QuickTime Video and AVI format. Those were the days of Macromedia Flash 4, which was a much simpler version than Adobe Flash Professional CS5. Exporting to video with Flash 4 required nothing more than choosing File > Export Movie and selecting either QuickTime or AVI video (depending on your operating system).

Exporting to video from Flash is very straightforward, but there are a few rules to follow, depending on your needs. If you are producing content that requires frame accuracy in Flash (generally content that will be exported to video or image sequence format), you must make sure all your animation is in sync with the main Timeline. Thus, you must avoid Movie Clip symbols. A Movie Clip Timeline is independent of the main Timeline and will only play within the Flash Player. It is recommended that you use Graphic symbols instead, especially when nesting animations and layering timelines. Graphic symbols are always in sync with the main Timeline and will export to video or an image sequence. If the animation plays inside the Flash IDE, it will also export to video.

### Document Setup

Let's take a look at how to set up a basic Flash document for video output in Flash CS5. Create a new document and then choose Modify > Document to open the Document Settings window. Here you can edit the dimensions of your document's Stage as well as its frame rate (**Figure 5.47**).

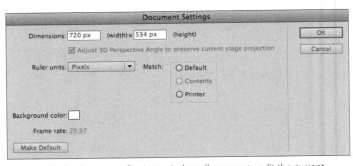

Figure 5.47 The Document Settings window allows you to edit the current document's dimensions and frame rate.

**NOTES**

Color is also an important issue when animating for broadcast. Some colors do not display well on television screens. You can find an NTSC color-safe palette at www.animonger.com/ntsc.html.

Even though NTSC and PAL both have a 4:3 ratio, pixels dimensions can vary based on the specific format (e.g., DV, D1DV, DVwide). Some formats use square pixels and others use rectangular pixels. For more on aspect ratios, see http://en.wikipedia.org/wiki/Pixel_aspect_ratio.

Adobe Flash CS5 provides premade templates that meet the NTSC (National Television System Committee) and PAL (Phase Alternating Line) broadcast standards. NTSC is used in North America and most of South America, whereas PAL is used outside of the Americas. NTSC uses a 4:3 aspect ratio and a frame rate of 29.97 (**Figure 5.48**). PAL uses a 4:3 aspect ratio and a frame rate of 25. The specific aspect ratio for PAL is 720 x 576 (**Figure 5.49**).

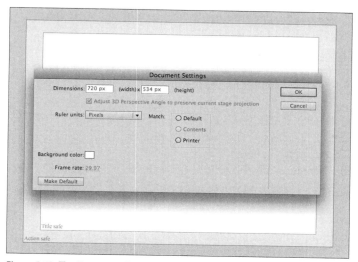

**Figure 5.48**  The Document Settings for an NTSC DV template.

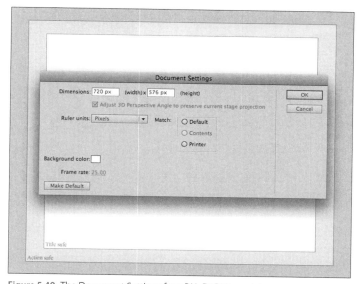

**Figure 5.49**  The Document Settings for a PAL D1DV template.

Most animators use a frame rate of 24 frames per second (fps) when using Flash, but that frame rate is converted during the export process based on which video standard is used. It is perfectly fine to use any frame rate when animating, because the software will calculate the conversion to the appropriate frame rate for video. Just keep in mind that animating at 24 or 30 (29.97) fps is recommended, because they are standard frame rates for animation.

### Exporting to PNG Sequence

In many situations, animation exported from Flash is often imported to Adobe After Effects for additional effects to be added. To ensure frame accuracy during the exporting and importing process, the PNG sequence is preferred among many postproduction professionals. When your animation in Flash is complete and you're ready to export it, there may be a few things you'll want to do first: For example, make sure you're using Graphic symbols (not Movie Clips) and turn off the visibility of your guide layers that contain graphics that you do not want exported in the final sequence. Be sure to hide any title and action safety layers, and any extraneous graphics (**Figure 5.50**).

**TIP**

Even though guide layers are not visible within the Flash Player, they will export to a PNG sequence unless their visibility is turned off as well. You could delete these layers, but it may be advantageous to keep them for future editing if the Flash document will be reused.

Figure 5.50 Turn off the visibility of any guide layers when exporting to a PNG sequence.

Depending on the length of your animation, a PNG sequence will contain several individual image files. The number of files can range from a few to several hundred or even thousands. It is best practice to break down your animation into different Flash documents based on scenes or even camera shots. It is typical to have several short animations as individual FLA files, as opposed to one long Flash document to avoid memory issues, crashes, and corrupt files. Based on our past experience, individual FLA files should range from two seconds to, at the most, one minute in duration. Each of these files can then be edited together using video editing software such as Adobe Premiere or Adobe After Effects.

**NOTES**

Some of the memory issues mentioned may be a thing of the past, since Flash CS5 has transitioned from a binary format to an open format based on XML, but it's better to be safe than sorry. Additionally, it is a good idea to back up your work frequently, because there's nothing more frustrating than losing hours of work.

To export your animation to a PNG sequence, follow these steps:

**1.** Choose File > Export > Export Movie (**Figure 5.51**).

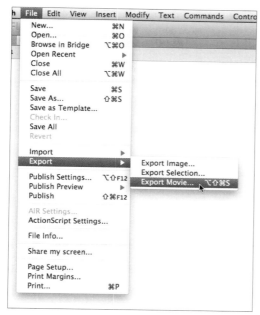

**Figure 5.51** The Export menu.

**2.** In the Format menu within the Export Movie dialog box, choose PNG Sequence (**Figure 5.52**).

**Figure 5.52** The Format menu within the Export Movie dialog box.

**3.** Create a new folder or select a folder already created for Flash to export the image to, and then click Save (**Figure 5.53**).

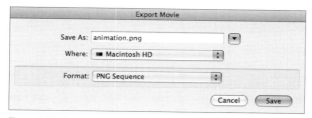

**Figure 5.53** Save to an empty folder using the Export Movie dialog box.

4. You will be prompted with PNG-specific encoding settings. Click OK to generate the image sequence (**Figure 5.54**).

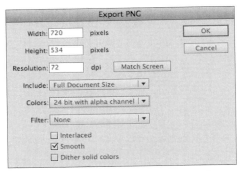

Figure 5.54 The PNG-specific export settings allow you to define the image encoding settings.

It is best practice to export each image sequence to its own folder. This helps keep each sequence organized and manageable (**Figure 5.55**).

Figure 5.55 The generated sequence of PNG files is stored in its own directory.

The export methods discussed so far work great for files that simply contain animation, but there may be some situations in which you'll need to export dynamically created (i.e., code-driven) animation to video.

## Exporting Dynamic Animation

Flash CS5's QuickTime Exporter supports ActionScript-generated content. As an example, let's create a simple animation that contains some ActionScript and export it to the QuickTime format.

1. Create a new ActionScript 3 document and save it as **dynamicAnimation.fla**.

2. Copy the Movie Clip instance of the driver running (the one used in the section "Building an Animated Preloader" earlier in this chapter, or copy it from run_cycle.fla in the Chapter 5/assets folder on the CD) and paste it onto the Stage in your dynamicAnimation document (**Figure 5.56**).

3. Give the Movie Clip an instance name of **runner** in the Properties panel (**Figure 5.57**).

4. Add a new layer named **actions**. Lock the actions layer and select the first frame.

5. Open the Actions panel (Window > Actions) and type in the following code:

```
runner.addEventListener(Event.ENTER_FRAME, run);
function run(e:Event) {
    runner.x += 10;
}
```

6. Save your document and test your movie to see the driver move horizontally to the right in 10-pixel increments. Now let's export this dynamic animation to a QuickTime movie.

7. Choose File > Export > Export Movie, and select Quick-Time in the Format menu (**Figure 5.58**).

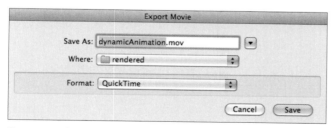

Figure 5.58 The Export Movie dialog box allows you to export a QuickTime movie.

8. Enter a filename for your QuickTime movie and the desired location to save it to. Then click OK.

Figure 5.56 The Sausage Kong driver Movie Clip on Stage.

Figure 5.57 The instance name applied in the Properties panel.

**TIP**

Before exporting to QuickTime, test your movie in the Flash Player and time it with a stopwatch. Because you are using dynamically generated content, its duration may not be as clear as that of frame-based content. You will need to enter the duration of your animation in terms of minutes and seconds during the export process.

9. In the QuickTime Export Settings dialog box, select "After time elapsed" and enter the duration of your animation. Type in a duration of **5** seconds (or **00:00:05**) (**Figure 5.59**).

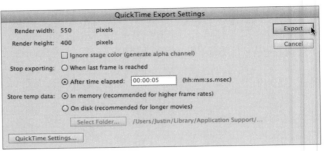

**Figure 5.59** The QuickTime Export Settings dialog box allows you to export your dynamic content based on elapsed time.

You can deselect the check box next to the Sound label to disable sound and reduce the file size on movies that contain no audio.

10. Click the QuickTime Settings button to open the Movie Settings dialog box. Here you can select the desired compression level for your movie's audio and video. You can leave the default video compression (set to Animation) and click OK (**Figure 5.60**).

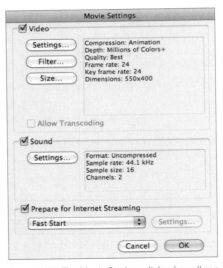

**Figure 5.60** The Movie Settings dialog box allows you to adjust audio and video compression.

**11.** Click Export to render your dynamic content to a true fixed-frame QuickTime file (**Figure 5.61**).

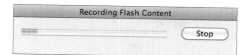

**Figure 5.61** Flash records the movie based on the time you entered and renders the compressed movie.

Now that you're familiar with the basics of exporting video, you can also apply this knowledge toward rendering videos that can be uploaded to the web.

### Exporting Files for Video Sharing Sites

Video sharing sites are another great way to show off your animation. There are plenty of well-established video sites on the web (YouTube, Vimeo, DailyMotion, to name a few), and more seem to be cropping up every day. You may decide that you want to post to YouTube because it has the widest audience, or you may choose to post to Vimeo because you like the design of the player. This decision is largely subjective.

Once you've decided where to share your video, you can create an account for that video-sharing website. You should then look up the recommended video settings for that particular site. Most of the sites have a guide for optimal video settings (e.g., www.vimeo.com/help/compression) that will help you avoid some frustrating trial-and-error attempts. These sites accept almost any video format, but they usually recompress the video to play on their site. You're likely to get the best results if you base your export settings on the site's recommendations.

Believe it or not, we have not yet run out of ways to share Flash content. Two more goodies are coming right up.

## Publishing to Mobile and Desktop

Flash has evolved from a simple web format into a rich platform that can run in almost any computing environment. Developing content in Flash effectively allows you to

**TIP**

The quality of the output from this method of capturing dynamic animation is heavily dependent on your machine's performance. It is recommended that you close any other open programs to free up memory.

**NOTES**

Some animators have had issues with the screen recording method of exporting video and still swear by SWF2Video from www.flashants.com.

**TIP**

To quickly locate instructions regarding optimal video settings for a particular site, try a web search with the site name and the words *upload* and *settings*.

be a mobile developer and a desktop developer, as well as a web developer. You can use the same familiar tools and techniques to deliver your content in a variety of settings and on a variety of devices.

For a detailed look at publishing to mobile and desktop, see the Chapter 5 subfolder on your book disc. Look for the pdf, "Chapter_5_Mobile_Desktop."

Not only can you create beautiful and dynamic content, but you can now also distribute it anywhere. Go forth and multiply (the number of places your animation can be seen, that is)!

# Index